AUTHOR: Richard Sterling

■ ■ ■

EDITOR: Maryanne Blacker

■ ■ ■

DESIGNERS: Paula Wooller, Robbylee Phelan

■ ■ ■

ASSISTANT EDITOR: Judy Newman

EDITORIAL COORDINATOR: Lara Quinlin

■ ■ ■

ILLUSTRATIONS: Marylouise Brammer

■ ■ ■

ACP PUBLISHER: Richard Walsh

ACP ASSOCIATE PUBLISHER: Bob Neil

■ ■ ■

Produced by The Australian Women's Weekly Home Library.
Typeset by Letter Perfect, Sydney. Printed by Dai Nippon Co., Ltd in Japan.
Published by Australian Consolidated Press,
54 Park Street Sydney.
♦ **AUSTRALIA:** Distributed by Network Distribution Company,
54 Park Street Sydney, (02) 282 8777.
♦ **UNITED KINGDOM:** Distributed in the U.K. by Australian Consolidated Press (UK) Ltd, 20 Galowhill Rd, Brackmills, Northampton NN4 OEE (0604) 760 456.
♦ **CANADA:** Distributed in Canada by Whitecap Books Ltd, 1086 West 3rd St,
North Vancouver V7P 3J6 (604) 980 9852.
♦ **NEW ZEALAND:** Distributed in New Zealand by Netlink Distribution Company, 17B Hargreaves St, Level 5,
College Hill, Auckland 1 (9) 302 7616.
♦ **SOUTH AFRICA:** Distributed in South Africa by Intermag,
PO Box 57394, Springfield 2137 (011) 493 3200.
ACN 000 031 747.

Sterling, Richard, 1927 –
Astrology the Richard Sterling Way
Includes index.
ISBN 0 949128 89 9

1. Astrology. I. Title. (Series : Australian Women's Weekly Home Library).
133.5

■ ■ ■

© A C P 1992
This publication is copyright. No part of it may be reproduced or transmitted in any form without the written permission of the publishers.

■ ■ ■

ASTROLOGY
the Richard Sterling way

Astrology is a fascinating science, in fact it's the oldest science known to mankind. Within these pages Richard Sterling gives you an insight into the intriguing and mysterious aspects of astrology. He explains the relationship between particular colours and your star sign, how the zodiac affects your choice of career and partner, the influence of the stars on your personality and that of your children. There is advice on getting the most out of your garden by planting according to the phases of the moon and hints on how to pick a winner at the races. You'll find chapters to inform, entertain amuse and, most of all, enjoy.

2	ASTROLOGY: PAST & PRESENT	78	HERBS OF THE ZODIAC
8	YOUR RISING STAR	82	ORIENTAL ASTROLOGY
24	STARRING PARTNERS	97	LIVING WITH NUMBERS
44	WORKING WITH THE STARS	103	WHICH DAY WAS IT?
53	CHILDREN OF THE STARS	109	AND THEY'RE RACING
58	COLOUR IN THE STARS	128	DATES OF THE STAR SIGNS
70	PLANTING BY THE MOON	128	INDEX

Astrology: Past & Present

Watching the sky, pondering the mysteries it holds,

has always held a fascination for mankind – day

following night, seasonal patterns and other dramatic,

unexplained events, such as eclipses, linked earth to

the heavens. No one knows for certain how or where

astrology first began, but, we do know that it is the

oldest science known to man because star charts

(horoscopes) have been found on clay tablets dating

back approximately 5200 years ago.

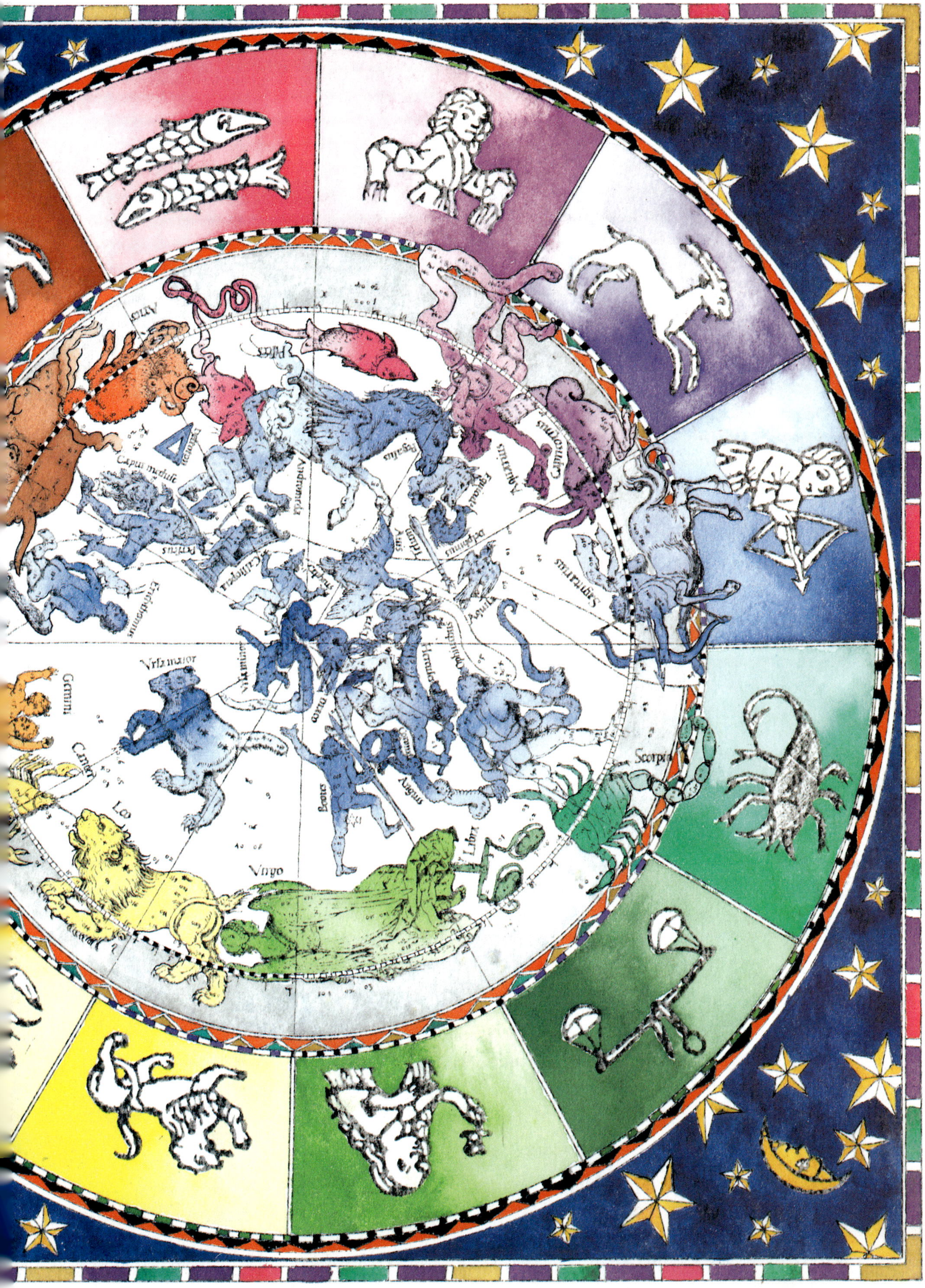

The priests of ancient Sumeria considered astrology to be part of religion. It was used to help the Sumerians choose auspicious days for religious ceremonies, important battles and the building of their temples; astrology played a significant and integral part of their lives. In this culture, unlike today, astrological predictions were applied to society as a whole rather than to individuals.

Astrology becomes a science

These first astrologers, known as Chaldeans, mapped the stars and later passed their knowledge on to the ancient Greeks who, during the 3rd century BC, developed astrology into a science with the use of mathematical aids and instruments to measure planetary movement. The Greeks were the first to cast individual horoscopes. They included planetary positions at the hour of birth, giving rise to many more variations and explaining why two people born on the same day could have very different personal characteristics and destinies. And, it was the Greeks who associated the four elements, earth, fire, water and air, with the signs of the zodiac.

With the development of astrology into a science, it became separate from religion; astrologers were professionals. Medicine was linked with astrology and Hippocrates insisted that study of the stars was essential for medical practitioning.

"Zodiac" can be translated from Greek to mean the "wheel of life" or "path of the animals". The Greeks not only had names for the 12 solar phases but had symbols for each; many correspond to the ones we use today, for example, the twins, the crab, the scorpion.

The symbol of a wheel divided into 12 sections has been found in various places from India and China to South America and Egypt. The ancient Egyptians were familiar with astrology, (which may also have originated from the Chaldeans); they hoped to learn how to predict the flooding of the Nile.

Ptolemy, who lived in Alexandria, in Egypt, catalogued stars and prepared horoscopes. His works, included comprehensive records of all astrological calculations to date and, for centuries to follow, were a valuable reference.

Astrological predictions

The Greeks passed on much of their knowledge to the Romans. During the 2nd century BC, Roman astrologers were primarily forecasters and were consulted frequently by rulers of the church and state. However, unfavourable predictions could result in the astrologer being cast out of Rome, or accused of being involved in subterfuge.

By the 3rd century AD, astrology existed with early Christianity. A harmonious co-existence was possible because it was considered that celestial bodies could foretell events, but did not determine the future —the stars seen by the shepherds at the time of Christ's birth were only predictions of his arrival. After the 4th century AD, Christianity strengthened and the popularity of astrology declined with Christian reluctance to support pagan beliefs.

The Middle Ages saw a revival in astrology, with courses being taught in universities and links established between the zodiac and herbs. Astrology was once again able to exist with the church, although many churchmen remained suspicious of astrologers.

Astrology at its peak

With the arrival of the 15th century, academics of the Renaissance movement looked to the past for knowledge; ancient philosophies were revived including astrology, and the arts and sciences developed. With the invention of printing, communication was vastly improved. Knowledge was no longer reserved for rulers and academics. Astrologers were held in high regard and were employed by leaders of church and state to give advice on omens and auspicious dates and to predict the future.

The famous prophet and astrologer Nostradamus lived during this period. Leonardo da Vinci portrayed aspects of astrology combined with geometry in his art. Writers of the time including Shakespeare, alluded to zodiacal influences.

During this time, the practical applications of astrology were many. Agricultural calenders indicating favourable planting times according to the phases of the moon

"Ancient astrologers were held in high regard and were employed by leaders of church and state to give advice..."

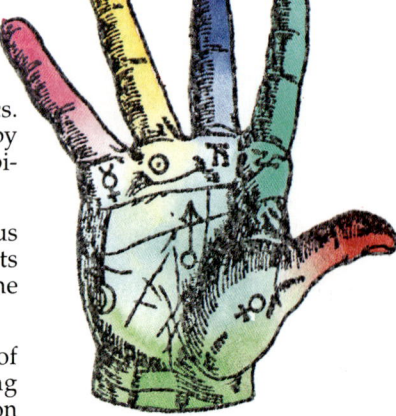

were introduced. Illness was linked with movements of celestial bodies. Each planet was thought to relate to particular parts of the body, and astrological analysis was often followed by bloodletting of the affected area. Emotional states and mental health problems were blamed on the planets. Eventually, new ways of thinking led to a split between astronomy and astrology. By the 17th century, science had developed to such a degree that astrology was no longer taken so seriously.

Ancient and modern systems of sign rulership

The ancients were obviously well aware of the 12 great constellations of fixed stars which encircle the ecliptic – the apparent path of the sun. Those constellations, which are made up of a multitude of great shining suns, have the same names as our now familiar signs of the zodiac – Aries, Taurus, Gemini, Cancer etc. Approximately 2000 years ago the positions of the constellations and the signs of the zodiac exactly coincided but because of a phenomenon known as the Precession of the Equinoxes (which is far too technical to explain here), the signs appear to be moving backwards against the backdrop of the constellations. This is not a problem because in the western system of astrology, the relationship between earth and the sun – (not the positions of the constellations) – determines the beginning and end of each of the 12 signs of the zodiac.

For example, twice each year the sun is directly above the equator. These dates mark the beginning of Aries (on March 21) and the start of Libra (on September 24).

Note. Because different countries have different time zones which can be as much as 12 hours ahead of GMT, the starting and ending dates of all the signs can vary by as much as a day, depending on where you live in the world. Therefore, American or English newspapers and magazines will give different dates from those which apply in Australia or New Zealand. This discrepancy has confused many people who were born "on the cusp" – the borderline which divides any two of the star signs.

Before the introduction of Uranus, Neptune and Pluto into modern horoscopes, the ancient astrologers devised a very clever way of giving each sign a ruling sphere. They worked on the principle of positive and negative polarities (similar to positive and negative electric currents) and applied these to the sun, moon and the five visible planets; Mercury, Venus, Mars, Jupiter and Saturn. They assigned the positive polarity to the sun and made it the ruler of the royal sign Leo. To the moon they allocated the negative polarity and made it the ruler of Cancer. Each of the five planets (like the children of the sun and moon) could be both positive and negative, giving 10 possible combinations to match the remaining 10 signs. If you look at the accompanying diagram over the page you will see that Mercury, the planet nearest to the sun, was given rulership over Gemini and Virgo, the two signs which happen to be nearest to Cancer and Leo. Mercury's positive polarity operates in Gemini and its negative one in Virgo. The next pair of signs are Taurus and Libra which are ruled by Venus, the next planet out from the sun; the negative current belongs in Taurus, the positive one in Libra. In this orderly progression in distance from the sun, Mars rules Aries in its positive phase, while Scorpio takes its negative polarity. Jupiter is the next planet out from the sun. It expresses its positive current in Sagittarius, while Pisces is in harmony with its negative polarity. Saturn is last of the five visible planets; it is positive in Aquarius and negative in Capricorn.

New planets, new inventions

Since those times, new planets have been discovered and new inventions have appeared. Astrology nowadays has a spiritual base and the individual search for self-knowledge is again linked with the zodiac. Uranus, Neptune and Pluto, follow on from Saturn in order of distance from the sun. In modern astrology, Uranus has replaced Saturn as ruler of Aquarius, Neptune is considered to be the ruler of Pisces rather than Jupiter, while Pluto, the higher octave of Mars has replaced that planet as the ruler of Scorpio.

In ancient times the combination of 12 signs and seven spheres was adequate for their needs; it is not the case today. The "Dictionary of Keywords" beginning on page 114 shows how new inventions have been attributed to specific planets. If, in the future, one or more new planets is discovered, there is no doubt that they will be associated with things of which we have not even dreamed.

"Each planet was thought to relate to particular parts of the body, and astrological analysis was often followed by bloodletting..."

The Ancient System of Sign Rulership

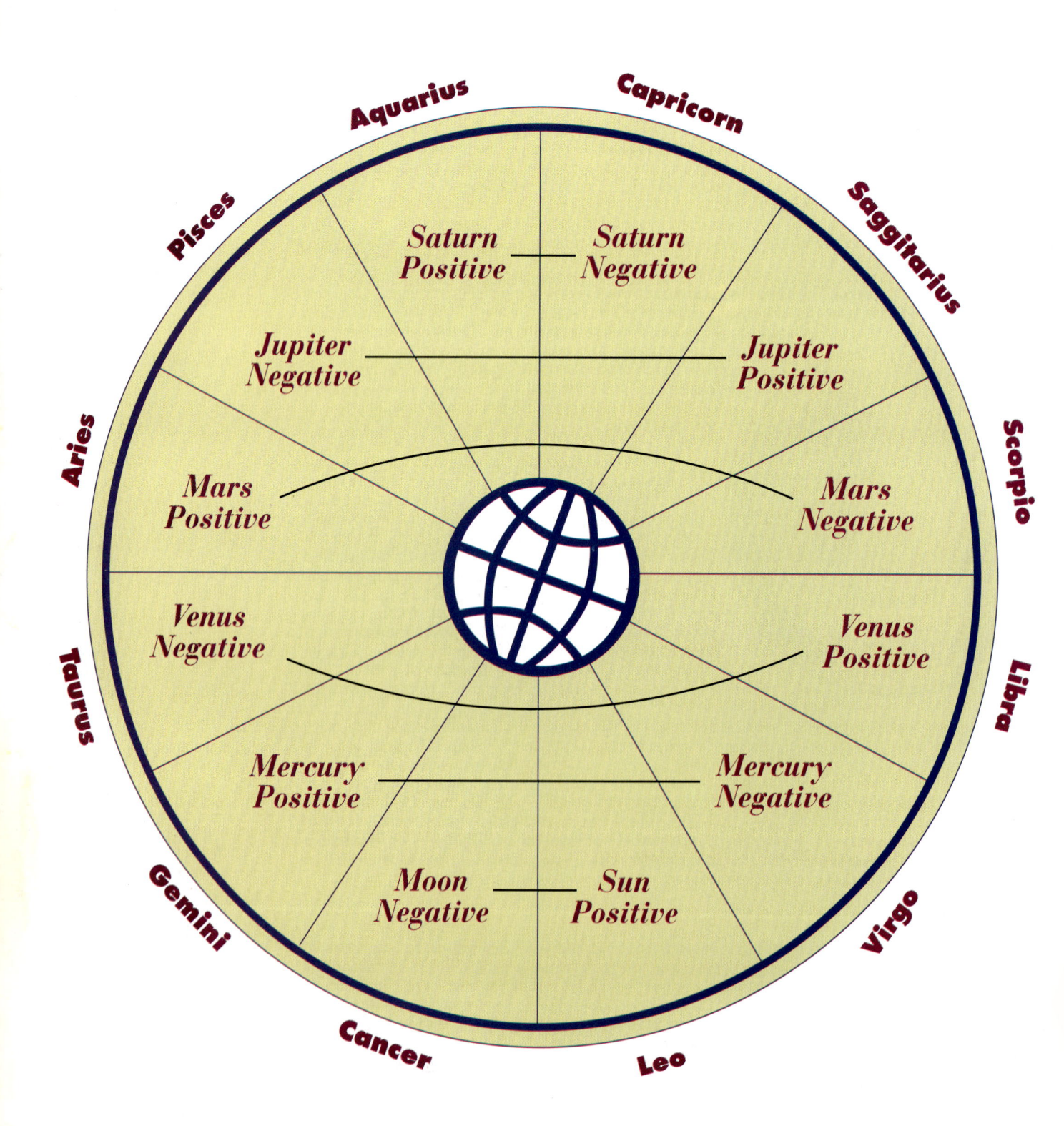

- Aquarius — Saturn Positive
- Capricorn — Saturn Negative
- Pisces — Jupiter Negative
- Sagittarius — Jupiter Positive
- Aries — Mars Positive
- Scorpio — Mars Negative
- Taurus — Venus Negative
- Libra — Venus Positive
- Gemini — Mercury Positive
- Virgo — Mercury Negative
- Cancer — Moon Negative
- Leo — Sun Positive

The Modern System of Sign Rulership

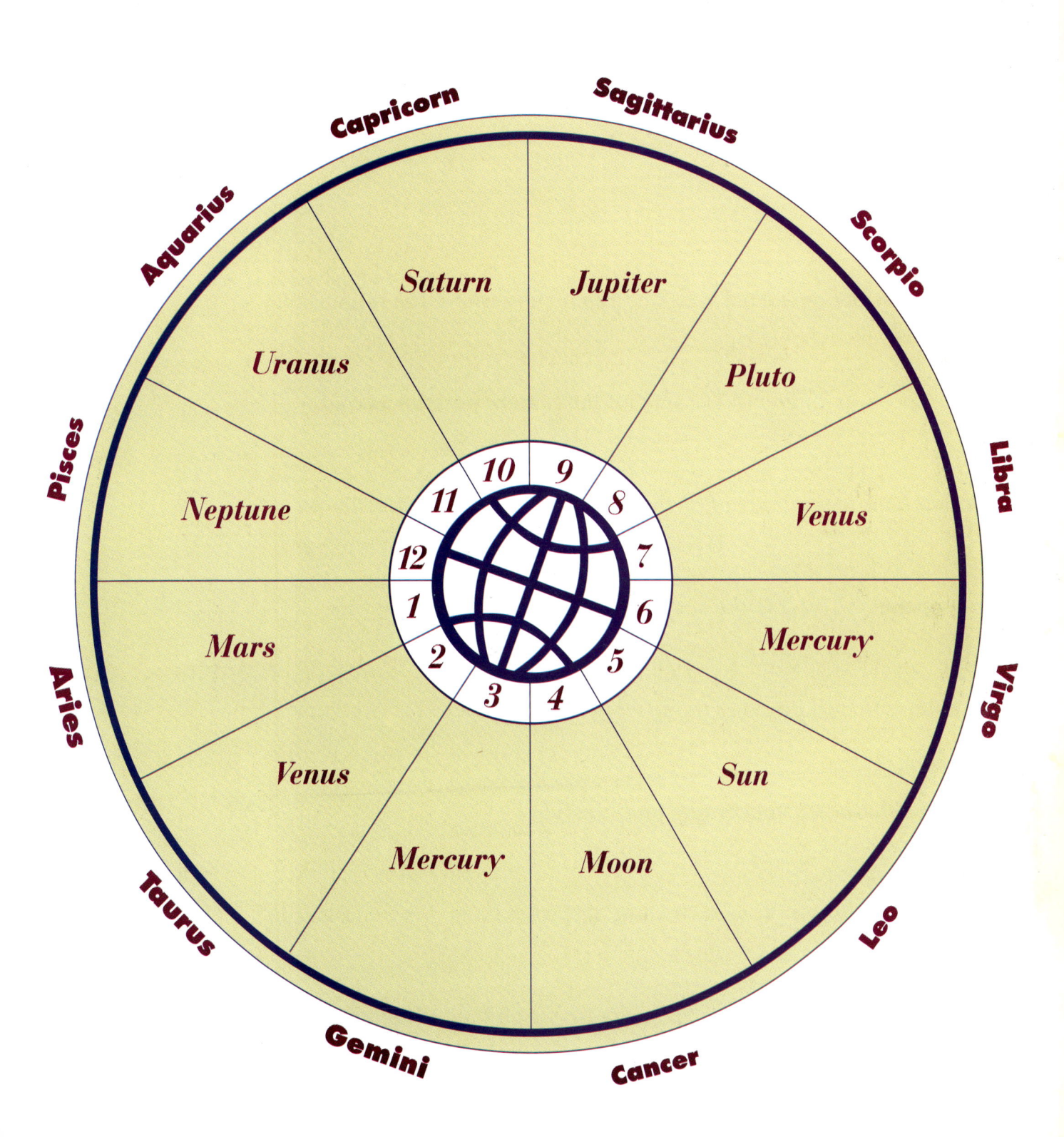

Your Rising Star

Have you ever wondered how two people who share the same star sign can be so different? The sign on the eastern horizon at the actual hour and minute of birth can have a powerful influence on your personality; it is the key to a complete horoscope. In this chapter you will discover the effect your own rising star can have on your character, appearance and lifestyle.

Firstly though, you'll need to know the exact hour, day and place of your birth; then simply use the zodiacscope on the following pages to work out your ascendant.

Southern Hemisphere

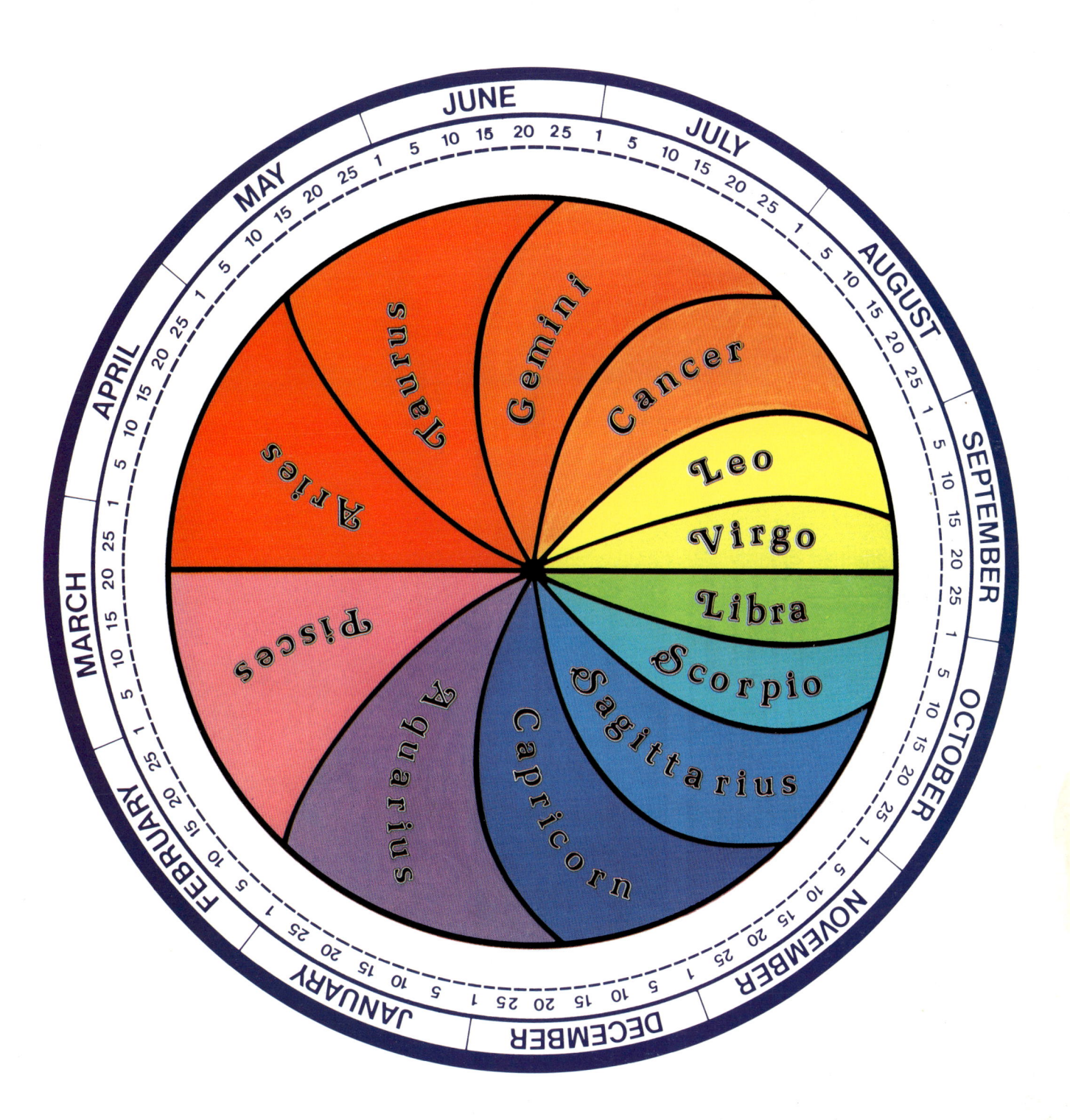

The Zodiascope

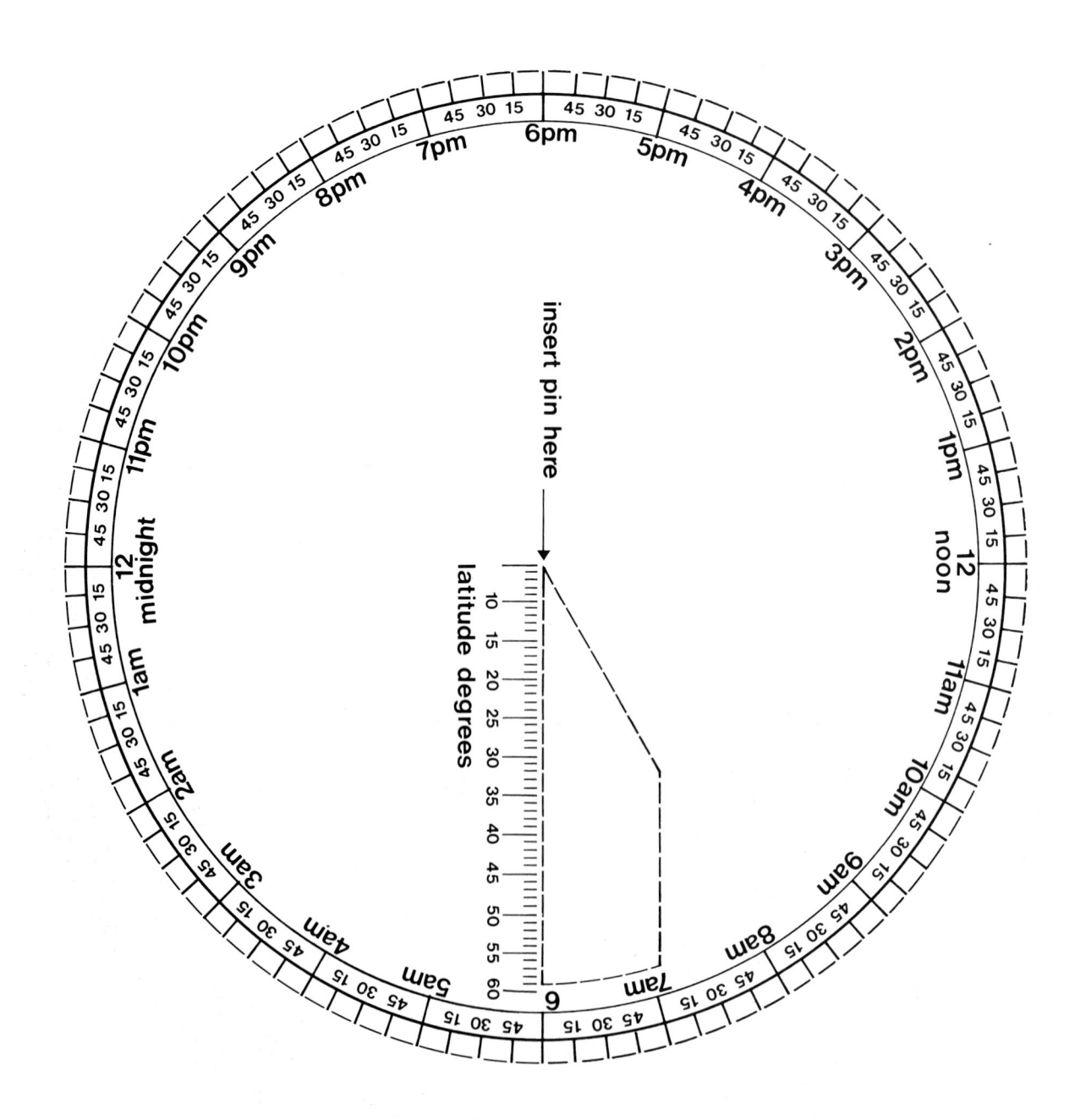

Photocopy this section of the zodiascope. Carefully cut along the dotted line around the zodiascope wheel so that it can be rotated to any position within the perimeter of either of the northern or southern hemisphere circles. Cut out the "window" exactly along the dotted line. The wheel can then be positioned onto the relevant hemisphere circle to reveal your rising star.

Northern Hemisphere

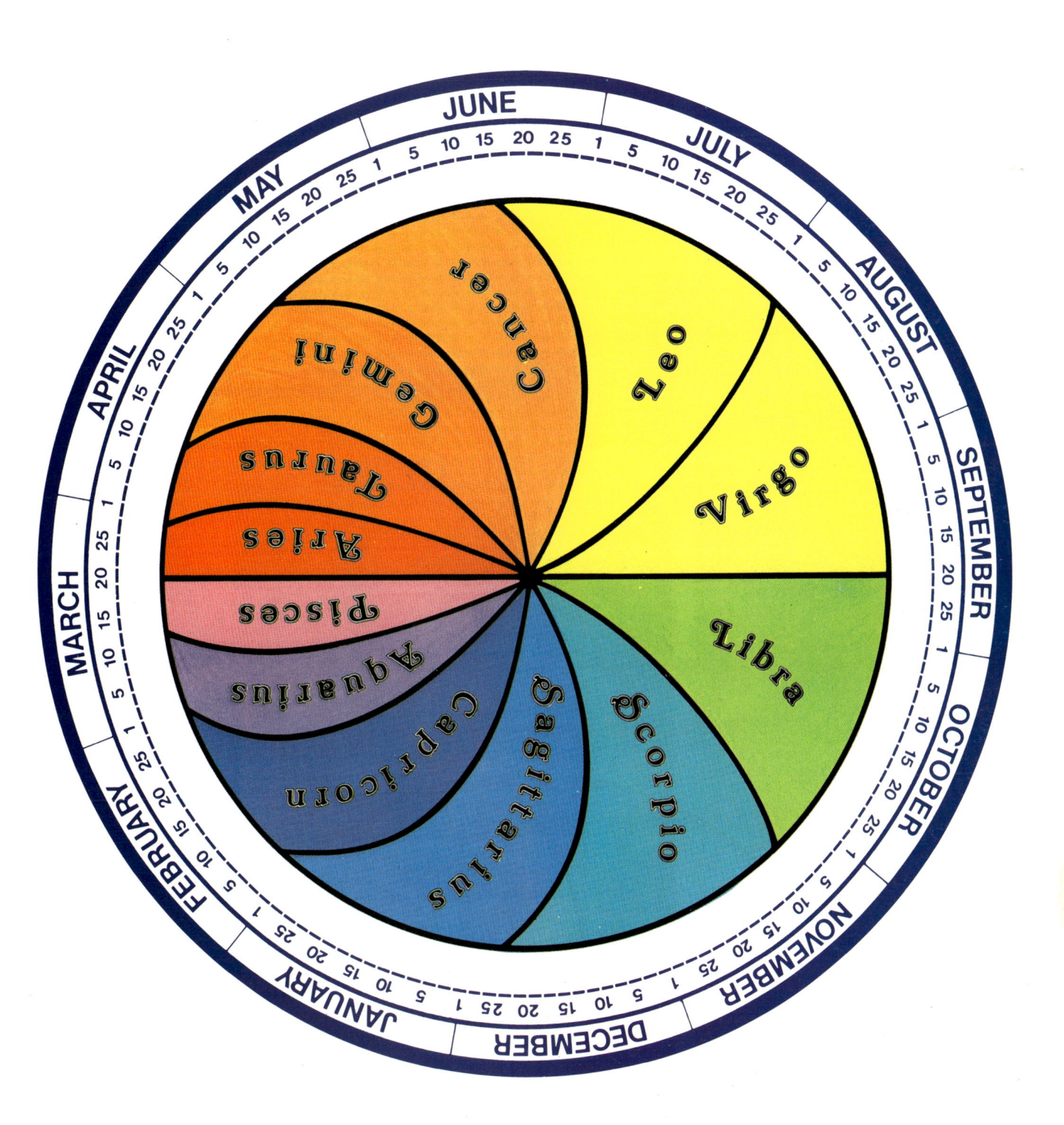

The eastern horizon is known as the ascendant and the zodiac sign which is on that horizon at the actual hour and minute of birth is called the rising sign or ascending sign. The ascendant can have a powerful impact on your character and destiny. Twelve people born approximately two hours apart on any particular day would share the same sun sign (also known as star sign) but all would have a different ascending sign. This is just one of the reasons why there can be so many variations in the personalities of people who are born in any one of the 12 zodiac signs.

On the day of your birth, the sun was in one of the 12 zodiac signs making you an Aries, Taurus, Gemini or so on. However, no analysis of your sign alone can give an accurate assessment of your character; this can only be done when an individual horoscope is calculated, using the actual date, hour and place of birth. This will give a complete picture, which considers all the variable factors, including the positions of the sun, moon, Mercury, Venus, Mars, Jupiter, Saturn, Uranus, Neptune and Pluto, plus the particular star sign which is on the ascendant.

Many people would like to know what their ascending sign is, so, to avoid all of the intricate mathematical calculations which an astrologer employs, I have devised a simplified method for you to follow using the zodiascope at the beginning of this chapter. You will need to know the approximate time of your birth.

When working out an ascending sign, you must know whether the birth occurred in the northern or southern hemisphere as this will determine which of the two larger circles you must use. The southern hemisphere circle is for people born in Australia, New Zealand and other places south of the equator. The northern hemisphere circle is only for people born in the United Kingdom, Europe, USA and other countries north of the equator.

Before using the zodiascope, there are two things you must know: firstly, the latitude of the birth place and, secondly, whether daylight saving was in force. I have listed the approximate latitude for many towns and cities in the world in the chart on page 23. Northern (N) and southern (S) hemispheres are also indicated. If your birthplace is not included, you can easily locate its latitude in a good atlas.

If the birth occurred during a period when daylight saving was being used, in most cases you must deduct one hour from the registered time of birth to obtain the standard time. Here, it is impossible to list the different time zones for every country in the world. In Australia, daylight saving was in operation during the periods listed below and opposite.

Daylight saving time in Australia

At 2am Standard Time at the beginning of the periods listed below, clocks are advanced one hour, making it 3am Daylight Saving Time. At the end of the daylight saving period, clocks are put back one hour at 3am, so that 3am Daylight Saving Time becomes 2am Standard Time.

The zodiascope is designed to operate on Standard Time in all countries and states. If you were born in Australia during any of the following periods, you must deduct one hour from your time of birth because it would have been recorded during daylight saving.

New South Wales, Victoria and South Australia

From January 1, 1917, to March 25, 1917; from January 1, 1942, to March 29, 1942; from September 27, 1942, to March 28, 1943; from October 3, 1943, to March 26, 1944; from October 31, 1971, to February 27, 1972; from October 29, 1972, to March 4, 1973; from October 28, 1973, to March 3, 1974; from October 27, 1974, to March 2, 1975; from October 26, 1975, to March 7, 1976; from October 31, 1976, to March 6, 1977; from October 30, 1977, to March 5, 1978; from October 29, 1978, to March 4, 1979; from October 28, 1979, to March 2, 1980; from October 26, 1980, to March 1, 1981; from October 25, 1981, to March 7, 1982 in western New South Wales, Victoria and South Australia, but in the rest of New South Wales and Tasmania it continued until April 4, 1982; from October 31, 1982, to March 6, 1983; from October 30, 1983, to March 4, 1984; from October 28, 1984 to March 3, 1985; from October 27, 1985 to March 16, 1986; from October 19, 1986, to March 15, 1987; from October 25, 1987, to March 20, 1988; from October 30, 1988, to March 19, 1989; from October 29, 1989, to March 4, 1990, in New South Wales and to March 18, 1990 in Victoria and South Australia; from October 28, 1990, to March 3, 1991 in New South Wales and to March 17, 1991, in Victoria and South Australia; and from October 27, 1991, to March 1, 1992.

Queensland

From January 1, 1917, to March 25, 1917; from January 1, 1942, to March 29, 1942; from September 27, 1942, to March 28, 1943; from October 3, 1943, to March 26, 1944; from October 31, 1971, to February 27, 1972; from

October 29, 1989, to March 4, 1990; from October 28, 1990, to March 3, 1991; and from October 27, 1991, to March 1, 1992.

Northern Territory

From January 1, 1917, to March 25, 1917; from January 1, 1942, to March 29, 1942; from September 27, 1942, to March 28, 1943; from October 3, 1943, to March 26, 1944; from then on, daylight saving was discontinued in the Northern Territory.

Western Australia

From January 1, 1917, to March 25, 1917; from January 1, 1942, to March 29, 1942; from September 27, 1942, to March 28, 1943; from October 3, 1943, to March 26, 1944; from October 27, 1974, to March 2, 1975; from October 30, 1983, to March 4, 1984; and from October 27, 1991, to March 1, 1992.

Tasmania

From October 1, 1916, to March 25, 1917; from October 28, 1917, to March 3, 1918; from October 27, 1918, to March 2, 1919; from January 1, 1942, to March 29, 1942; from September 27, 1942, to March 28, 1943; from October 3, 1943, to March 26, 1944; from October 1, 1967, to March 31, 1968; from October 27, 1968, to March 9, 1969; from October 26, 1969, to March 8, 1970; from October 25, 1970, to March 14, 1971; from October 31, 1971, to February 27, 1972; from October 29, 1972, to March 4, 1973; from October 28, 1973, to March 3, 1974; from October 27, 1974, to March 2, 1975; from October 26, 1975, to March 7, 1976; from October 31, 1976, to March 6, 1977; from October 30, 1977, to March 5, 1978; from October 29, 1978, to March 4, 1979; from October 28, 1979, to March 2, 1980; from October 26, 1980, to March 1, 1981; from October 25, 1981, to March 28, 1982; from October 31, 1982, to March 27, 1983; from October 30, 1983, to March 4, 1984; from October 28, 1984, to March 3, 1985; from October 27, 1985, to March 2, 1986; October 19, 1986, to March 15, 1987; from October 25, 1987, to March 20, 1988; from October 30, 1988, to March 19, 1989; from October 29, 1989, to March 18, 1990; from October 28, 1990, to March 17, 1991; from October 6, 1991, to March 29, 1992.

Reading the zodiascope

Assuming you now know the latitude of your birth place and the hour of your birth (in the Standard Time for that locality), the rest is easy. Place the small wheel of the zodiascope over the larger circle of the relevant hemisphere; insert a pin through the centre of both circles.

Find the point around the rim of the small wheel which corresponds with your time of birth (to the hour and minute, if this is known), being careful to select either am or pm. Now rotate that time of birth until it is aligned with the day and month of your birth shown around the outer rim of the large wheel. Next, locate the latitude of your place of birth along the section marked **latitude degrees** on the small inner wheel.

As you look through the window in the smaller wheel, the particular zodiac sign which lies exactly along the cross bar on that degree of latitude is the one which was rising over the eastern horizon at the hour of your birth. This is the star sign which was on your ascendant at the time you were born and in the following pages you can find out how it affects your life. In some cases the degree of latitude will lie exactly over the borderline between two zodiac signs. When this happens, you probably will be able to decide which one applies to you by reading the interpretation given for each of the signs.

Aries on the ascendant

Some of the keywords of Aries are energy, activity, audacity and enterprise, so your nature will be fiery and impulsive with a constant desire to be busy and on the go.

You have abundant self confidence in your ability to succeed and no obstacle is too big to tackle, for you have a courageous spirit and will not allow anything to daunt you. You are frank, forthright and outspoken, sometimes to the point of becoming rather blunt.

You are the type who can quickly become enthusiastic over a new idea but, unless other factors in the horoscope lend persistence, you soon find that you have lost this initial enthusiasm and the idea no longer appeals. Consequently, there is likely to be a lot of unfinished business in your life things which you have begun on impulse but which are still waiting to be completed. Try to cultivate the habit of tying up loose ends and finishing one thing before you begin something else.

Aries on the ascendant, when not overpowered by heavy restrictions elsewhere in the horoscope, makes you bold and impulsive with plenty of on-the-surface self confidence,

"Aries is aggressive and combative and thoroughly enjoys a battle of wits. You come alive when pitted against a rival..."

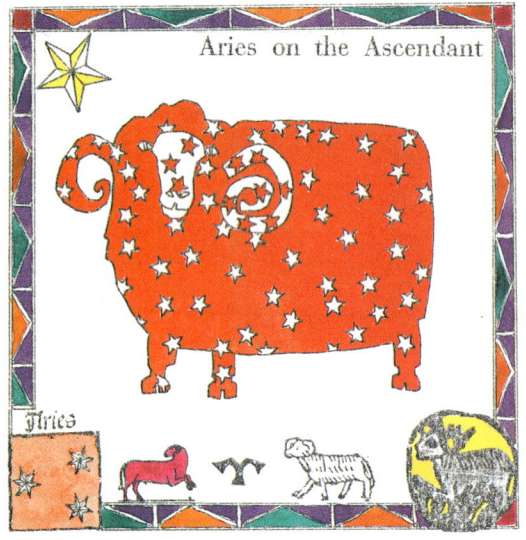

so that wherever you go, you create an impression. However, some withdrawn people may find you overwhelming.

"A storm in a teacup" is a phrase which fits this type of Aries temperament. Impulsive, quick and impetuous, you are happiest doing things on the spur of the moment. You become bored with long-range plans. An excess of recklessness, impatience and lack of forethought may lead to personal calamity, so you should train yourself always to think before you act.

You may have an abundance of physical vitality but your makeup is better suited to quick, short bursts of activity than to prolonged strain. There is often a surplus of tension and heat in the body, with the result that an Aries on the ascendant often suffers from headaches, insomnia and fever. If you are so stricken, the secret of overcoming the trouble is to learn to relax.

Forceful and determined to get your own way, you can become indignant and even hot tempered when opposed, although you soon forget an argument or a grudge.

Aries is aggressive and combative and thoroughly enjoys a battle of wits. You come alive when pitted against a rival in debating, sport, business competition – even in marriage. You like to be first off the mark and prefer to lead.

Since you are fond of having your own way, enjoy independence and are happy when in command, you may not be suited for occupations where you have to subjugate your own desires. There is definitely ability to take command in executive positions but it is essential that you have a backup to maintain a check on your reins, complete what you leave unfinished and also to rectify some of your more impulsive actions.

You have a marvellous ability to rise to the occasion in times of emergency but you usually do not have the endurance that is required to cope with prolonged hardships.

Mars, your ruling planet, signifies vitality and strength and so, from a health point of view, you do have excellent recuperative powers. However, try to avoid burning yourself out through too much activity and constantly driving yourself.

You are fond of red; it is probably your favourite colour. You will get on well with most people who were born in the sun sign Aries.

Taurus on the ascendant

A most noticeable characteristic of this zodiacal influence is a dislike of too many changes. A stable and sometimes inflexible mind complements a settled and predictable existence. So any sudden, unpredicted changes really upset your love of peace and harmony.

You have a loving nature and are almost certainly fond of beauty, music, colour and artistic surroundings. You like pleasure, luxury living and have a definite attraction to good food. Since regular physical activity does not appeal to you, Taurus on the ascendant may contribute to weight gain in middle age. Taurus is solid by nature and, when found on the ascendant, it produces a substantial physique.

Like the bull, you are slow to anger but, when finally stirred up, you are capable of violent outbursts. You are stubborn in the face of all opposition, resisting any compromise.

You are thorough in your work because you are practical and pragmatic. For this reason you may judge things from a purely materialistic point of view. Being very down to earth you prefer facts and reality to idealism and flights of fancy. However, if by chance your work brings you into touch with fantasy, you will use it not because you believe in it but because of the financial returns and business success it brings.

You are possessive of the things and the people you love because you derive much pleasure from collecting and owning beautiful things. However, should you feel you are losing your possessive grip, you may experience jealousy and unhappiness.

Taurus on the ascendant makes for a quiet, inflexible nature. Consequently, you have a steadfast determination to plod on and persevere without making too much fuss. Add to this the fact that you are consistent and methodical and it is easy to see that this zodiacal influence is one indication of worldly success in life. Of course, the solar, lunar and planetary positions in your complete horoscope either add to or detract from this indication.

Troubles and difficulties in life may result from your unreasonable resistance and stubborn inflexibility both in matters of human relationships and in business. After all, strong prejudices are fixed thoughts and opinions which control you and your lifestyle. To counteract this, you must guard against allowing yourself to think and live in a groove; it is easy for a person born with Taurus on the ascendant to get into a rut.

This zodiac sign is related to the neck and throat, so you could have some problems in that part of the body, particularly in early life.

Colours such as pink, hot pink, red, orange and flame will appeal to you. You usually get on well with people born with the sun in Taurus.

Gemini on the ascendant

One of the most noticeable effects of this influence is a restlessness which can be seen in the quick manner of walking and in continuous movements of the hands while talking. It also can produce the irritating habit of constant chatter and comment.

You have a versatile mind which you use to learn a little about a lot of things, so there is the danger of becoming a "Jack of all trades but master of none" unless you make a deliberate effort to stick at something long enough to master it.

Gemini on the ascendant can give a brilliant, ingenious mind but this very ingenuity, when combined with restlessness, also can cause you to be inconsistent and lack continuity of purpose. You should guard against letting yourself be satisfied with a superficial knowledge about things by learning to concentrate on a single thing at a time.

Usually the nervous system is highly strung, making you feel a constant need to be busy, running here and there, phoning someone, jotting down notes and so on. In fact, your mind always seems to be far ahead of your body. You must learn to be calm, to give your mind and your nervous system a chance to unwind. Learn to sit still, perfectly relaxed, until you reach the point where you do not feel any need to talk and chatter or move your hands around restlessly.

You have the twin or double influence of Gemini in so far as you are kind, humane and sympathetic in an intellectual kind of way. Emotionally, you lack real depth of feeling when compared with the scale of emotional response possible for some of the other star sign personalities. Perhaps this is one reason why a fair percentage of people born with Gemini on the ascendant have problems in marriage.

Gemini usually gives fluency in speech and/or writing and, since it is an intellectual sign, you probably enjoy and could become quite proficient at writing, literature or science. Gemini is closely linked with communication, both mental and physical, so your subconscious urge is to make contact with others. Curiosity is one of your keywords and you enjoy investigating things and experimenting with new ideas.

The restless qualities of Gemini give you a love of change and variety and, where hobbies, career or other interests are concerned, this influence is likely to bring about many changes during your lifetime.

Gemini on the ascendant can indicate a variety of respiratory problems such as bronchitis, pneumonia or weak lungs. These types of health problems are particularly noticeable in the early part of life.

Warm colours such as orange appeal to you. There is a natural affinity for people born in the sun sign Gemini.

Cancer on the ascendant

A noticeable feature of this zodiacal influence is sensitivity. Your emotional reactions to other people can make you brood over even a small insult or remark until your imagination builds it up to gigantic proportions.

Cancer, having such sensitive, impressionable qualities, is likely to make you timid and retiring and so, cramp your initiative in making radical changes. You prefer the tested conservative line of thought and action; when you are confronted with the need to introduce unusual or unconventional innovations into your life you tend to procrastinate.

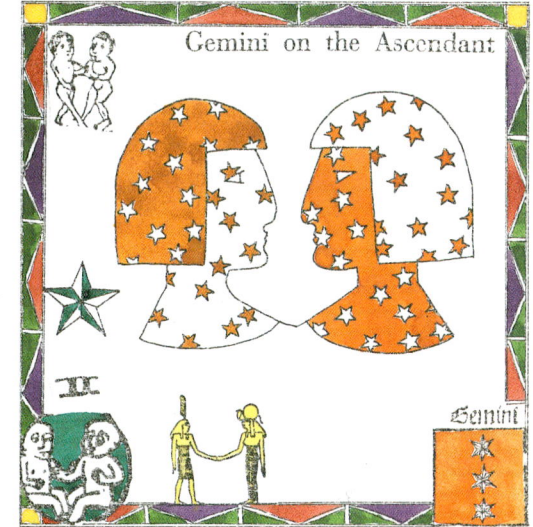

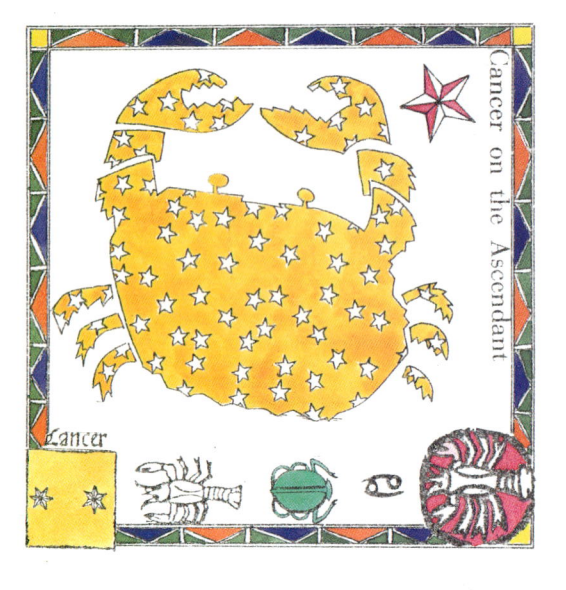

You like the security of a home base because your home, domestic and family life is of prime importance. A career or other interests are all very well but you need a home life to achieve complete fulfillment. Cancer is the sign of the home lover and homemaker.

This zodiacal influence, when taken alone and analysed, does not give a very robust constitution and often points to faulty action of the digestive system or the stomach, especially in early childhood. Of course, this influence will be modified or accentuated by the positions of the sun, moon and planets and the star patterns they form between themselves.

Cancer, like the ocean tides which it governs, is changeable and fluctuating. These qualities will manifest in your life as moods which are up one day and down the next. You must be careful that this moodiness does not develop extreme tendencies. Try to maintain an even balance and remember that moderation in all that you do is best.

You are good at adapting to changing conditions because you have the knack of being able to sense an atmosphere and consequently you know how to respond accordingly. This ability links up with Cancer's affinity with water which always will adapt itself to the shape of the container which holds it.

You are sympathetic towards people in distress and it is remarkable how many times Cancer on the ascendant brings contact with sufferings and troubles of others. Perhaps this is because you have some of the martyr in your nature!

You are sentimental, especially where family ties and links with home and parents are concerned, so you are the type who always remembers birthdays and anniversaries. Close friends and family are very important and you enjoy nothing more than an evening at home with good company.

Although you can be timid and shy of taking the initiative, especially in physical matters, you can be extraordinarily brave in your mental and moral attitudes and convictions.

Being born with Cancer on the ascendant means you would derive much pleasure and satisfaction from living close to water or in a home with a view of the sea. White and pastel sunny colours such as pale orange and apricot appeal to you. You will probably get on well with most people who were born in the sign of Cancer.

Leo on the ascendant

Leo is known as the royal sign of the zodiac; when found on the ascendant it gives a noble dignity to both personality and appearance, provided, of course, that there are no serious planetary afflictions in the other parts of your horoscope.

Your magnetic qualities enable you to command both the respect and attention of others around you.

The sign of Leo is ruled by the sun and, just as it has control of all the planets and satellites in the solar system, so you've inherited definite desires and the ability to lead, control and organise. You have some of the power and masterful qualities of the sun, such as self confidence and self possession, and these factors may take you far up the ladder towards success.

Leo is akin to grandeur and largess, so you prefer to do things on a lavish scale. You think big and cannot tolerate pettiness or meanness in others. You are frank, open-hearted and ambitious. Unless nipped in the bud, these characteristics can degenerate into a tendency to show off.

Excesses of pride and vanity are also some of the less favourable effects produced by Leo on the ascendant; if these characteristics begin to manifest, they will stem from an inborn desire to be the centre of attention which, for one reason or another, has been frustrated. In spite of the fact that you are self reliant and self possessed, your ascendant sign, perhaps more than any other, makes you thrive on appreciation, approbation and flattery. You are at your best, give of your best and feel a sense of fulfillment, when you receive recognition and appreciation but, if this is not forthcoming, you are likely to resort to using the negative side of Leo to attract attention. The less favourable aspects of Leo can range from ostentation, overdressing and boasting, through to egotism, pomposity, arrogance and conceit.

You succeed best in a position of authority where you can exercise your organisational and administrative skills. You prefer to lead rather than follow and in your social sphere you should be popular. However, because of these very abilities and your inborn magnetic power, it is all too easy for you to slip into the habit of dominating other people, especially weaker types who look to you for assistance.

You are inclined to resent authority, but, if the person in charge shows his or her appreciation of your capabilities, you are more than willing to comply with instructions.

You are both warm-hearted and generous, particularly towards the people you love, and will give abundantly and unstintingly to people who need your support. In some cases Leo on the ascendant can cause an excess of these qualities and as a result you become generous to a fault.

You normally have plenty of faith and hope and are not the type who gives in easily to fits of depression and despondency. You are fond of pleasure and luxury and, no matter how limited your resources may be, you have a flair for making something ordinary appear to be rather swish. This is because you know the value of presentation. Your sense of the dramatic helps you to make the most of things by accentuating the highlights. This applies to your personality, home, way of entertaining and management of business affairs; Leo, more than any other, is the sign of the showman.

You are attracted by bright colours such as yellow, gold and sunny, radiant tones and there usually will be a touch of splendour in your furnishings, decor and clothes. Mirrors, chandeliers and even gilded furniture could be just your cup of tea. Leos will be among your favourite companions.

Virgo on the ascendant

Virgo, more than any other sign, is suited to serve others. There are two reasons for this: you are quiet, reserved, methodical and practical; and you can be relied on to carry out instructions to the letter with care and attention to every detail.

You have keen powers of discrimination and these, combined with your cool, clear intellectual abilities, give you accurate insight into most problems and situations. You are a born critic, and you are choosy when it comes to associates. You can stand apart and objectively sum up a person or situation in a detached way; normally you do not allow yourself to be carried away by emotions, so your analysis of any situation is clear cut and unbiased. Your decisions and opinions will be based on reality.

You enjoy gaining knowledge and can do so without difficulty. When a job has to be done, your careful analysis of it usually leads you to a clever solution of any problem.

A combination of tact and diplomacy will help you achieve success, and in business affairs you pay attention to every detail.

Virgo on the ascendant usually indicates great interest in health matters but when you are not feeling well you should try to avoid imagining yourself to be worse off than you are. This inborn interest in health complements your hygienic habits. You keep yourself, your clothes, home and surroundings scrupulously clean.

You are modest and conservative and you do not particularly like the limelight, especially when it brings you into close contact with other people. One noticeable feature which you derive from this position of Virgo on the ascendant is a dislike of being touched by other people. This somewhat virgin-like quality makes you almost indifferent to physical passion and violent emotions and probably accounts for the fact that quite a high percentage of people who are born with Virgo on the ascendant prefer to remain single.

Another characteristic is your intense love of detail. In everything you do, each separate item will receive proper attention.

This position of Virgo also favours work which involves small component parts such as in watchmaking, jewellery, needlework, instrument-making, electrical circuits, microscopic analysis and so on.

Virgo has a sensible and healthy scepticism – it is not bigoted or unreasonable but more along the lines of discrimination between what is practicable, workable and reasonable, and what is nonsense.

If you allow the negative side of Virgo to develop, your critical and discriminative faculties will degenerate into constant displays of nagging and fault finding. Your emphasis on detail also must be kept well under control in order to avoid overfastidiousness.

Virgo is much more interested in mental accomplishments than in physical prowess. Because of this, most people who have Virgo on the ascendant are inclined to neglect physical exercise after youth has passed and this leads to sluggish activity of the intestinal tract and subsequent poor elimination. Once a true-to-type Virgo person becomes chronically ill, it almost becomes a status symbol to continue that way and there is, sometimes, a tendency to derive a morbid enjoyment from talking about "my illness".

Colours such as pale green, lime, olive and some mixtures of yellow and green appeal to you. You get on well with people born under the star sign of Virgo.

Libra on the ascendant

Since the symbol of this sign is the balance, one of the most noticeable features about you is your liking of things in proportion. This rule applies to everything, so that you prefer paintings which are in perspective and well balanced, music which is harmonious rather than discordant, architecture which is symmetrical, clothes which balance and complement your looks and personality and so on. Your environment influences you greatly and you will not be happy unless it is harmonious and elegant.

Even in your thinking and planning you like to take time to balance things out, weighing one thing against another and taking a good look at both sides of the situation. For this reason you appear to be indecisive to those who make snap decisions and they may lose patience with you, especially if you procrastinate as you can do when you are not satisfied with the relationship of all the factors involved.

Just as the balance can tip easily from one side of the scale to the other, so you can be changeable in both your ideas and your moods. You may be giving all of your attention to a particular hobby or line of thought and then almost without warning you can drop it, forget all about it as though it never existed and take up a new hobby or entirely different point of view. When the pendulum swings it does so completely – there are no half measures for Libra.

You can be very tactful when occasion demands and certainly diplomacy and strategy are strong points. This stems from your inborn ability to see both sides of the question. With this knowledge you can cleverly steer your course and manipulate your plan of campaign and, when combined with your charm, this enables you to achieve your goals before people even realize how you have done so.

You have a strong sense of justice and will never allow a wrong to go uncorrected. This sometimes can result in other people thinking of you as callous whereas, in reality, you are just being fair-minded. If you extend a courtesy to a friend or do a good deed for someone, you expect the person concerned to return the favour.

You are pleasant, with a charming disposition, and to be happy you must have peace and harmony around you. In fact peace at any price could well be the motto of Libra on the ascendant.

Libra makes you naturally artistic, with a good eye for design, so your home always will be tastefully decorated. Beauty and elegance are important to you and you will spare no expense when buying anything which accentuates these qualities.

You are affectionate and make friends easily, so your social life is not only likely to be interesting but also profitable, providing opportunities for furthering your success. As you have an intense dislike of conflict, tension and discord, most people find it easy to get along with you.

Having a well-balanced mind gives you that rare quality of being able to judge something impartially, because your mind and emotions function together as a unit instead of as opposites.

Green appeals to you and may well be your favourite colour and many of your favourite people will be Librans.

Scorpio on the ascendant

You have an intensely emotional nature and are capable of deep feelings. As long as your love life runs smoothly, all is well. But if your loved one should ever deceive you in any way, not only are you never likely to forget it – it is also most unlikely you will ever forgive. At such times you are your own worst enemy because you can suffer agonies of jealousy and resentment – even hatred.

This zodiacal influence gives you a concentrated, intense nature in which tenacity is a fundamental. You have plenty of determination and unflinching courage to achieve your goals. Your thoroughness, drive and fixed purpose will take you far along the road to success but there is perhaps one drawback to being so intense – you tend to look on life as a battle to be won. Just be careful that your self discipline does not replace all the lighthearted fun.

No problem is too formidable for you to tackle; a challenge or an obstacle creates an outlet for your dynamic constructive or destructive abilities. You know what you want and will not allow anyone or anything to stand in your way.

You have strong likes and dislikes and cannot be persuaded easily to change plans or opinions. Scorpio has an inflexible willpower with great self reliance and this may be one of the reasons why you tend not to trust or rely on other people.

You are willing to work hard and long to achieve your goal and, being secretive, you do not normally divulge all your plans. You may tell some of the facts but you always keep your trump card hidden.

You demand the utmost from yourself and, when in a position of authority, you expect the same from others. So, you are likely to come up against some harsh criticism unless you learn to relax the reins of discipline and become more tolerant.

Any troubles you may experience in life are likely to be the result of too much emotional intensity or jealousy, for you are capable of experiencing the extremes of love and hate and your emotions can tear you to pieces. Unless nipped in the bud, this zodiacal influence can lead you to treat other people harshly, especially those who serve you or who are subordinate.

Scorpio is closely related to the principle of death and destruction and it is remarkable how many times I have seen children with this ascendant sign take a delight in dealing sadistically with insects, animals and their own possessions. This influence occasionally can turn in on itself, just as the scorpion can sting itself, and the result is a person who subconsciously wishes to destroy his or her own success or happiness.

In the physical body, Scorpio is related to the sexual organs and reproduction and, when this sign is on the ascendant, it can indicate an over emphasis on sex or even some type of physical problem involving the reproductive organs.

Colours such as turquoise, the bluish-green of the ocean, shades of aqua or a mixture of blue and green appeal to you and complement your water sign ascendant. You usually get on well with people born under the star sign of Scorpio.

Sagittarius on the ascendant

A strong desire for expansion is one of the hallmarks of your nature. The avenues through which you will seek this expansion will depend on other factors in your horoscope but it will be on one or more of these three levels: your physical environment and surroundings; your mental interests, knowledge and learning; spiritual development, unfolding and expansion of the consciousness.

Another strongly-marked characteristic which naturally accompanies your driving urge to expand is a strong sense of independence and a great love of freedom. You will not tolerate anyone or anything restricting your freedom or placing limitations on your thoughts or activities.

Quite a high percentage of people who have Sagittarius on the ascendant enjoy sport, and this stems once again from a love of freedom because the wide-open spaces, sunshine and fresh air are synonymous with unrestricted and unhampered activity.

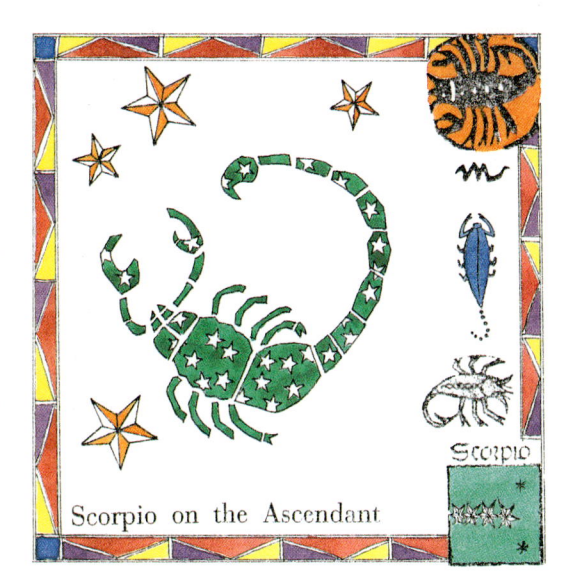

Where close relationships are concerned, this influence of Sagittarius can cause problems, unless they are recognised early and then handled carefully. The reason is that when marriage or any other close partnership is entered into, it automatically imposes a tie and a certain amount of restriction on your freedom and independence. After the initial romance has faded and your marriage has become a practical affair, you can begin to resent the fact that you are no longer independent. Unless you take full control of this Sagittarian characteristic, it can lead to a broken marriage. As a matter of fact, this particular zodiacal influence on the ascendant is found in many people who have married more than once.

Of course, it also can cause the other extreme where the person refuses to give up his or her freedom and does not marry at all. Naturally, where the success or failure of marriage is concerned, the influence of the sun, moon and planets must be considered. Certainly, not every person with Sagittarius on the ascendant is destined for a broken marriage but, nevertheless, it is an influence which needs careful handling.

You have a keen intelligence and a rather colourful, enthusiastic personality but you must watch the tendency to be over-optimistic and over-confident, especially in business and financial affairs where practical and realistic thinking is essential.

You are open and candid and, although sometimes abrupt in your manner as a result of the fiery, impulsive qualities of Sagittarius, you generally like people to act in a "proper" manner, since you usually behave according to the rules of etiquette. Sagittarius makes you generous, just and honest and you cannot tolerate people who are underhanded or deceive you in any way.

Just as the archer aims straight for his target, so you like to go straight to the point. You do not like to equivocate either in your methods or your manner of speech.

Because of the dual nature of Sagittarius you sometimes become edgy and irritable for no apparent reason. When this happens it is because the two opposing forces of the sign are coming into play at once, causing internal conflict.

You are an able manager and administrator of financial affairs and since you have a philosophical turn of mind you are likely, at some period of your life, to take an interest in religion, the law, any of the occult subjects such as astrology, the philosophies and so on.

Sciatica, rheumatic pains, liver troubles and varicose veins are some of the possible ailments associated with Sagittarius on the ascendant; other planetary factors will either modify or accentuate these tendencies. This sign also rules the hips and thighs so these areas could be affected by falls, cuts, bruises; your thighs may be longer or heavier than usual.

Blue is probably one of your favourite colours. You usually enjoy the company of other Sagittarians.

Capricorn on the ascendant

Capricorn gives you a great sense of purpose and much ambition to achieve something really lasting and worthwhile in life. You have two vital characteristics which are essential to success – self control and strength of will – and whatever you undertake you will do to the best of your ability.

Perseverance is a keyword of your nature, with the result that once you decide to reach a goal you will persist until you do so. It may take some time for you to decide just what you want to do in life but, once you reach a decision, your steadfast determination will help you to achieve almost anything you set your mind to.

You place much importance on the opinions which other people hold of you and you value their trust, confidence and respect. Yet, strangely, you do not take many people into your confidence. Where others are concerned you sometimes will slip into the habit of being suspicious of their motives and so you do not make many friends, preferring one or two trusted and loyal acquaintances to whom you always will be faithful.

You are not the type who lives just for the moment; you plan for the future, are economical and wherever possible, your financial affairs are organised to ensure comfort and security in both your prime of life and your later years.

Being influenced by Capricorn, you are neither flippant nor superficial but rather serious minded, patient, thrifty and stable. These are excellent qualities but be careful not to allow over-cautious attitudes to cramp initiative and so prevent you from taking a chance to expand.

Your rather reserved manner sometimes will be misconstrued as aloofness or snobbishness. The reason for this is that you have a keen sense of dignity and formality in that you make distinctions between people according to their rank and position in life and, unless you guard against it, you can be quite harsh towards people whom you regard as far beneath you. Not only are you impressed by people who have achieved recognition – you sometimes will deliberately say or do something to impress another person for the purpose of gaining respect.

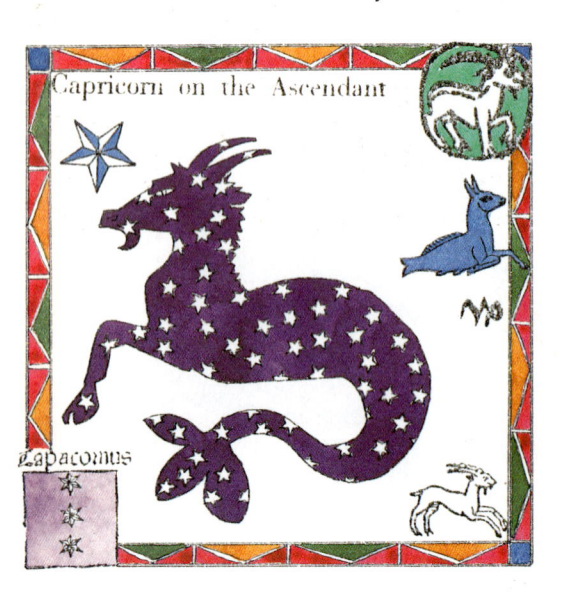

Your outlook is practical and down to earth and there is likely to be a lack of imagination and fun in your nature. Cultivate your sense of humour and do not allow Capricorn's over-serious and pessimistic outlook to overrule the joy of living.

You must learn to be more tolerant of other people whose ideas are not in line with your own. A little more sympathy and understanding may be needed and this will help to soften and broaden Capricorn's tendency to be narrow minded.

You have a disposition which ensures success in anything which requires discipline, both of yourself and of others – although your subordinates are more likely to respect you than to hold affection for you.

Ambition, executive ability and love of power are some of the basic qualities of your Capricornian temperament. Combine these qualities with your ability to work hard and long, your intensity and concentration, your careful planning and practical ideas and you have many of the basic ingredients for success. However, what you do with these ingredients will depend on all the other factors in your horoscope.

Capricorn rules the skeletal system, the skin and the knees. Typical Capricorns are often subject to rheumatic pains, broken bones, skin problems or a weakness in one or even both of the knee joints. You, too, could suffer these symptoms.

Dark colours appeal to you, particularly dark blue, navy or a bluish shade of violet. You get on well with Capricorns.

Aquarius on the ascendant

Aquarius is one of the great signs of the zodiac, containing as it does the seeds of a highly-evolved humanity. In its present stage of evolution, humanity is not able to respond to the full scale of influence hidden within Aquarius, so if discrepancies appear and you feel some of these characteristics do not seem to apply to you, it is because you are as yet unable to tune in to the heart of the sign.

Aquarius is the most humane of all the 12 zodiacal signs, with the result that you are a genial person, capable of complete sincerity of purpose and dedication to any particular person or cause. You are not an extremist but your understanding is so broad as to give you the necessary patience and kindness to tolerate other people's foibles and idiosyncrasies.

You have a straightforward temperament and disposition which is liked by most people. An easy and genuine friendliness comes naturally to you and your friendships are often long and many in number. Yet, strangely, no matter how well or how long a person has been associated with you, he or she never comes to know you completely. This stems from the complex and unfathomed depths which are latent in the grand sign of Aquarius. Of course, the average person does not realise this and interprets it simply as a pleasant aloofness in your nature. You give the impression of being slightly detached but manage to do this without appearing unfriendly or unsympathetic.

You have a strong will and definite opinions; you are not easily swayed by others and will keep to your own ideas with an unshakable determination.

Aquarius is one of the anchor points in the zodiac where things are kept under control, so there is normally a self-contained and tranquil serenity about you which helps you to cope with problems, tensions and other adverse circumstances. It also causes you to dislike having to rush around and you will never make snap decisions unless they are unavoidable. You dislike shoddiness and no matter what your interest you always will be prepared to spend sufficient time to gain a thorough comprehension of it. You have an inventive and somewhat scientific way of looking at things and, unless other factors in the horoscope nullify it, you have the ability to reason clearly and logically. Some of your ideas may be considered a little too radical but Aquarius is a progressive sign and you should not allow others to prevent you from capitalising on the opportunities which it presents.

While Aquarius makes you altruistic, to other people you often seem to be a contradiction because you are at once naturally friendly and a loner. There are times when you feel a misfit because in some ways you are ahead of your time.

You could suffer from sprained, weak or swollen ankles.

Shades of violet, purple, mauve, lilac and lavender are probably your favourite colours. People born under the sign of Aquarius will be among your companions.

Pisces on the ascendant

Few people can live up to the inherent possibilities and potentials of Pisces, one of the very complex signs of the zodiac. This influence causes a degree of self confusion and you find self mastery difficult to achieve. The dualistic nature of the sign pulls you in opposite directions with the result that you can be very undecided about what to do or what you really want. Also, this confusion sometimes makes you feel that things are all wrong but when you try to pinpoint exactly what is wrong it is difficult, since the confusion is psychological and intangible. This can cause a great deal of frustration in your life.

You are extremely sensitive and impressionable, with the result that you can sense an atmosphere when you walk into a room. The only trouble is that you readily pick up and absorb other people's influences, so it is important for you to associate with the right kinds of people, otherwise you could slip into the habit of doing as others do and thinking as others think, rather than being true to yourself.

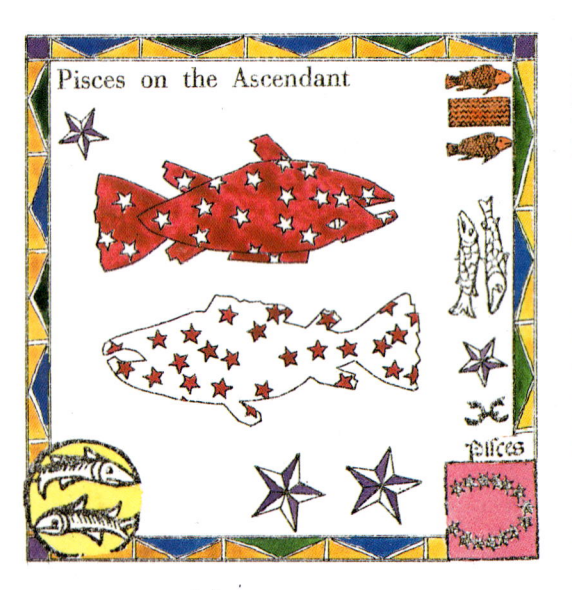

Pisces makes you very emotional and your feelings play a dominant role in your reactions, both to people and to situations. It also gives you an intuitive, even psychic, nature so you either like or dislike a person without having to reason out their good and bad points. Logical analysis and reasoning do not play a large part in your judgement – rather, you sense things.

You are extremely sympathetic and unlikely to do anything to harm others. However, you should realize that it is sometimes necessary to be cruel in order to be kind.

One of the keynotes of Pisces is completeness, which is another way of expressing perfection, and whenever you see a person in trouble or lacking happiness, health and so on, your desire to assist comes strongly to the fore. You sense their lack of completeness, their lack of perfection, and it is the nature of Pisces to supply these qualities. Your intentions are good but you are likely to be at a loss when it comes to the best way of giving practical assistance.

You have a strongly-developed imagination and are essentially an idealist, tending to escape from the sordid world of harsh reality into your private world of dreams. It is no wonder that many great poets, authors and musicians were born with Pisces on the ascendant.

You have some wonderful ideas and your imagination is always at work; however, ideas are useless unless they are put into practice. This is where the influence of Pisces can be a drawback because you lack self confidence and do not like to push yourself into the limelight. You become disheartened at the slightest rebuff and, unless you make a determined effort to overcome your timidity, you will miss out on the rewards which the realization of your ideas would bring you.

The whole nature of Pisces is receptive and negative; to counteract this you must train yourself to be more forceful, outgoing, practical and positive. Once you can do this you will have the best of both worlds: reality and romance.

You have a restless, changeable disposition, a longing for perfection; in short, you are a creature of many and varied moods. You dislike having to make important decisions and generally will ask another person what to do.

While other people are out enjoying sports or other busy activities, you prefer peace and quiet, harmony and leisure. Unless you guard against this tendency, it can develop into laziness and indifference. Water is likely to hold a special fascination for you, although other factors in the horoscope easily can modify or cancel out this affinity.

Any work or interest which allows you plenty of freedom to use your imagination will be in harmony with your natural disposition.

Because Pisces rules the feet, you could have problems associated with them, such as corns, bunions, fallen arches and sore, cold, aching or swollen feet.

Shadowy, translucent and deep, mysterious colours appeal to you. You will feel empathy towards people born under the sign of Pisces.

Latitudes of some major cities and towns

A
Acapulco, Mexico 17N
Adelaide, SA 35S
Albury, NSW 36S
Alexandria, Egypt 31N
Algiers, Algeria 37N
Alice Springs, NT 24S
Amsterdam, Holland 52N
Ankara, Turkey 40N
Antwerp, Belgium 51N
Armidale, NSW 31S
Athens, Greece 38N
Atherton, Qld 17S
Auckland, NZ 37S

B
Bairnsdale, Victoria 38S
Ballarat, Victoria 38S
Bangkok, Thailand 14N
Barcelona, Spain 41N
Bathurst, NSW 33S
Bega, NSW 37S
Belfast,
    Northern Ireland 55N
Belgrade, Yugoslavia 45N
Bendigo, Victoria 37S
Berlin, Germany 53N
Birmingham, England ... 52N
Blaxland, NSW 34S
Bombay, India 19N
Boston, USA 42N
Bourke, NSW 30S
Bowen, Qld 20S
Brisbane, Qld 27S
Broken Hill, NSW 32S
Brussels, Belgium 51N
Bucharest, Romania 44N
Budapest, Hungary 47N
Buenos Aires, Argentina 35S
Byron Bay, NSW 29S

C, D, E
Cairns, Qld 17S
Cairo, Egypt 30N
Calcutta, India 22N
Canberra, ACT 35S
Cape Town,
    South Africa 34S
Casino, NSW 29S
Charters Towers, Qld 20S
Chicago, USA 42N
Christchurch, NZ 44S
Cloncurry, Qld 21S
Coffs Harbour, NSW 30S
Colombo, Sri Lanka 7N
Copenhagen, Denmark .. 56N
Cooktown, Qld 15S
Cowra, NSW 34S
Darwin, NT 12S
Derby, WA 17S
Dresden, Germany 51N
Dubbo, NSW 32S
Dublin, Eire 53N
Eden NSW 37S
Edinburgh, Scotland 56N
Esperance, WA 34S

F, G, H
Florence, Italy 44N
Forbes, NSW 33S
Geelong, Vic 38S
Geneva, Switzerland 46N
Genoa, Italy 44N
Geraldton, WA 29S
Glasgow, Scotland 56N
Glen Innes, NSW 30S
Gosford, NSW 33S
Goteborg, Sweden 58N
Goulburn, NSW 35S
Grafton, NSW 30S
Gundagai, NSW 35S
Gunnedah, NSW 31S
Gympie, Qld 26S
Hamburg, Germany 54N
Hamilton, NZ 38S
Hanover, Germany 52N
Hastings, England 51N
Hastings, NZ 40S
Havana, Cuba 23N
Hay, NSW 34S
Helsinki, Finland 60N
Hobart, Tas 43S
Hong Kong 22N
Honolulu, Hawaii 21N

I
Innisfail, Qld 18S
Inverell, NSW 30S
Ipswich, Qld 28S
Istanbul, Turkey 41N
Ivanhoe, NSW 33S
Jerusalem, Israel 32N
Johannesburg,
    South Africa 26S
Kalgoorlie, WA 31S
Karachi, Pakistan 25N
Katoomba, NSW 34S
Kempsey, NSW 31S
Krakow, Poland 50N

L
Latrobe, Tas 41S
Launceston, Tas 41S
Lawson, NSW 34S
Leeds, England 54N
Leicester, England 53N
Leipzig, Germany 51N
Leningrad, Russia 60N
Leonora, WA 29S
Lima, Peru 12S
Lisbon, Portugal 39N
Lismore, NSW 29S
Lithgow, NSW 33S
Liverpool, England 53N
Lord Howe Island 32S
London, England 52N
Longreach, Qld 23S
Los Angeles, USA 34N

Lucerne, Switzerland 47N

M
Mackay, Qld 21S
Madras, India 13N
Madrid, Spain 40N
Maitland, NSW 33S
Manchester, England 53N
Marble Bar, WA 21S
Maryborough, Qld 26S
Melbourne, Vic 38S
Mexico City, Mexico 19N
Michigan, USA 42N
Milan, Italy 45N
Mildura, Vic 34S
Montreal, Canada 46N
Moree, NSW 29S
Moscow, Russia 56N
Mount Isa, Qld 21S
Munich, Germany 48N

N
Napier, NZ 39S
Naples, Italy 41N
Narrabri, NSW 35S
Narromine, NSW 32S
Nelson, NZ 41S
Newcastle, NSW 33S
New Delhi, India 28N
New Orleans, USA 30N
New Plymouth, NZ 39S
New York, USA 41N
Norfolk Island, ... 29S
Nottingham, England ... 53N
Nowra, NSW 35S
Nyngan, NSW 32S
Oodnadatta, SA 28S
Orange, NSW 33S
Orbost, Vic 38S
Oslo, Norway 60N
Ottawa, Canada 45N

P, Q
Palermo, Italy 38N
Palmerston North, NZ ... 45S
Paris, France 49N
Parkes, NSW 33S
Peak Hill, NSW 33S
Peking, China 40N
Penrith, NSW 34S
Perth, WA 32S
Philadelphia, USA 40N
Port Macquarie, NSW ... 31S
Port Moresby, PNG 9S
Port Pirie, SA 33S
Proserpine, Qld 20S
Queanbeyan, NSW 35S
Quebec, Canada 47N
Queenstown, NZ 45S

R, S
Rangoon,
    Myanmar (Burma) ... 17N
Ravensthorpe, WA 34S

Reggio Calabria, Italy ... 38N
Renmark, SA 34S
Rio de Janeiro, Brazil 23S
Rochester, England 51N
Rockhampton, Qld 23S
Rome, Italy 42N
Rotterdam, Holland 52N
San Francisco, USA 38N
Santa Cruz, Bolivia 18S
Sao Paulo, Brazil 24S
Seymour, Vic 37S
Shepparton, Vic 36S
Singleton, NSW 33S
Sofia, Bulgaria 43N
Springwood, NSW 34S
Stockholm, Sweden 59N
Stuttgart, Germany 49N
Swan Hill, Vic 35S
Sydney, NSW 34S

T
Taiping, China 23N
Tamworth, NSW 31S
Taree, NSW 32S
Tel Aviv, Israel 32N
Tennant Creek, NT 20S
The Hague, Holland 52N
Thredbo, NSW 36S
Tokyo, Japan 36N
Toowoomba, Qld 28S
Turin, Italy 45N
Townsville, Qld 19S
Trento, Italy 46N
Trieste, Italy 46N
Tripoli, Lebanon 34N
Tripoli, Libya 33N
Tunis, Tunisia 37N
Tumut, NSW 35S
Tweed Heads, NSW 28S

U, V, W, Y, Z
Ulladulla, NSW 35S
Utrecht, Holland 52N
Valencia, Spain 39N
Valletta, Malta 36N
Vancouver, Canada 49N
Venice, Italy 45N
Ventspils, Latvia 57N
Vienna, Austria 48N
Vladivostok, Russia 43N
Wagga Wagga, NSW 35S
Walgett, NSW 30S
Wangaratta, Vic 36S
Warrnambool, Vic 38S
Warsaw, Poland 52N
Washington DC, USA 39N
Wellington, NZ 41S
Wollongong, NSW 34S
Yallourn, Vic 38S
Yass, NSW 35S
Young, NSW 34S
Zagreb, Yugoslavia 46N
Zeehan, Tas 42S
Zurich, Switzerland 47N

Starring Partners

The mysteries of compatibility have intrigued mankind for ages, and yet astrology, the oldest science known, can supply many answers to the puzzle. When two people come together, inevitable questions arise – will it last, will we always be together, will we drive each other mad if we live in the same house? There are no definitive answers, but the stars do offer some pointers on partnership in all its shapes and forms.

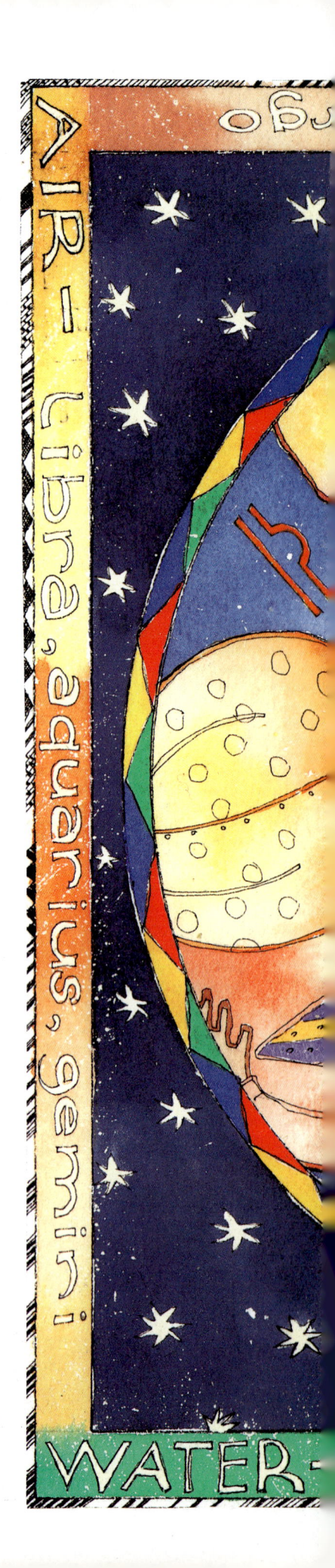

EARTH – Capricorn, Taurus, Virgo

FIRE – aries, leo, sagittarius

Cancer, Scorpio, Pisces

Before considering the potential for compatibility between the 12 sun signs it is important to know about your circadian rhythms. These will be of little significance in your relationship with friends, neighbours, relatives or business associates, but they will play a vital role in intimate unions, such as lovers or marriage partners. It is now well researched and documented that circadian rhythms can and will affect close relationships. In simple terms, these rhythms define your inbuilt biological clocks.

Some people like to get up early in the morning because their peak of energy and efficiency occurs during the first half of the day; they like to go to bed early; they can be described as "morning people". On the other side of the coin there are the "night people" who stay up late, do their best work at night and who hate to get up early.

Two people who live together as lovers or marriage partners will have a much happier relationship if they are both "night people" or "morning people". If your star signs are a perfect match but one is a "morning person" and the other is a "night person", be warned, it will not be plain sailing! It's an excellent idea to check these instinctive preferences before you become involved.

Undoubtedly, there is "chemistry" when two people meet – intuitive feeling or a physical response which either attracts or repels. Sometimes, you will feel an instant rapport with one person at first meeting and, for no apparent reason, others will turn you off.

No star sign horoscope is complete without the equally important information gleaned from the positions of the moon, the planets and the ascendant sign; this complete picture can only be gained by having an astrologer chart your individual horoscope. However an analysis of the star signs of two people can reveal much about how they will interact.

Before analysing the 78 possible combinations of the 12 star signs, let us look at some of the fundamental characteristics of each sign because they will play a significant role in determining compatibility when two people share a friendship, a business partnership, a family link, a marriage or a love affair. Also check what the ancient Chinese have to say about the compatibility or otherwise between the 12 animals in the Oriental Astrology chapter.

If you find that your star sign, your Chinese animal and your circadian rhythm is in tune with a friend, business partner, neighbour, relative, lover or marriage mate, you can be sure that you have someone special in your life.

Aries

If I had to choose two words to describe the driving force of Aries, they would be: "I begin". Far more than anything else, you get a kick out of starting new ventures or trying new ideas on for size. When you become excited about a project you just cannot wait to get cracking; it has to be done immediately or you lose interest.

Aries is a good and happy leader because you can inspire interest and enthusiasm in others. However, if you have to be a follower for long periods, you can become discontented and down in the dumps.

Basically, you are quick and decisive in your actions and thinking. If prolonged hindrances cross your path, you can become impatient, even aggressive.

You can and do get things done quickly and efficiently. But you cannot tolerate people who dither. Unsolicited advice is not appreciated because you are independent, with a fiery, untamable spirit. Although you can organise others, you dislike other people organising you. You are frank, loyal and straightforward. Your keyword is action. Give you a challenge and a bit of combat – verbal, commercial or emotional – and you will sparkle as long as there is something or someone to conquer.

Taurus

Taureans place great importance on physical, financial and emotional security. You derive much pleasure and satisfaction from your possessions.

Taurus is famous for its solid, steadfast, reliable, practical qualities. To a greater or lesser degree you will have these characteristics and you also will look for them in others and in the things you buy. You generally are conservative, preferring fact and reality to fantasy. Taurus is a doer, not a dreamer, and you will look at what ever you do from a practical and realistic point of view. You usually take your time to make a decision, but once your plans are made you will be persistent and determined. Your stubbornness can be infuriating to more flexible people!

Taureans can have fixed ideas and when this is combined with your rather conservative, materialistic outlook it is not difficult to see how you can restrict yourself. Conservatism is fine as long as it does not squash initiative or deny you the right to take a chance.

> *"Aries is a good and happy leader because you can inspire interest and enthusiasm in others."*

You are kind, affectionate, seldom moody and not easily offended. But you fail to understand temperamental, volatile, unpredictable people. You like to feel settled and secure.

Gemini

Gemini people are like the bubbles in champagne – without them life would be flat and dull, but like the sparkling fizziness they are here one minute and gone the next.

You are highly strung, restless, excitable, a lover of change and variety and sometimes quite scatterbrained. You have a keen, versatile mind and like to dabble in a variety of interests. You may not be such a profound thinker but you certainly are clever and capable. "You have your wits about you" must surely have been written about a Gemini. Your ruling planet Mercury is the symbol of communication, so you are at your best when you can share interesting ideas and discussions.

Where love is concerned you are more likely to be lightheartedly affectionate than deeply emotional and intensely passionate. You like to share your affection with many people.

You are adaptable and find little difficulty in adjusting to variety and changes of scene – in fact, you somehow thrive on such things. Because of this constant desire to change it will be unusual if you go through life without changing your business, career or profession at least once – probably more often. Your dexterous hands and versatile mind are your greatest assets. Make the most of them.

Cancer

Cancer gives you a sensitive, impressionable nature which means that you feel things strongly. This is particularly true where your family or a loved one is concerned and you can worry yourself sick when pettiness or disputes upset harmony in the home. A house is not enough for you until you make it into a home which says welcome. You will sacrifice your own interests for the sake of your family.

You are a born worrier and in this sense you are your own worst enemy. When someone says or does some little thing which hurts you, you will brood about it for hours. You are hypersensitive when it comes to little slights, hurts or insinuations.

Where love is concerned you are very romantic and sentimental. You store memories and never forget many of those little things which happened long ago.

You are naturally timid, perhaps shy, but patience and tenacity are two of your strong points, so that once you decide on a goal you can show remarkable persistence. You sense how other people feel, and if they are in trouble you are quick to give sympathy. You have a strong instinctive urge to protect the ones you love, but when things go wrong in relationships you become moody or over emotional. You often are guided more by your feelings than you are by facts.

Leo

Under normal conditions Leo people will think big and act big. You cannot tolerate pettiness of any type and you cannot be bothered with the small details of any activity or undertaking. This is because you have breadth of vision and comprehend the overall picture. Fussiness irritates you!

Your obvious qualities are your air of authority, desire to organise and control a situation and inborn leadership skills. You inspire confidence and respect in others because they sense your strength of purpose and tremendous capacity for achievement.

You are warm hearted and generous, always willing to help others less fortunate than you. You often will do a good turn to attract the admiration and affection which you need so much. In some cases, if this is not forthcoming, Leo people can resort to boasting or showing off – pushing themselves forward to be noticed. You are not happy in a subordinate position for long; whatever your sphere, you don't fancy second place.

You are loyal, sincere and frankly honest, but others will often hurt or try to take advantage of you. You love beauty and splendour and have a marvellous sense of presentation, preferring to entertain lavishly.

Virgo

A true Virgo person will be analytical, practical, methodical and critical, possessing a shrewd, keen mind with an instinctive ability and desire to discriminate. Neatness and attention to detail make you a perfectionist. If these characteristics are carried to excess, however, you can become an exaggerated fusspot.

You base your actions on sound, practical commonsense and so your life usually is

Cancer: "Where love is concerned you are very romantic and sentimental. You store memories and never forget many of those little things..."

well planned and pigeonholed. When these characteristics are combined with a natural reserve and tendency to be critical of failings in others, it is not surprising that marriage can prove a problem unless you choose a partner whose characteristics and outlook on life are in harmony with your own.

You are modest, retiring and not inclined to seek the limelight if it brings you into close contact with too many people. Health and hygiene are very important to you, so your home and office will be scrupulously clean. You don't understand real passion, and violent emotions may either upset or even possibly revolt you. Fair criticism of others is fine, but do not allow constant fault-finding or nagging to spoil your associations.

Libra

You need peace and harmony in your surroundings and personal relationships; disputes and conflicts upset you. Libra seeks fulfillment through union and partnership. This not only includes marriage but can apply to friendship or business associations. You constantly think in terms of the other person because the keynote of Libra is relating to others.

Your instinct is to compare, so you constantly weigh up the pros and cons of situations. You usually can see both sides. Because you like to judge things from all angles you can be hesitant about a conclusion. Tact and diplomacy are strong points, endowing you with the qualities of a born strategist who can manage to achieve objectives subtly and unobtrusively.

Venus, your ruler, gives you a love of colour, beauty, art, music and luxury. Librans generally are easy to get along with. You hate to hurt people's feelings, and since "peace at any price" is your motto, you often have trouble saying no.

Nothing gives you more pleasure than sharing something beautiful with someone you love. Life is not the same for you if you are alone.

Scorpio

Scorpio has tremendous drive, determination and intensity in every aspect of life, whether work, play or love. You are never satisfied with half measures because, for Scorpio, it is "all or nothing". You possess an intense, concentrated outlook on life and a high degree of physical magnetism. You can exercise a peculiar fascination over other people who happen to tune in to your wavelength.

Where love life is concerned, emotional intensity, passion and desire are definite qualities. The urge to possess your partner, body and soul, also will be strong. Unless you choose the right person to complement your nature you can suffer agonies of jealousy, frustration and unhappiness.

Your assets are power, purpose, penetrative insight, shrewd judgement and fierce determination. But this zeal and intensity can take you up or down, depending on how you use it. You demand much of yourself and expect the same from others but you should remember that they may not always have it to give.

Scorpio may bring an unconscious desire for destruction – perhaps even self-destructive tendencies. Sometimes you try to punish yourself by martyrdom in extremely harsh and difficult circumstances.

You enjoy research because superficial knowledge does not give you satisfaction. You want all the facts.

Sagittarius

Sagittarius is the sign of expansion and this plays a dominant role in all aspects of your life. Consequently, you cannot tolerate any restriction or limitation because you need plenty of freedom and independence to be genuinely happy.

Where marriage is concerned, this desire for freedom can create a problem unless you accept the marriage ties without irritation. With the right partner all will be well, but troubles arise with someone who is too possessive, jealous or suspicious.

You are basically a happy, optimistic person with a cheerful and hopeful outlook on life at large. You can be frank and outspoken because you are honest and straight to the point. Consequently, you often put your foot in it.

Sagittarius is an enthusiastic sign and you can bubble with enjoyment when your spirits are high. Exaggeration in speech, action or behaviour can be a failing, however.

You enjoy natural interests and pleasures in preference to the tinsel and glitter of sophisticated society. Outdoors and open spaces appeal more than high-density areas. You love to take a chance because you have a resilient confidence in what the future holds.

"Scorpio has tremendous drive, determination and intensity in every aspect of life, whether work, play or love."

Capricorn

Capricorn is related to the most elevated point in the heavens. Consequently, it symbolises the highest peak of achievement to which one can aspire. Onward and upward in a practical sense is your aim, and in striving to achieve your goals you become the organiser and manipulator of people and circumstances.

You will use your environment, opportunities and even the people around you as stepping stones. Unfortunately, this can lead to ruthlessness and selfishness. Personal prestige, social status and position in life are very important to you. There is a tendency to be cautious and conservative and you are inclined to overemphasise economy and self-discipline, responsibility, respectability and the deadly serious business of just living. Unless you offset these characteristics with a little sparkle, spontaneous fun and gaiety, you can miss out on happiness and severely limit your self-expression.

Thoroughness in the things that matter is the hallmark of Capricorn. You are unwilling to take big risks on the spur of the moment because you are very deliberate, always preferring to look before you leap.

Your emotional and romantic self-expression is often stifled by your practical commonsense and reason.

Your main assets are prudence, maturity, dedication, tenacity and thoroughness. Your faults are general lack of sentiment, pessimism, apprehension and selfishness.

Capricorn: "...in striving to achieve your goals you become the organiser and manipulator of people and circumstances."

Aquarius

Aquarius is one of the most enigmatic signs of the zodiac; it can be difficult for people born in other signs to understand your outlook and motives.

Aquarius has a detached, elusive quality which other people can never pin down. You can be friendly and remote at the same time. Close, fussy, personal relationships may bother you because Aquarius is the sign of the humanitarian, giving you the nature of a universal lover rather than a personal lover.

You can be temperamental when people or circumstances come into conflict with your ideas. You can be tenacious when you decide on something and consider carefully and deliberately anything you do. But the unpredictable quality of Uranus (your ruling planet) pops up unexpectedly and precipitates a sudden change which surprises you and others in your orbit.

Aquarius is the sign of the reformer and this means that you are interested in new ideas, originality, shortcuts and unorthodox trends. Involvement with a group, organization or cause gives you more satisfaction than functioning within the confines of a personal relationship. Your ideals find expression through friendship and humanity. You also need independence and the freedom to withdraw from the restricting demands of one particular close, intimate association.

Pisces

Pisces makes you very sensitive and also impressionable to outside influences. Your actions and decisions are motivated more by feelings, emotions, impressions and intuition than by cold, hard facts and logical analysis. There are both advantages and disadvantages in being so sensitive. On one hand it gives you hunches and intuitive knowledge about people and situations – in fact, some Pisceans have a keenly developed psychic ability and sixth sense.

The drawback is that you are made vulnerable to every influence in the environment. Your whole being is receptive to changes of atmosphere. Consequently, undesirable associations can have an adverse effect.

Pisces is the most flexible sign of all, making you very adaptable. You can adjust to changes without great difficulty because you are especially changeable. You are sentimental, romantic and easily give way to worry and fretting. You have loads of sympathy and compassion for people in trouble but you flounder when it comes to positive action.

Some of the weaknesses of Pisces are a timid, self-effacing attitude and a tendency to apologise or constantly make excuses. You also can become too dependent on others. Indecision is a Piscean failing; you put things off or miss opportunities. How often have you missed the bus?

You are a born idealist, with a vivid imagination, so you often have your head in the clouds. Being so sensitive you are likely to find it difficult to cope with the harsh realities of this materialistic world, with its fierce competition, tensions and struggle to survive.

12 signs and 4 elements

The ancients divided the 12 signs of the zodiac into four groups corresponding with the four elements: fire, earth, air and water, in that order. The rapport between any two people *partly* depends on the way in which their ruling elements interact.

However, when checking out my interpretation of the various combinations of signs and elements, remember that there is no infallible rule when these principles are applied in such a general way to the abbreviated star sign horoscope.

It is important to know to which of the elements your star sign belongs and how it interacts with the others.

The **zodiac chart** pictured at right clearly illustrates the layout of the 12 elements.

Fire signs

Air is compatible with fire and with air except in the case of the opposite pairs which you can easily locate in the zodiac chart. These are Aries – Libra, Leo – Aquarius, Sagittarius – Gemini. There can be a strong initial attraction between opposite signs, but after a while the pendulum can swing the other way and friction may result. Fire does not easily combine with water nor with earth.

Air signs

Air is compatible with air and with fire, although initial affinity between the opposite pairs Gemini – Sagittarius, Libra – Aries, Aquarius – Leo, can sometimes revert to conflict later on. Air does not have much in common with water nor with earth.

Water signs

Water is compatible with water and with earth except in some cases when the pairs of signs are on opposite sides of the zodiac chart. These are Cancer – Capricorn, Scorpio – Taurus, Pisces – Virgo. Water has little affinity with fire or air.

Earth signs

Earth is compatible with earth and with water, although some conflict may develop with a water sign if it is opposite your earth sign on the zodiac chart. These pairs are Capricorn – Cancer, Taurus – Scorpio, Virgo – Pisces. Earth does not easily combine with fire nor with air.

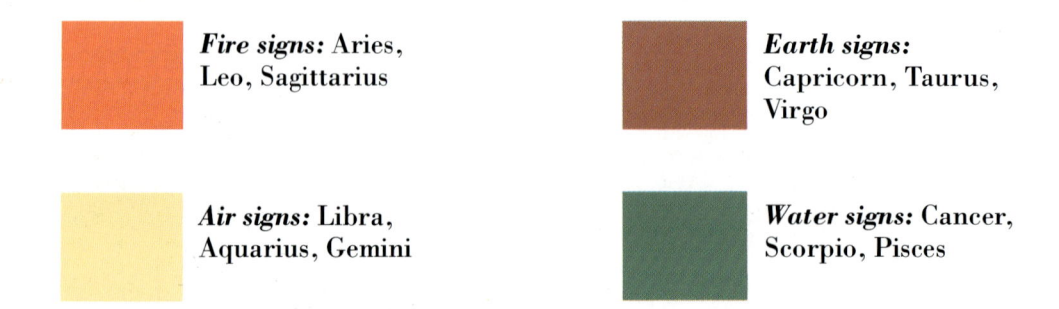

Fire signs: Aries, Leo, Sagittarius

Earth signs: Capricorn, Taurus, Virgo

Air signs: Libra, Aquarius, Gemini

Water signs: Cancer, Scorpio, Pisces

The Zodiac Chart

31

" Aries cannot be bothered with all methods, fuss and attention to detail which comes so naturally to a thorough Virgo..."

For People Born on The Cusp

This term applies to people born during the first three days and the last three days of any particular sign, in which case you have a much more complex nature because you come under the influence of two adjoining signs and their corresponding elements. Therefore, your compatibility ratings cover a wider range of possibilities because you will be a mixture of either water plus fire, fire plus earth, earth plus air or air plus water.

Here is the complete list of on the cusp birthdays:

★ *March 18 to 23 combines Pisces – Aries, water plus fire.*

★ *April 18 to 23 combines Aries – Taurus, fire plus earth.*

★ *May 19 to 24 combines Taurus – Gemini, earth plus air.*

★ *June 19 to 24 combines Gemini – Cancer, air plus water.*

★ *July 20 to 25 combines Cancer – Leo, water plus fire.*

★ *August 21 to 26 combines Leo – Virgo, fire plus earth.*

★ *September 21 to 26 combines Virgo – Libra, earth plus air.*

★ *October 21 to 26 combines Libra – Scorpio, air plus water.*

★ *November 20 to 25 combines Scorpio – Sagittarius, water plus fire.*

★ *December 19 to 24 combines Sagittarius – Capricorn, fire plus earth.*

★ *January 18 to 23 combines Capricorn – Aquarius, earth plus air.*

★ *February 17 to 22 combines Aquarius – Pisces, air plus water.*

Now let us see how the star signs and their elements will combine when people come together in human relationships.

The following reactions will not be obvious in passing acquaintances because it takes time for two people to get to know one another. However, you will be able to see how the chemistry of the zodiac affects marriage, friendships, love affairs, family relationships and business partnerships. All possible combinations of the 12 signs of the zodiac are listed, giving a total of 78 pairs.

Aries with Aries

Fire with fire is a compatible combination, although it produces a volatile, dynamic, exciting and sometimes stressful atmosphere. Peace, quiet, serenity and relaxation will be difficult to achieve. If both people try to rule the roost or compete with one another, flare-ups, disputes and tension will occur. When necessary, each will defend the other. Your arch enemy – boredom – will seldom arise in this duo because you both like to be active.

Aries with Taurus

Fire with earth is not an easy combination, and since the needs, natures, likes and dislikes of these two signs are so very different there will be difficulties unless a compromise is reached. Aries needs the stimulus of new enterprises or challenges, whereas Taurus prefers quiet stability. Aries becomes irritated or impatient with the Taurean's slowness, stubbornness and stay-put attitude.

Aries with Gemini

Fire with air is a very agreeable combination, and since you both generate a busy, lively atmosphere, life is not boring. Gemini's wits can match the Aries fighting spirit. Both enjoy variety, action, discovering, doing new things – a happy relationship if you share your interests.

Aries with Cancer

Fire with water can create problems unless you search for a common ground on which to meet. Cancer is very sensitive so is often hurt by Aries frank, abrupt or even abrasive ways. Aries does not appreciate Cancer's sentimentality and emotional moods.

Aries with Leo

Fire with fire is a very positive combination, and providing both people do not try to be the boss this can be a stimulating duo.

Leo can appreciate the Aries drive and initiative, while Aries is not overwhelmed by the big ideas, power and largess of Leo. Both signs are outgoing, extroverted, warm, zealous and vibrant.

Aries with Virgo

Fire is volatile and impetuous, whereas earth is practical, stable and self-controlled, so there is a great contrast of temperaments here.

Aries cannot be bothered with all the method, fuss and attention to detail which comes so naturally to thorough Virgo, although Aries appreciates the end results. Widely different emotional natures, so a good mental affinity will be necessary.

Aries with Libra

Fire has a natural affinity with air, but since these signs are opposite each other in the zodiac they can attract but also repel, so a variable association likely. If conflicts arise Aries triumphs while Libra gets upset or leaves. Initially, there is often a strong physical or emotional attraction between these two.

Aries with Scorpio

Fire with water creates a highly charged association to say the least, but since Mars rules both signs there can be mutual appreciation of the other's strength and capability or, alternatively, fierce competition.

Forthright Aries does not suspect the devious, secretive ways of Scorpio. Excellent for teamwork if goals agree but both will demand much of each other.

Aries with Sagittarius

Fire does not conflict with fire, but because you are both highly independent you must allow each other the freedom to come and go and be yourselves. Sagittarius encourages enthusiastic, active Aries who appreciates the former's optimistic outlook and frank honesty.

A fast tempo combination so not much peace, quiet or relaxation in this union. Neither will tolerate the other being bossy.

Aries with Capricorn

This combination of fire with earth can be a stressful one, especially since Aries' ruling planet Mars is impatient and fiery whereas Capricorn's ruler Saturn is cautious, sombre, slow and deliberate. Capricorn likes to plan ahead and can play a waiting game, but Aries acts now and hates to wait. Unless both people are willing to exercise tolerance, your extremely different viewpoints can bring tension or even bitterness. Capricorn often unwittingly squashes Aries.

Aries with Aquarius

Fire is compatible with air, but the interaction of your ruling planets, Mars for Aries and Uranus for Aquarius, can generate tremendous power, so much will depend on whether it is used constructively or not. Aquarius will not dampen the initiative and independence of Aries, while the latter appreciates a friend in Aquarius. Aries loves anything new so is interested in the Aquarian's off-beat ways, but if Aquarius turns unpredictable at an inopportune moment, Aries becomes irritated and impatient.

Aries with Pisces

Your ruling planets, fiery Mars and watery Neptune, are entirely different in nature, so if you are true to your sign type you are worlds apart and it will be difficult to find common ground.

Positive, active Aries cannot fathom the nebulous, mysterious substance of Pisces who often irritates Aries by appearing to be negative or indecisive.

Taurus with Taurus

Earth with earth produces a very stable, conservative, down-to-earth association and your relationship has enduring qualities because you both have a desire to maintain the status quo.

Naturally, this can lead to some degree of being "in a rut" or following a lifestyle which appears stodgy to more adventurous types. When provoked, both can be jealous and possessive. Because both people have a cautious, security-conscious outlook, this team lacks dynamic initiative.

Taurus with Gemini

Taurus is the most earthy sign of all, while airy Gemini is extremely restless, volatile and changeable, so your basic needs and motives are worlds apart. Gemini's love of constant change and variety can be unsettling for Taurus who likes to stay put.

It will be "mission impossible" if Taurus should ever try to possess Gemini.

Taurus with Cancer

There is a natural affinity between earth and water, so you will have much in common. Feelings, emotions and affections are of paramount importance to both signs and Taurus appreciates the attention and protection which Cancer enjoys giving.

You are both basically conservative and conventional so conflicts are unlikely to be caused by radical extremism or widely divergent interests. Commonsense plus logical discussions are the best antidotes when over-emotionalism develops.

Taurus with Leo

Earth with fire in two such strong-willed signs can cause conflict and opposition unless you both learn to compromise and practice some give and take. Leo thrives on the attention and affection which Taurus can so naturally give. The latter is often willing to tolerate being dominated by Leo until one day Taurus revolts! Leo's big ideas can be very disturbing to conservative Taurus.

Taurus with Virgo

Earth with earth means that you can see eye to eye in many ways and you are both practical, realistic, capable and thorough in the things you do. However, your emotional natures are very dissimilar. Taurus, being deeply emotional and possessive, can sometimes smother Virgo whose feelings are more under control.

Your down-to earth goals will have much in common because you both desire material success and security.

Taurus with Libra

Although there is little affinity between earth and air, Venus creates a strong link because it rules both signs. Your bond depends on feelings, affection or the mutual appreciation of beauty and the finer things of life. Because peace and harmony are very important to both signs, neither one is likely to provoke conflict in the relationship. Diplomatic Libra can tactfully manipulate stubborn Taurus. You both need your pleasures and little luxuries so more than a shoe-string budget will be necessary.

Taurus with Scorpio

Although earth is compatible with water, these are opposite signs in the zodiac. In love relationships this factor often brings irresistible physical attraction initially but, when this diminishes, the pendulum can swing the other way unless you have other things in common. Both are jealous and possessive, so mutual trust is essential. Such intense feelings can sometimes bring a love-hate relationship.

Taurus with Sagittarius

This combination of earth and fire is as different as chalk and cheese. Taurus is one of the most stable, down-to-earth signs and you only feel safe and secure when life is settled. Your strong desire to stay put and possess your loved one will often be at odds with the Sagittarian need to feel free and independent. This fire sign is restless, enjoys change, likes distant horizons, far away places and needs plenty of room to move around both mentally and physically. Too much of this will be very unsettling for Taurus.

Sagittarius takes a wide-angled view of life so could find Taurus too restricting. True love can transcend all these differences.

Taurus with Capricorn

This combination of earth with earth is compatible because security-conscious Taurus will appreciate Capricorn's practical, basic attitudes, perseverance, realistic approach and ambition to achieve success. Both are conservative, down-to-earth, patient and willing to share responsibility.

Neither one places any real importance on superficial pleasures, so life could be too serious at times unless you deliberately add some light-hearted fun.

Taurus with Aquarius

There is little in common between earth and air in this combination of two very determined signs which are basically worlds apart in nature and in needs. Taurus will not understand the Aquarian's unpredictability which pops up for no apparent reason. When Aquarius wants to be free and aloof he/she finds Taurus too possessive. One or the other has to give in, but who? Aquarius has a natural desire to share affection with many people but Taurus is much more exclusive where feelings are concerned.

Taurus with Pisces

This combination of earth and water is very compatible because your ruling planets, Venus and Neptune, do not clash. Lots of friendship, affection or love can be shared and you both appreciate beauty, artistry, pleasures and the good things in life. Each can help to balance the other because Taurus is down-to-earth, whereas Pisces is often up in the clouds. The realist complements the dreamer. When problems arise, clear thinking is clouded by too much emotion.

Gemini with Gemini

This double dose of such a highly strung, restless air sign ensures that life will never be dull or dreary but depending on what each person is like the relationship can be either lively, excitable, scatterbrained, gossipy, intellectually stimulating, multi-purpose and full of change, variety, interest or nervous tension. Who is going to pay the phone bill?

Gemini with Cancer

The air sign Gemini is mentally orientated, whereas the water element of Cancer emphasises the emotions, so there is a marked contrast in your natures. All that variety which is the spice of life to Gemini can make Cancer feel unsettled or uneasy. Cancer's sentimentality and over-emotionalism will not evoke a deep response in Gemini, who in turn never has time to fathom Cancer's moodiness. Gemini is busy doing so many things that Cancer will sometimes feel neglected.

Gemini with Leo

Air with fire will help to maintain interest between these two signs, particularly on a mental or intellectual level. Leo likes to be the centre of attention but you will often feel neglected when Gemini becomes absorbed in those many interests or activities. Leo's "think big, act big, grand scale" modus operandi appeals to Gemini's mind. Leo's desire to be the boss and take control can sometimes be too overpowering for Gemini's free spirit. If each person is happy to allow the other to do his/her own thing this can be a sparkling combination.

Gemini with Virgo

Although air has little affinity with earth, Mercury rules both signs and this can act as a stimulating catalyst. Neither one is over-emotional so your common ground will include practical, social, mental or business interests. Realistic, systematic Virgo will not always go along with Gemini's multitude of plans or scatterbrained ideas. Although variety is the spice of life to Gemini, Virgo is more concentrated and one-pointed.

Gemini with Libra

Air with air is compatible in this combination which blends Mercury, the planet of the mind, with Venus, the symbol of love and emotion thus creating a mutual appreciation of all that is refined, artistic, beautiful, sociable, interesting, informative. Gemini likes to communicate so is happy to share ideas with Libra, who in turn is not fulfilled nor complete when alone.

Gemini with Scorpio

Air and water will not be easy to mix in this combination of signs which are as different as black and white. The deep emotional intensity of Scorpio is lacking in Gemini who will be overwhelmed by it. Gemini's free spirit will feel stifled if Scorpio becomes jealous and possessive.

Gemini with Sagittarius

Air with fire is a stimulating combination but since these are opposite signs in the zodiac they can not only attract but also repel one another. Gemini is self-contained enough to allow Sagittarius his/her beloved freedom and independence. Both are naturally busy, active people who like to fill their lives with interest, so a mutual exchange comes easily.

Gemini with Capricorn

Although air and earth are very different, the young at heart spirit of Gemini can complement the wisdom and experience of Capricorn, providing both are willing to communicate. Sometimes you will have to agree to disagree because Gemini often changes direction, whereas Capricorn will pursue a goal to its conclusion. Capricorn who is steady and controlled does not always understand the highly strung, quicksilver ways of Gemini. Although very different, each can enrich the other with their unique gifts.

Gemini with Aquarius

Air with air is compatible but your ruling planets Mercury and Uranus give very different natures and viewpoints. Gemini can accept it when Aquarius goes into a detached or unpredictable mood. Gemini is mentally stimulated by the Aquarian's originality, inventiveness or way-out ideas. The unconventional, changeable quality of this relationship keeps it interesting.

Gemini with Pisces

The marked contrast between air and water is clearly illustrated here. Gemini is logical, factual and mentally orientated, whereas Pisces is imaginative, dreamy, sensitive and lives by feelings, emotions, impressions and intuition. Gemini will often be unable to see reason in the illogical ways of Pisces. However, both signs are reasonably adaptable and tolerant of other people's ideas, so although you will seldom understand the whys and wherefores of each other, you will usually accept the inevitable. Gemini is practical, quick, handy and efficient whereas Pisces often dithers around or is indecisive.

Cancer with Cancer

The emotional nature is related to your element which is water so two Cancerians will produce a relationship in which feelings and emotions play a dominant role. If you agree, this combination will bring great happiness, but the reverse can also occur. Each is very sym-

---

"Gemini likes to communicate so is happy to share ideas with Libra, who in turn is not fulfilled nor complete when alone."

pathetic and compassionate, so will help the other in times of trouble. Emotions can make clear thinking difficult, so some really upsetting or muddled situations could occur when things go wrong.

Cancer with Leo

Although water is not compatible with fire, your respective rulers the moon and sun do complement each other, so despite your very different natures there will be a strong bond. Cancer will often have to give way to dominant Leo, but the latter has qualities which make Cancer's moon shine brighter. Leo needs the appreciation and attention which Cancer is happy to give.

Cancer with Virgo

Water, being compatible with earth, enhances the merits of this combination. Cancer is sincere, loyal and conscientious so will appreciate the hallmarks of Virgo which are care, attention to detail and thoroughness. Cancer is patient, therefore willing to accept the fact that Virgo will not be happy with quick, shoddy, or slap-happy work. Virgo is too much of a perfectionist to do things in a hurry. Cancer is hyper-sensitive and very easily hurt so Virgo should curb the tendency to criticise when Cancer errs. Cancer, who is very emotional, should remember that Virgo is not overly demonstrative when it comes to expressing feelings of love or affection.

Cancer with Libra

Although water and air are not very compatible, your respective rulers the Moon and Venus have much in common and they do harmonise. Cancer is easily hurt but unless peaceloving Libra is provoked he/she is unlikely to do anything to deliberately cause conflict. Cancer's natural desire to love and protect will be appreciated by Libra although the latter will sometimes impose on the Cancerian's generosity. Libra likes a balance between emotion and reason, so may be disturbed by Cancer's excess of emotion.

Cancer with Scorpio

Water with water is compatible but since this element is related to feelings and emotions, these, rather than facts, logic and reason, will predominate in this relationship. When harmony reigns this is a very constructive duo, but if conflicts arise, emotions get out of control and distort clear thinking. Each one is intuitive and can sense what is going on, so mutual trust is essential. Cancer has its own way of understanding that Scorpio can sometimes be tough and ruthless.

Cancer with Sagittarius

This combination of water with fire highlights the great differences in your natures, so unless there is good communication plus give and take in close personal relationships, you could feel that you sometimes live in two different worlds. Sagittarius is far too wayward and freedom-loving to be domesticated like Cancer. Sagittarius is mentally, emotionally and physically independent which can make Cancer feel insecure. Both are generous. Cancer is inclined to cling and too much of this will cause Sagittarius to feel smothered.

Cancer with Capricorn

Water is compatible with earth, but because these are opposite signs in the zodiac the combination can be complementary *and* competitive. If Capricorn gives top priority to ambition and success, sensitive Cancer will feel left out, hurt or neglected. The moon child admires and benefits from Capricorn's sense of duty and responsibility but Capricorn sometimes lacks the sentiment, warmth and loving care which is so important to Cancer.

Cancer with Aquarius

Long periods together will soon reveal that your respective rulers the watery moon and airy Uranus, have very little in common. Cancer's sensitive feelings and clinging emotions can disturb Aquarius who needs time to be independent, detached, even impersonal as well as feeling free to do his/her own thing. In a way, Aquarius is a universal rather than a personal lover who likes to share interests and affections with friends and humanity, but Cancer is much more emotionally exclusive.

Cancer with Pisces

This unites two water signs and since the water element is related to feelings, emotions and intuition, these will always take priority over logic, reason and analysis in this combination. Consequently, some of the practical necessities of life will often become muddled or confused. You both feel things very deeply so each can evoke a sympathetic response in the other without a word being spoken. Both people are very romantic and need to love and be loved.

Leo with Leo

Fire with fire in two such positive, strong-willed people can be very good or very bad. If both are true to type there could be too many chiefs and not enough Indians. Mutual give and take will be necessary if this combination is to work. Alternatively, one will have to play second fiddle, but who? There is nothing you could not achieve if your goals and methods agree.

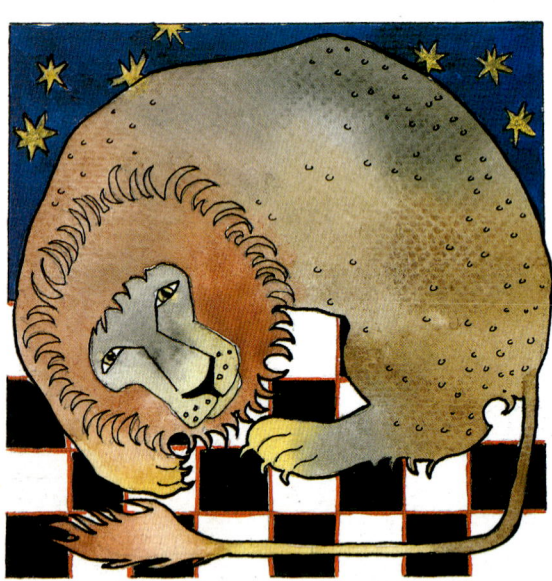

Leo with Virgo

Fiery Leo is extroverted, dominant and likes to be in control, whereas earthy Virgo is modest and retiring, so the success or failure of this combination in close personal relationships will depend on who is male and who is female. In business associations it is better when Leo leads and Virgo follows. Leo's ardent emotions will sometimes overwhelm self-controlled Virgo, but the latter will seldom show it.

Leo with Libra

Fire is compatible with air and since both signs have a natural ability for enjoying many of the good things in life you will be able to share lots of happy times together. Libra who likes to keep things balanced may think that the Sun child is either too extravagant, generous, flamboyant or lavish. Although Leo likes to be the boss, Libra gets what Libra wants through tactfully manipulating the Lion.

Leo with Scorpio

Fire with water in two such strong-willed signs can prove a stormy combination unless you agree to disagree or practise give and take without one trying to dominate the other. There is no limit to what this team can achieve if your goals coincide. Frank Leo will not understand Scorpio's secret, manoeuvres and may disapprove of them.

Leo with Sagittarius

This combination of fire with fire will work well because your respective rulers, the sun and Jupiter, are positive, optimistic and take a wide-angled viewpoint and because both signs are frank, generous and openhearted you can enrich one another by coming together. Independent Sagittarius will rebel if Leo tries too much bossing or controlling. The little lion will fret or feel neglected if Sagittarius is too eager for freedom and wider horizons.

Leo with Capricorn

Fire with earth highlights the great difference between these two signs and their respective rulers, the brilliant, grandiose sun and conservative, austere Saturn. Leo could feel too hemmed in by Capricorn, who in turn will feel that Leo's ways are either too generous, flamboyant, lavish or demonstrative. Leo likes to live life to the full, right here and now, whereas Capricorn, being more cautious and conservative, likes to plan for the future. Capricorn, who is emotionally reserved and fairly undemonstrative, seldom realises that Leo can feel starved unless given lots of love, affection, attention and appreciation.

Leo with Aquarius

Even though fire has a natural affinity with air, these signs are opposite each other in the zodiac, so although there can be a strong initial attraction, this can sometimes be transformed into equally strong opposition when the pendulum swings the other way. You both have extremely fixed opinions, strong determination and minds of your own, so unless one or both are willing to compromise there will be a clash of wills at times. Being a Leo you feel justified in claiming most of your partner's attention so you will find it difficult to accept the fact that Aquarius likes to share interests, activities, ideals and affections with more than just one person. Leo will not understand why Aquarius should be so unpredictable, detached and uncatchable at the most unexpected times and for no apparent reason.

Leo with Pisces

Fire with water highlights the great difference between these two where Leo is one of the most frank, open, extrovert signs, whereas Pisces has deep, mysterious and elusive qualities which are almost unfathomable to most people. Leo never really knows what Pisces is made of, but the latter admires the strength and purpose of Leo. Pisces often needs to be more organised and Leo is just the one to do it. You live in two different worlds but those who manage to bridge the gap will learn from and benefit each other in ways you never dreamed of.

Virgo with Virgo

Earth is compatible with earth but it does double up on the practical, down-to-earth, realistic qualities of your sign. Because of this, plus the fact that each likes to have an organised routine, it would be easy to get into a rut. Neither will make impossible emotional demands on the other but avoid mutual nagging or fault finding.

Virgo with Libra

The marked contrast between earth and air is not so apparent in this combination because your respective rulers Mercury and Venus, being the planets of mind and emotion, do complement each other. You are both fastidious and seek to achieve some degree of perfection. Libra aims to achieve harmony, balance, beauty and to keep the peace, so is not likely to provoke the critical, fault finding side of Virgo.

Virgo with Scorpio

In practical or intellectual areas this combination of earth with water will work well, but emotionally these two signs are worlds apart. Scorpio has intense feelings, burning desires and is often at the mercy of his/her own emotions, whereas Virgo believes in keeping them under control. Scorpio demands much of self and others so will appreciate Virgo's reliable, conscientious qualities.

Virgo with Sagittarius

Earthy Virgo is careful, methodical self-controlled and analytical, whereas fiery Sagittarius is impulsive, quick, independent and sometimes reckless or extravagant. Virgo is mentally equipped to specialise or concentrate on one thing at a time, handle small details and live in the present, whereas Sagittarius is mentally wide-angled, optimistic and always looks to the future. The self-expression of these two signs flows through very different channels.

Virgo with Capricorn

These signs belong to the element earth, so you both have your feet on the ground and you appreciate the practical, realistic necessities of life and work. Both are very conscientious with a strong sense of duty and responsibility but you should avoid the rut of all work and no play. Your ruling planets, intellectual Mercury and wise, self-disciplined Saturn, are well matched for business and practical matters, but there could be a lack of feeling, warm emotions and romantic sparkle. Capricorn admires the systematic, methodical, well-ordered ways of Virgo while the latter is sufficiently self-contained and logical not to be cut to the quick by Capricorn's selfish ways.

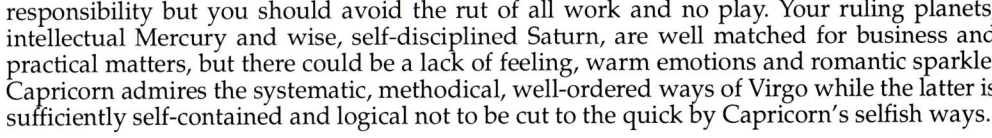

Virgo with Aquarius

Earth with air highlights the great difference between these two signs. The combination of your respective rulers Mercury and Uranus emphasises a mental and intellectual affinity rather than a deep emotional bond. Virgo is sensible, rational, analytical and sometimes cool, while Aquarius can be dispassionate, detached and uninvolved when it suits. However, Virgo is careful, self-controlled and orthodox, whereas Aquarius can be unpredictable, temperamental and unconventional at times. Virgo's logical mind has difficulty deciphering the enigma of Aquarius.

Virgo with Pisces

Although earth has an affinity with water and these opposite signs in the zodiac can complement each other, you both see things through very different eyes and each will always be a bit of a mystery to the other. Virgo is motivated by reason, analysis, facts and logic, whereas Pisces is guided by feelings, emotions, intuition and that strange ability to "sense" what is what. Virgo brings the method into Pisces' madness! Romantic, imaginative Pisces can add a touch of intangible magic to Virgo's life.

Libra with Libra

There is no conflict when air mixes with air and since you are both ruled by Venus, the planet of peace, harmony, balance and beauty, it will be easy to agree on most things. Any type of discord or conflict really upsets Libra so anything which is likely to cause this will be avoided or left unfinished. You are both easy-going and lack the fighting spirit, so it is not a very progressive team. Your environment will certainly reflect the elegance and attractiveness which is so important to Libra.

Libra with Scorpio

This is a case where air will mix with water because your rulers, feminine Venus and masculine Mars, can create a very strong physical, emotional and sexual attraction. However, gentle Libra may find the intensity and severity of Scorpio somewhat overwhelming at times. The secret of happiness in this duo is to find something to share which gives pleasure and satisfaction to both. Libra is tactful enough not to provoke Scorpio's sting. There is a mutual attraction between Libra's charming allure and Scorpio's magnetic sex appeal.

Libra with Sagittarius

Air will harmonise very well with fire in this combination because the union of your ruling planets Venus and Jupiter increases their qualities of love, happiness, success, pleasure and the ability to enjoy life. Although Libra needs to share things with someone special, you are tactful enough to allow Sagittarius that much loved freedom and independence. Sagittarius is generous enough to allow Libra to indulge in those much loved pleasures, little luxuries and the good things in life.

Libra with Capricorn

Air does not easily combine with earth so there is likely to be some type of purpose or destiny when these signs form a long-term association. Capricorn does not wear his/her heart on the sleeve and is unlikely to openly demonstrate the warmth of love and affection which Libra needs. The latter enjoys ease, luxury and self-indulgence, whereas Capricorn takes life very seriously, attracts responsibility and can cope with austerity much better than Libra when this is necessary. Capricorn should remember that the sharing of love, affection and beautiful things is as necessary to Libra as food and water.

Libra with Aquarius

Air harmonises with air and since these two signs are naturally friendly and need the company of other people, you can share these pleasures together. In a way, Libra is the epitome of the personal lover, whereas Aquarius is the universal lover who needs to share interests and affections with lots of people. When Aquarius becomes aloof or unpredictable, Libra employs tact and diplomacy rather than anger to handle the situation. Neither will make impossible demands on the other and yet you can share a feeling of togetherness providing Libra allows Aquarius the freedom to do his/her own thing.

Libra with Pisces

The harmony between your ruling planets Venus and Neptune helps to bridge the gap between air and water, so although you are very different in nature there can be an affinity because you both appreciate beauty, art, music, refinement, entertainment, harmony, gentleness, love, affection, togetherness and the magic of romance. Libra's innate sense of balance and good judgement will help to counteract the Piscean confusion, indecision and impracticality.

Scorpio with Scorpio

This double combination of the emotional element water will intensify the already intense feelings, desires, emotions and passions which are either latent or active in every Scorpio. There are no half measures with this sign. It is all or nothing, so two people with such intensity of purpose and powerful driving force will achieve great things if your goals agree. If not, violent clashes are likely. There is a touch of both saint and devil in this combination.

Scorpio with Sagittarius

Unless you either compromise or agree to disagree, this combination of water with fire in a close relationship can create problems. The Sagittarian's independence and need to feel free will arouse Scorpio's jealousy when the latter's desire to own and possess is denied. Scorpio demands much of self and others but Sagittarius will rebel against being controlled, dominated or forced in any way. Sagittarian's enthusiasm can bring out the best in Scorpio, who, being somewhat secretive, seldom divulges all that he/she thinks, feels, possesses and desires. This trait will either fascinate, irritate or mystify Sagittarius who is naturally so frank and open.

Scorpio with Capricorn

Water harmonises with earth but since your rulers are the "tough" planets Mars and Saturn, neither of you expect life to be an easy road, full of fun and games. Both signs can be totally dedicated, determined and hard working when it comes to achieving important goals, so in serious, responsible and practical matters you make a good team providing your objectives coincide. When conflicts arise you can be deadly enemies and since neither of you readily give up or give in, serious rifts will not be quickly nor easily resolved.

Scorpio with Aquarius

The lack of affinity between water and air points up the great difference between these two signs. You are both strong-willed and very determined, so if you can find a way to channel your combined forces into a common goal, great achievements are possible. Scorpio is intensely emotional and naturally possessive, whereas Aquarius likes to feel uncluttered and free to share interests, activities and affections with friends, groups, social causes and even humanitarian ideals. Therefore, if Scorpio tries to possess and to dominate the indomitable Aquarian, the latter will eventually rebel and when a serious rift develops Aquarius can separate very quickly and cut the losses. For Scorpio, love is an intensely personal matter, whereas Aquarius sees love in broader, universal terms. Unless this important difference in emotional attitudes is clearly understood, Scorpio will feel that Aquarius is too impersonal and detached.

Scorpio with Pisces

There is a magnetic attraction between these two water signs and in combination they will generate an intensely emotional relationship. Scorpio has an inborn desire to dominate or conquer something or someone, so needs to have others who will succumb to his/her will. Pisces can give the impression of being submissive although in reality it is often a devious manoeuvre. Pisces can soothe and anaesthetise the inner tensions, compelling desires and compulsive strivings within Scorpio. Each intuitively senses the other's moods, needs, fears and faults. When things go wrong an over-abundance of emotion will cloud the issue.

Sagittarius with Sagittarius

This combination of fire with fire in two such active, enthusiastic, optimistic, happy-go-lucky people creates a very lively team. Together you generate an atmosphere of restless activity and excitement so that life will often be like living in a whirlwind. You both like freedom and independence so unless you pull together and constantly reinforce the partnership, there's a chance you will drift further apart. Monotony and too many restricting ties are your enemies.

Sagittarius with Capricorn

The marked contrast between fire and earth is very evident in this combination because Capricorn is cautious, conservative, prudent, serious-minded and sometimes pessimistic, whereas Sagittarius is exuberant, optimistic, impulsive, broadminded and happy-go-lucky. Even your ruling planets are opposites because Jupiter symbolises expansion and increase, whereas Saturn, the ruler of Capricorn relates to contraction, decrease and limitation.

Although opposites can attract, the wide differences in your natures and outlook will certainly manifest at times. Independent, freedom-loving Sagittarius will not take kindly to being repressed or restricted by Capricorn, who in turn will not understand the Sagittarian's inner longings, high ideals and impossible dreams. If you can bridge the gap, each will certainly benefit in the long term.

Sagittarius with Aquarius

There is a strong affinity between fire and air as well as between your rulers Jupiter, the god of thunder, and Uranus the lord of lightning. Each sign makes a strong impact on the other and yet when necessary you are willing to leave each other alone. You both have an independent streak and need freedom to do your own thing so neither should trespass on the other's territory. Both signs have high ideals which transcend the purely personal level. These two signs are naturally very friendly so you will attract many people and share the pleasures and reciprocal benefits which are an integral part of good friendships and social intercourse.

Sagittarius with Pisces

This combination of fire with water is full of complexities and it presents a multitude of possibilities within some types of human relationships, such as marriage, friendship, family. For some, compatibility will be found in a mutual appreciation of philosophy, religion, philanthropic pursuits, charitable causes, travel, humanitarian or other lofty ideals. For others, there will be long periods of confusion, uncertainty or wishful thinking. In some cases, each person may live in their own private world, untouched and unnoticed by the other.

Pisces' vivid imagination will conjure up the worst picture when Sagittarius feels the need to be independent and free to do his/her own thing. Although Sagittarius is basically kind, helpful and generous, it lacks the softness and tender, loving care so essential to hyper-sensitive Pisces. The latter's tendency to be indecisive and disorganised will exasperate Sagittarius who is basically a positive person who likes to get things done quickly and efficiently.

Capricorn with Capricorn

This double dose of earthy Capricorn multiplies your cautious, conservative, realistic, down-to-earth approach to life. For this reason it is important to have contact with other types of people, otherwise you will both take things so seriously that you will miss out on many of the more lighthearted pleasures of life.

If you are both working towards achieving the same objectives, your combined ambitions and perseverance will ensure success. However, if one tries to use the other for selfish ends it can lead to much bitterness and resentment.

Outsiders who are more adventurous and lighthearted are likely to find this Capricorn duo too serious, formal and conservative. Avoid the tendency of becoming more and more isolated by keeping your lines of communication open, not only between your selves but especially with other people.

Capricorn with Aquarius

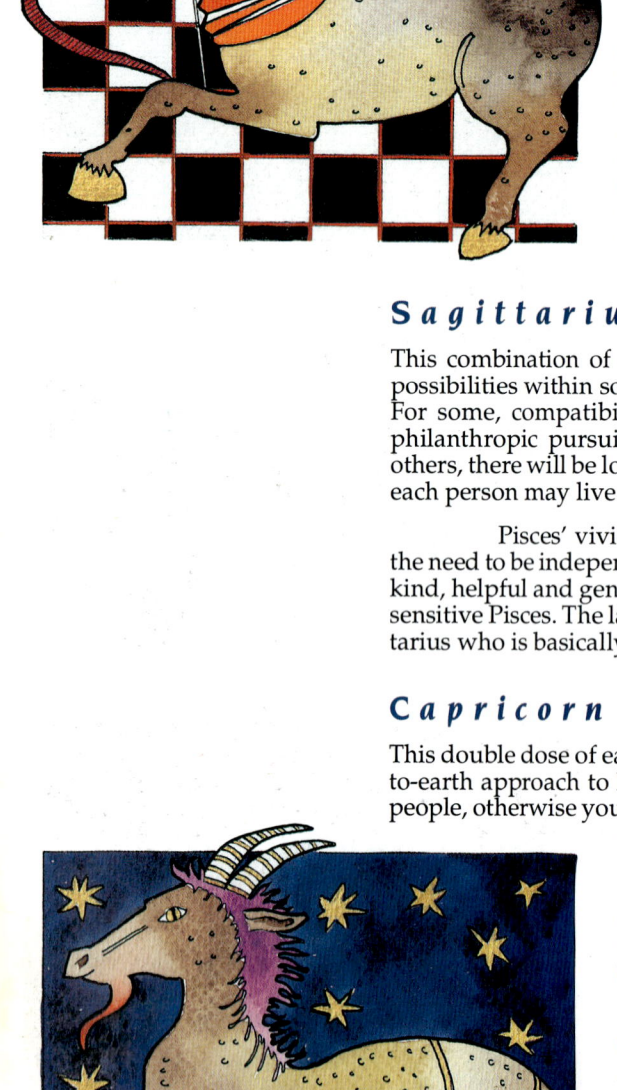

There is little in common between earth and air, nor between your respective rulers, cautious, conservative Saturn and unpredictable, wayward, unorthodox Uranus. This relationship will often be subject to ups and down, differences of opinion, changes of mood, routine and attitudes. Personal readjustments will have to be made; these may not be easy to achieve because Aquarius is independent and particularly stubborn where personal ideas are concerned while Capricorn is extremely tenacious and holds on tight to goals and convictions. Capricorn will never be able to fathom why Aquarius sometimes becomes unpredictable and capricious, shooting off on some odd tangent for no apparent reason. This behaviour undermines Capricorn's desire for stability and security. Sometimes Aquarius likes the thrill of a new, exciting experiment, regardless of the consequences. For Capricorn, this is totally unnecessary. Capricorn is self-controlled and disciplined, whereas Aquarius is a wayward, free spirit.

Capricorn with Pisces

Earth has an affinity with water and although there is a great difference between these two signs, they do complement each other. Pisces finds it easy to amalgamate and can adapt to people and situations which are safe and secure. Capricorn is the epitome of safety and security. Pisces is intensely sensitive, emotional, romantic, and sentimental so may feel sad or hurt when Capricorn hides his/her true feelings. Pisces is not one of the aggressively competitive signs so it offers no apparent threat to Capricorn's ambitions and long range plans to climb the ladder of success. Capricorn's sense of management and excellent practical abilities will shelter sensitive Pisces from some of the harsh realities of worldly life.

Aquarius with Aquarius

The air sign Aquarius is ruled by Uranus, the planet of all that is new, original, unique, inventive, erratic, unusual, unpredictable, unorthodox or rebellious. Therefore, outsiders may not be able to fathom this complex Aquarian wavelength because in a way it takes one Aquarian to know another. Much will depend on which facets of this sign each person reflects, but sooner or later unusual, surprising, disruptive or changing conditions will affect this partnership.

Aquarius with Pisces

It would be hard to find a more unusual combination than airy Aquarius with watery Pisces, for the simple reason that your respective rulers Uranus and Neptune are "out of this world", beyond the boundary lines of Saturn. Consequently, they transcend the limits of purely personal ideals and give you unique qualities which others do not possess. You are both "different" from most people, except other Aquarians and Pisceans. There will be at least two sides to this combination. Firstly, the outward, superficial layers of the association which can appear quite ordinary. Secondly, the unseen, hidden interplay of psychological forces which make this a very obscure and complex relationship. Each person can sense unfathomable depths in the other which are seldom plumbed, even in the long-term.

Pisces with Pisces

Because Pisces is a water sign, feelings, emotions, intuition, daydreams, imagination and hyper-sensitivity to "atmospheres" will always dominate and take precedence over logic, rational analysis and cold, hard, material facts. You each have your own private world of make-believe to escape to. You sense things about people, including each other, without a word being spoken. Both can become disorganised and indecisive, so there will be periods when time is wasted and confusion reigns in practical matters. Because you are so emotional and sentimental, you cry when you are happy and you cry when you are sad.

Working with the Stars

In order to gain fulfilment and self-esteem, we all need a purpose in life. Many people gain this through their work, providing the job they choose suits their talents and temperament! In fact, if these factors are not harmonious, frustration and unhappiness can result.

Be guided by your star sign; it can give you many pointers to a suitable, and successful, career path.

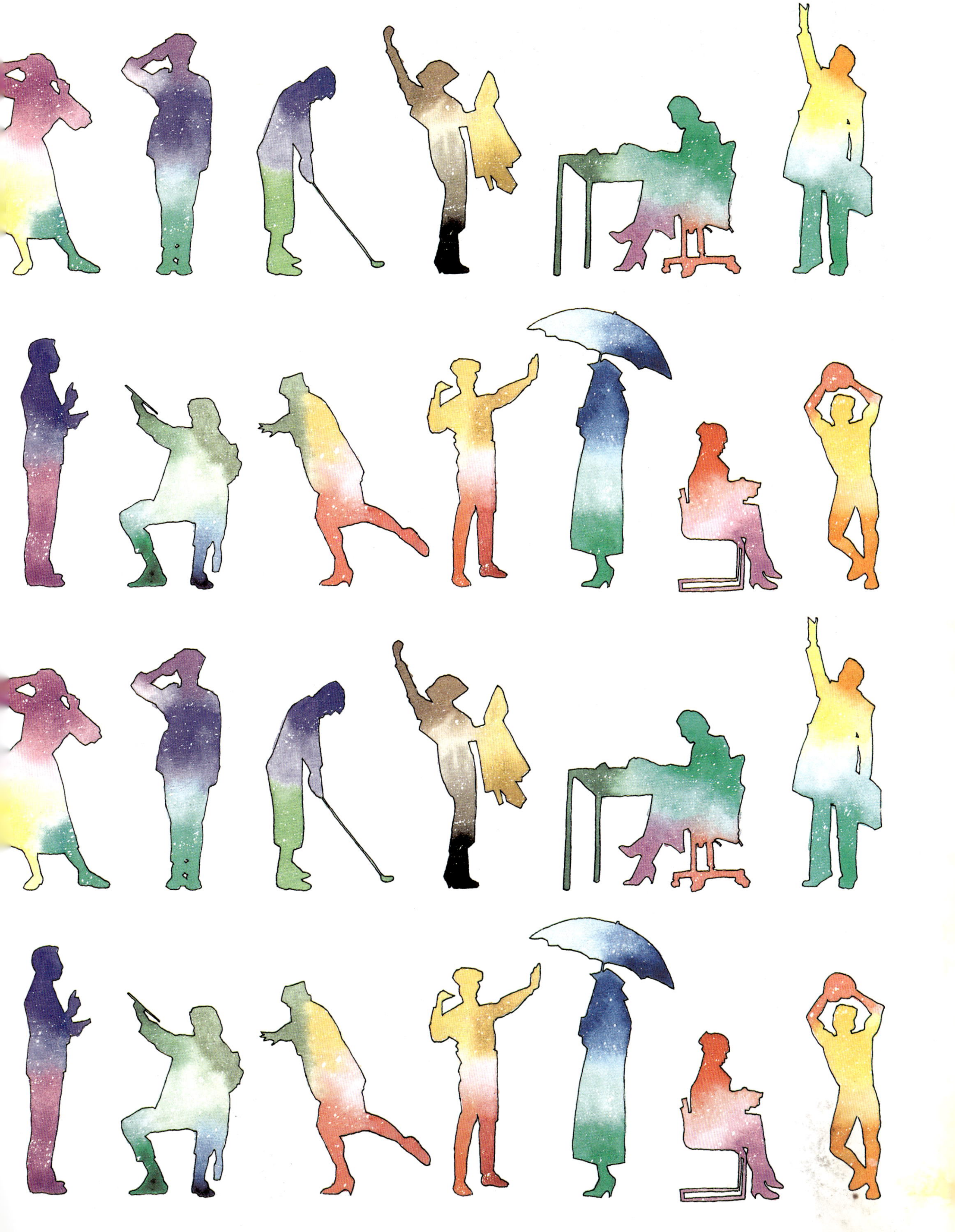

Aries

First and foremost, you like to be active, either mentally or physically, and you become bored with a dreary, monotonous routine. You have plenty of initiative, so you should avoid any occupation which is slow-moving and tedious or which places limitations on your enterprising abilities and your desire to forge ahead.

You like to get the job done as quickly as possible and you can be a little slap-dash at times. Therefore, a career where precision and perfection is essential would hardly be suitable. However, if you are working for yourself, the result would be different because Aries does bestow a high degree of self-esteem. You believe in "I, me and mine".

Running your own business is good for many Aries people for two reasons: you are a leader rather than a follower; being your own boss means that you are in control, and secondly, it offers a challenge which always brings out the best in you.

If you work for a large company, you'll be happy if you can rapidly work your way up the ladder, perhaps to the head of a particular department. However, if you have to wait years to achieve this, you will be tempted to move on to something else.

You are impetuous and become very enthusiastic about new interests, activities or projects, and inclined to jump into a new career without considering all the implications and consequences. Many Aries people, especially men, are attracted to, and fascinated by, danger.

You have lots of self-confidence and are in your element when you can show other people what to do. A good example would be a coach who guides, teaches or trains others.

Occupations which involve action, adventure, competition, construction or destruction, crime, cuts, burns, scars or surgery, emergencies, firearms, hot or sharp tools, leadership, machinery, metal, motivation, physical effort, sport, stamina, stress or the armed forces, will be in tune with the nature and qualities of Aries.

Taurus

There are two very different sides of Taurus when it comes to a suitable occupation.

Firstly, Taurus is a very physical, sensuous, earthy sign of the zodiac, so you are not afraid of hard, physical work and you do not shy away from getting your hands dirty. For example, farming, gardening, horticulture and landscaping fit into this earthy category, as does plumbing and drainage. There are many Taurean women who work with crops, gardens, nurseries, plants and the soil. Many Taurean men are physically strong, robust and muscular, making them well suited for those types of activities. They are the ones who love nature, the outdoors, the simple things in life and plenty of good, nutritious food. Some of them derive great satisfaction from bricklaying, building and mining, especially for precious gems.

Secondly, Taurus (via its connection with Venus) is associated with everything which is beautiful, elegant, colourful, refined, artistic, attractive, decorative, luxurious and ornamental. There is a very long list of occupations which suit people who appreciate these qualities. For example: artists, beauticians, boutique and gift shop workers, confectioners, craftspeople, etiquette specialists, fashion designers, florists, furnishings specialists, hairdressers, interior decorators, jewellers, milliners, models, musicians, photographers, resort workers and singers.

Some Taureans are plodders whose motto could be "slow but sure". You are cautious, down-to-earth, practical and very thorough in everything you do, so whatever your career or occupation, you will be very conscientious. You will want it to endure because stability and security in all aspects of your life are of paramount importance to you.

Taurus is a normally patient, placid and conservative sign, so you are quite content to work in one of the many occupations which are of a routine, ordinary nature.

You will not feel at ease in a career in the fast lane where there is no respite from pressure and the rapid tempo of work. You would be much happier and healthier in an occupation where you can operate carefully and at your own speed.

Taurus is one of the financial signs of the zodiac – (the other being Scorpio) – so many of you could derive much pleasure and satisfaction in a career which involves dealing with money. There are several avenues in the economics field to consider such as accountancy, banking, cashiering, financial and investment advice, insurance, the mint, the stock market, treasury or perhaps even in government!

Gemini

Because "variety is the spice of life" for Gemini people, it is very likely you will have more than one career or occupation during your lifetime. Being a Gemini, I have had two careers – an astrologer and a pianist – and in true Gemini fashion I was actively engaged in doing both at the same time for a few years. And would you believe it? – I'm at it again – writing this book and preparing more music for another recording.

Gemini means you are a versatile person who likes to have several fingers in several pies. There is a danger you will flit from one job to another without ever mastering or specialising in anything. Of course there are many exceptions to this rule.

Gemini gives you a sharp mind which can function well in almost any type of "brainy" rather than "brawny" career. There are two essential points to consider in your choice of work. Firstly, it must be mentally stimulating and preferably offer some degree of variety. Secondly, it should bring you into touch with other people or ideas. This is important because Gemini, the hallmark of communication, needs to be "in contact", either physically, mentally, verbally or through travel, correspondence, books, papers and magazines.

There are many careers and occupations which involve various types of communication. Consider work as a courier, driver, journalist, lecturer, public speaker, sales representative, secretary, teacher, travel consultant or a writer.

Geminis do not enjoy housework but you will give all your attention to those tasks which require manual dexterity because you are just so good with anything involving the use of your hands. Maybe this is one of the reasons why many Geminis make excellent commercial artists, craftspeople, designers, engravers, manicurists, organists, osteopaths, sculptors, and surgeons. These are just a few of the multitude of occupations which allow you to express yourself through the use of your hands.

As is the case with all the star signs, Geminis will be found in almost every type of career or occupation, so it is quite inappropriate to say that you must only do this or that type of work. You are far too versatile to have those types of limitations placed upon you.

Cancer

Cancer, being one of the "water" signs, ruled by the gentle moon, makes you a sensitive, deeply emotional person to whom caring for and about others comes so naturally. What a wonderful gift to have in your heart. Although you possess this beautiful softness and tenderness, there is also a very tenacious streak in your nature, so that once you decide on some particular goal, you will persevere until it is achieved; once you commit yourself to a specific occupation you will stick to it and give it all you've got. It is in this way that you can be tough and inflexible.

Speaking in a general sense, Cancer is probably suited more than the other signs to cope with housework, running the domestic front and organising everything to do with the family unit. After all, Cancer rules the home, so you have an instinctive knack of knowing how, what, when, where and why to do all those dozens of things which are necessary in maintaining the home and family.

Many Cancerians enjoy looking at homes and other types of property, so you may like a career in real estate, the building industry or house renovation. No matter what you do, your intuition will always be a guide because you get a "feeling" when something is either right or wrong.

Your natural desire to care for other people would be an invaluable asset for occupations involving care of children or the elderly, housekeeping, missionary work, nursing and many other avenues which give you the opportunity to help others. Cancerian people have a strong maternal or paternal instinct so will derive a great sense of pleasure and satisfaction in a career which allows expression of these natural feelings.

"Gemini gives you a sharp mind which can function well in almost any type of 'brainy' rather than 'brawny' career."

Cancer is related to nutrition and all aspects of the food and beverage industries. Consider your suitability as a chef, dietitian or manager of one of the many types of food stores or restaurants. A Cancerian would probably also enjoy being a farmer, market gardener or a wholesaler or retailer of food.

You are a naturally protective, conservative and careful person. These attributes equip you well for any type of career that involves managing money. In fact some very successful financiers have been Cancerians. Of course, there are many other occupations which are related to various types of money management. For this same reason you can be very good at business administration.

Although not always obvious, you have tremendous inner strength and determination, so once you set yourself a goal, you are unlikely to give up until you achieve it.

Leo

It is from your ruler, the all powerful sun (which gives life to the entire solar system), that you inherit your qualities of leadership, authority and organizational abilities.

In order to derive satisfaction from your career, you must eventually become one of the leaders, the person who is in a position of responsibility and authority. You will never be really happy if you have to play second fiddle or be a subordinate to others for a long time. Therefore, choose a career which offers a high level of success. You are definitely not a stay-put, stodgy, submissive person. You are an achiever and you need the right type of occupation which will enable you to do just that.

In many ways, Leo is the ideal sign for people who want to run their own business, because you are then your own boss, answerable only to yourself. There are dozens of possibilities which fit into this category.

Many Leo people are creative, artistic and have a sense of style, with the bonus of knowing just what to do to make a big impression on others. There's a touch of "showmanship" in these Leos, so if you like to do things on a grand scale to create an impact these areas will appeal: acting, architecture, art, landscaping, music, stage and costume design, the performing arts, television or film industries, theatrical production and direction, window dressing and other jobs based on the principles of "display" and "presentation".

You are an excellent organiser and because you have a natural air of authority and self-confidence, you inspire respect (and sometimes, envy) in other people. You have the ability to see the overall picture of any project. However, you can't be bothered fussing with the minor details involved in achieving an end result. Consequently, in a career which is compatible with your nature and broad vision, you need to be in position where you can delegate those details to other people while you remain at the helm and in control.

Housework may not be your cup of tea but, if, like most people, you have to do it, you will generally end up making your home look wonderful because you have a talent for beautiful presentation. For the same reason you would be the ideal type of person to run a jewellery store, a boutique or a shop which sells spectacular lighting, ornaments or decorative items. Your ruler, the sun, is radiant and its "brilliance" often shines through in the things which many Leo people do.

Virgo

Most Virgo people are practical and methodical, with a natural ability to deal with routine work and fine details. Your judgment is much more likely to be influenced by facts and logic rather than by fantasy because you like to have a down-to-earth reason for doing something. Consequently, in choosing a career, you will usually go for something where the ultimate goals are realistic and achievable. For you, pipedreams are too uncertain and too much of a gamble. You are very sensible about money so you are good in most types of business where you can keep a watchful eye on what is going on. It is unlikely that you will want to build a huge empire where too many things can get out of control or become messy and complicated.

In many ways, Virgo is a follower rather than a leader and because you are reliable and extremely thorough in your work, you are an invaluable asset to any employer who wants a job done well. Just so long as you feel safe and secure in your chosen occupation you are happy to carry out the duties assigned to you. As a matter of interest, a well known, successful business woman in Sydney would seldom employ anyone unless that person was born in the sign Virgo. This says a lot for her appreciation of your particular aptitudes as a member of the work force.

Attention to detail is one of the hallmarks of the sign. It can be put to good use in accountancy, clerical work, computer programming, design and drawing, electronics, engraving, languages, libraries, mapping, mathematics, micro-surgery, microscopic analysis, pathology, proof reading, statistics and watch-making plus a multitude of other activities

"Many Leo people are creative, artistic and have a sense of style with the bonus of knowing just what to do to make a big impression ..."

which involve small components or fine detail. One thing is certain – Virgo people always read the fine print on important documents.

This sign is specifically related to health and hygiene. Most of you are particularly fussy about what you eat, how it is prepared and cooked and you like to know what chemicals, artificial colours, flavours and preservatives are in our modern foods. Consequently, you may feel comfortable working in a health food store, a health resort, compiling facts and statistics or even writing about various aspects of health. For those Virgoans who are attuned to such matters, a career as a chemist, chiropractor, dietitian, herbalist, naturopath, nurse, osteopath, physician or any other type of healer could be very rewarding.

Whether we like it or not, almost everyone has a part-time or full-time career as a homemaker. Virgo, being one of the "earth" signs puts you ahead of most of us when it comes to being organised and efficient, and this important aspect of daily life is no exception. With your insistence on cleanliness, the place will usually be spotless.

Libra

Because Libra is the symbol of balance and equilibrium, it is appropriate that the Libran period occurs at a time of year when day and night are almost equal. Because of this principle of balance, there are very few extremes in the Libran nature. Harmony in all aspects of your life is of paramount importance, especially in the home, in partnership, with family and close friends, and also in your work place.

You were not born with the strident, competitive, aggressive, striving qualities which are so evident in some of the other star sign types, so in choosing a career it is most important that you do not put yourself into a position where high pressures, discord, fierce competition and " a life in the fast lane" are prerequisites because these will eventually irritate and exhaust you. In saying this, I do not mean to infer that you are weak. In fact, you are quite the opposite, as anyone who crosses you will soon discover. You intensely dislike conflict and rather than provoke it, you will often run away from an argument or a confrontation. However, Libra is also the sign of justice, so when the chips are down, your quiet, inner strength will come to the surface and demand retribution.

The "scales of justice" – a Libran symbol – is also associated with the legal profession. You are a born strategist, with a natural flair for tact and diplomacy and you can excel in almost any type of arbitration. Therefore, many Librans will do well if they feel attracted to a career in law or any of its subsidiaries. In this realm, and with your natural understanding of partnership and its implications, you could be the ideal person to act as a marriage guidance counsellor, a legal aid worker, an arbitrator in family or neighbourly disputes, or as a go-between wherever opposing parties are involved. You have a natural ability to smooth the way over troubled waters.

Libra is the sign of partnership – in love, marriage or business – so providing you have a compatible associate, you will feel more complete if you can work with another person rather than going it solo.

The combination of Libra and your ruling planet Venus is the hallmark of beauty, colour, symmetry, artistry in all its forms, music, luxuries, romance, partnership and pleasure. In terms of careers and occupations, Librans have a smorgasbord from which to choose. Consider working in a boutique or gift shop, a music shop, an art gallery or a dating agency. A Libran would do well as an artist, architect, beautician, collector dealing in antiques, objects d'art, coins, stamps, dolls and other specialty items, designer, dancer, hairdresser, interior decorator, jeweller, musician, photographic or fashion model, producer or director in ballet or working with clothes, fabrics or furnishings.

Librans are perfectionists in almost everything they do, so even as a housewife or house husband, the home will always look immaculate. Within the limits of a budget they will create an atmosphere of peace, harmony, beauty and comfort.

Scorpio

There is an old, yet valid description of Scorpio which says: "You put a great deal of intensity into everything you do, whether it is working, playing or loving". In terms of a career this means that there is almost nothing you cannot achieve, once you set your mind to it.

Of the 12 signs of the zodiac, Scorpio is the most fiercely determined, the one who will never give up or give in. You frequently put yourself to the test, sometimes overtaxing yourself and demanding as much from others as you do from number one.

Some Scorpios excel in ferreting out hidden facts and secret information. This type of ability would be necessary in fields such as archaeology, astronomy or astrology, botany, clairvoyance, geology, government or industrial espionage, industrial chemistry, invention, private investigation, psychiatry, reporting especially where gossip is involved, science and many other occupations which involve the unravelling of hidden, secret or unknown facts.

Scorpio is specifically related to sex, so the exploitation of this as a theme, either overtly, covertly or symbolically can work well for many Scorpio people. Sex has been and always will be a money spinner (in advertising, books, fashion and swimwear design, magazines, modelling, photography, television, films and videos), but, of course a career in these domains may not appeal to all Scorpio people.

Another fact of life related to Scorpio is death. Everything which has a beginning also has an end. There are many workers in this area: abattoir workers, butchers who deal in carcasses, coroners, farmers who raise livestock, fishing industry workers and funeral directors plus others working in that industry. All these occupations and others of a similar nature are related to Scorpio.

Any career which involves challenge, danger or excitement is like a honey pot to a bee for certain Scorpios. The idea of something being impossible to achieve is inconceivable to Scorpios. Maybe this is the reason why some of the greatest athletes, explorers, scientists, surgeons and virtuoso performers have a strong Scorpio influence in their horoscopes.

Being a "water" sign (and a secret one at that), it fits well with a career involving plumbing, drainage, dam building and maintenance or working underground in mines, caves, lakes, rivers and the sea. (Note the element of danger).

For obvious reasons, most Scorpio people will not find complete fulfillment and satisfaction in a career based solely on housework and domestic duties.

Sagittarius

Sagittarians are basically optimistic and outgoing, they need freedom and independence. Being restricted or dominated does not bring out the best in you so in choosing a career or any type of partnership, it is imperative that you have "room to move" – mentally, physically, emotionally, spiritually and financially. You also like to do things quickly.

In any type of profession, try not to put yourself into a situation where you have to work alone in cramped quarters for long periods of time, because working in isolation within those four square walls will eventually make you feel like a prisoner; a telephone or fax to the outside world would help to alleviate this problem! Find a job which allows you to enjoy the wide open spaces or travel, and the "free spirit" within you will be happy.

A few career possibilities for Sagittarius: air hostess or steward, athlete, farmer, freelance photographer, gardener, golf caddy, green-keeper, journalist, pilot, sports professional, surfer, tour operator, train driver, travel agent, travelling salesperson.

Many Sagittarians excel in fields which expand the mind and broaden horizons: astronomy, foreign affairs, foreign correspondence, law, literature, metaphysics, overseas travel, philosophy, publishing, religion, science and the shipping industry.

You are a "high flyer", ever optimistic, always aiming for a lofty target which takes you onward and upward. If you can find a career which satisfies your high expectations, you will feel on top of the world until you find the next mountain to climb and, as you know, there will *always* be another mountain. You have a restless soul and you seldom settle at the end of one achievement; this can be a source of much frustration.

You are generally full of enthusiasm, high spirits and energy, so don't take up an occupation which is slow moving or dreary. Above all else, you love to be active.

Capricorn

Capricorn is a down-to-earth person to whom the basic fundamentals of life are important. You like to build your career, home, family, financial situation and overall lifestyle on a solid foundation. You feel very uneasy when conditions are unstable, unpredictable or insecure. Therefore, in choosing a career or job, aim for something safe and soundly based which is also practical, realistic, and achievable. You are not likely to be attracted to highly idealistic occupations which involve fantasy, imagination and impossible dreams unless you can see good financial rewards and practical reasons for doing so.

You are an excellent organiser and administrator and could do very well in most types of business where good management, executive ability and careful planning are prerequisites. Capricorn, being an earth sign, is related to farming, agriculture, mining and most rural industries, so if you enjoy life on the land you could derive a sense of satisfaction from such activities. You also have the necessary toughness and perseverance to carry them out.

You thrive on responsibility and because you are an ambitious person you need to have a real purpose in life. Consequently, you will always strive for bigger and better things.

You will seldom rush into anything important because you like to think things out carefully, but once you decide on your goal you will not let anyone or anything get in your way. It is then that your amazing tenacity, patience and self-discipline will become evident. It is no wonder that so many Capricorn people eventually climb high up the ladders of career, material and financial success.

Any type of occupation which has lasting qualities and which offers good long-term prospects and opportunities for promotion will appeal to you. However, you would be wise to avoid an occupation which involves working in cold temperatures for long periods of time because this could trigger off rheumatic or arthritic pains.

Some of the other fields of employment which are specifically related to Capricorn are architecture, bricklaying, building, chiropractics, civil engineering, civil service, clock making, crystallography, economics, care of the elderly, excavation, government, mathematics, osteopathy, plastering, politics, pottery, quarrying, real estate, refrigeration, restoration or repair, sculpture, second-hand dealing and stone masonry.

"The best is yet to come" applies to Capricorn, because like a good wine, your career and lifestyle improves with age. As a bonus you will probably be able to enjoy your work and favourite activities for a very long time because Capricorn is the sign of longevity and you usually live much longer than people born in the other signs.

Aquarius

Aquarius is one of the most enigmatic signs of the zodiac with the result that very few people will ever understand your motives, your nature or your needs. In many ways you are a law unto yourself and although you can be very friendly, you don't like to become too deeply entangled with other people, even those close to you, so you will feel more at ease in an occupation where you can keep your distance from others in the work place. You are somewhat of a loner and you treasure your inner freedom far too much to be willing to surrender your independence to anyone.

You often surprise people by doing unusual or unexpected things, revealing the unpredictable nature of Aquarius. No wonder your career and lifestyle can undergo sudden or dramatic changes.

In no way could you be described as conventional so it is natural that many Aquarians choose a career which is different or unorthodox. Some of you even love to do things which other people would never think of doing. For example, astrology is a truly

"Of the 12 signs of the zodiac, Scorpio is the most fiercely determined, the one who will never give up or give in. You frequently put yourself to the test..."

Aquarian subject, but not too many people think of becoming astrologers.

Some other fields of employment which have a relationship with this sign are aeronautics, aviation, broadcasting, computer programming, electroplating, exploring, faith healing, invention, new age teaching, nuclear physics, psychotherapy, radiology, research, science and space technology.

In a way, some of those occupations reflect the fact that many Aquarians are ahead of their time. This does not apply to everyone born in the sign of the water carrier, but for those of you who are strongly in tune with your ruling planet Uranus, there is certainly an element of the "avant garde" in your nature and you do not fit any standard mould. Therefore, you are fiercely independent and a radical nonconformist who prefers to blaze new trails and experiment with new gadgets, methods or ideas and carve an original career.

For the less unconventional Aquarians, any of the following employment fields may appeal to you: antique dealing, aviation, counselling, electrics and electronics, photography, radar, sonar or television, research, selling specialised commodities, selling unusual books, specialist hobbies or working in a social club or co-operative society.

For obvious reasons, most Aquarians will not find housework a very satisfying career, even if you have to do it.

Pisces

Piscean people have a marvellous ability to adapt to almost any situation. Consequently, Pisceans will be found in all walks of life and in every conceivable type of occupation. This does not necessarily mean that you will all enjoy what you are doing because, being so sensitive, impressionable and responsive to external conditions means that, you pick up and absorb the influences around you. If the vibrations are happy, harmonious and constructive, you will respond to and reflect them.

However, if they are discordant or destructive, your reaction to them will be very disturbing. For this reason it is very important that you mix with people who are good for you and that you work in an atmosphere and an occupation which is conducive to peace, harmony and cooperation and which gives you a degree of soul satisfaction. In many ways you were not made to cope with the harsh, ruthless realities of the materialistic world.

You have a wonderful imagination and this, combined with your vision and inner source of inspiration, means that you can excel in most types of careers which involve fantasy, sensitivity, idealism, mystery, creative imagination and romanticism. It is no wonder that some of the world's greatest poets, artists, writers and composers (such as Frederic Chopin) were born under the sign of Pisces. You have a wonderful gift to give those people who can appreciate it. Such is the nature of mystical Pisces.

Your inherent talents can blossom in a wide variety of fields, some of which are acting, art, clothing, dance, fabrics, furnishings, garden art, gifts, jewellery, music, literature, paintings, perfume, pets, photography, puzzles, souvenirs, stage and costume design, theatre, television and film industry, and almost any work which involves imagination, mystery or romance.

Pisces and your ruling planet Neptune is the most psychic of all zodiac combinations. For a few, this bestows a rare ability to transcend the limits of time and space. You intuitively "know" or "sense" certain things without a word being spoken.

Neptune's realm is the ocean, so you may feel at home in one of the many occupations which will put you in touch with water; the element of Pisces.

Children of the Stars

The time of birth is, astrologically, the most significant moment in your child's life. The alignment of the planets at the time of birth will influence your child's character and destiny. So from the earliest age, the zodiac can give you clues about your child's needs, strengths, personality and future.

Sagittarius baby

Capricorn baby

Aquarius baby

Pisces baby

Aries child

Aries is one of the most positive, forthright and dynamic signs of the zodiac, so your child will always be active, both mentally and physically. Because he/she will be strong willed and determined to have his/her own way, the parents will need to know how to exercise some tactful but firm discipline, otherwise this child will soon be running the household.

Mars (the mythological god of war) rules this star sign, so don't expect your child to be peace loving or meek and mild. There is a forceful, aggressive quality about Mars. If your baby is a girl, don't be surprised if she is not interested in many of the things which appeal to most little girls. She is also likely to go through a tomboy stage as she grows up.

This star sign gives an abundance of vitality, enthusiasm and stamina. He/she must find an outlet in a variety of exciting activities. Aries is at its best when faced with a challenge, but there is usually an intense dislike of anything slow, dreary or monotonous. Parents should be alert to the fact that many Aries children are attracted to danger, so it is essential that they be carefully educated in all aspects of safety.

There is a natural enthusiasm for starting new projects and having new things to play with, but the novelty soon wears off. Your child has a natural inclination to rule the roost and when opposed or thwarted, the Aries impatience and hot temper will rise to the surface.

Taurus child

Because Taurus is the most "earthy" of the 12 signs, your child has a very stable nature and a contented disposition unless subjected to constant changes. Too much change is undesirable because it will produce feelings of instability and insecurity. A Taurean child is a determined plodder who does most things in life slowly but surely and according to the book of rules.

Venus (the mythological goddess of love and beauty) rules Taurus, so these factors together with peace, tranquillity, harmony and affection will be very important to this child.

As parents will quickly realise, you have a very strong-willed, stubborn child on your hands whose determination "to dig their heels in" is so inflexible that it will often overcome any resistance. Once the child realises that you will give in, you will find it extremely difficult to reverse the situation. Therefore, start off as you wish to continue.

These children have a natural artistic sense, whether it is for beauty, design, music, art or nature, so when buying books, playthings or clothes for him/her, be sure that they are appealing and offer a means of artistic or creative self-expression.

Taurus has a strong desire to own and possess things; this child will be very reluctant to part with toys or other possessions which he/she treasures so much. The Taurean child will also be quite possessive of special childhood friends and this characteristic will continue on into adulthood.

In true Taurean style this child will learn to appreciate the value of money and even when quite young will derive a great deal of satisfaction from having a personal bank account.

Gemini child

Gemini is related to the mind and all mental faculties, so a child born under this star sign will often have above average intelligence and a quick, alert, enquiring mind (avoid too much baby talk). However, the duality of Gemini (symbolised by the twins) gives a love of variety and change. It also confers a high degree of versatility, so there is the tendency to flit from one interest to another.

Mercury (the mythological winged messenger of the gods) is the planet which rules Gemini, so you will find that communication in all its forms will always be a vital factor in this child's life. For this reason parents should give the child plenty of books, magazines, pens, pencils, paper, a toy telephone or typewriter. Manual dexterity comes naturally; the child likes to fix or make things, take things apart to see how they work or play a musical instrument.

A Gemini child is usually more restless than other star sign types and since the nervous system is highly strung they need regular periods of peace, quiet and relaxation in order to give their system a chance to unwind. At times your child will be a walking question mark, always asking how, when, where, why. Gemini children naturally share their thoughts, friendship and affection with just about everyone they know because they have an innate need to mix with other people.

Cancer child

The moon, Cancer's ruling sphere, is intimately related to feelings and all that is gentle, homely, sensitive, responsive, familiar and protective, so this little person really needs to know that he/she is loved and wanted. To your moonchild, the family circle and the safe,

"The Taurean child will be quite possessive of special childhood friends and this characteristic will continue on into adulthood."

familiar home environment is of paramount importance, so never do anything to make a Cancerian child feel cut off, rejected or unloved. Constant reassurance will be necessary, especially during the early stages of any big change such as moving house or starting school.

Cancerians are very loyal, diligent, resilient and resolute. In fact, they can surprise many people because their strength of purpose is not always obvious.

This is one of the most emotional of all the zodiac signs and their feelings are easily hurt. Even a slight rebuke or a criticism made by a friend, teacher or parent will upset the gentle Cancerian; there is no-one who is more expert at making mountains out of molehills. When parents play any type of mental or physical games with this child, let the child win often because this will help to boost his or her self-confidence and allay the fear of insecurity. The maternal (and paternal) instinct is very strong so give these children something to care for such as a pet, a doll or a plant.

Leo child

The sun, which has control over the entire solar system, is the ruler of Leo. This explains why so many people born in this star sign are natural leaders in their particular field. This basic characteristic is evident even in the very early years, so little Leos like to be big bosses taking control of other children and childhood situations. Although this air of authority and power is appropriate in some settings it can become a real problem; Leo likes to be number one.

Your child is warm hearted, outgoing and fun-loving, with plenty of self-confidence, but he/she does need to be noticed, appreciated, praised and loved. When this is not forthcoming your child will start showing off and doing all sorts of naughty things in order to attract attention. This is where parents need to exercise some discipline because if this tendency is allowed to go unchecked the child can become absolutely obnoxious.

Leos usually want the best of everything. However, if the Leo child receives too much, too easily, it will not be valued nor appreciated. Therefore, parents should educate their little one from a very early age about the dangers of "easy come, easy go".

Leo is known as the royal star sign because its ruler, the sun, is the "king" of the solar system. From childhood through adulthood to old age, he/she will be like a ray of sunshine, bringing joy, light and some degree of splendour, pomp and ceremony wherever he/she goes. A Leo child is impressed by success, strength, prestige and self-confidence in others, so never let your own faults, fears and weaknesses become too obvious.

Virgo child

Virgo, being one of the earth signs, is very practical, realistic and down-to-earth. He or she appreciates commonsense and needs to have a logical explanation for all of life's activities. You can expect your Virgo child to be always asking how, when, where or why.

Mercury (the planet of the intellect) rules Virgo, so this child has a keen, sharp, analytical mind. Therefore, a Virgoan is usually a diligent student and develops into a reliable, responsible citizen. This star sign is certainly the hallmark of a perfectionist. Method, order and system also belong to Virgo so a messy household will subconsciously disturb this child. Attention to detail and a natural ability to work with small items are typical qualities of this star sign. He or she notices all the little things which others fail to see and don't be surprised if your child often picks faults in various ways and in other people.

Virgo is inclined to build a protective shell around itself, so unless parents, by example, encourage the child to give open expression to feelings and emotions, the loving nature will gradually become more and more reserved, cool and even inhibited. Having an attainable purpose in life is of paramount importance to a Virgoan, so parents should encourage the child to do some of the easy chores around the house. Because the nature is reserved, modest and somewhat timid, this child will not seek the limelight.

Libra child

Venus (the mythological goddess of love and beauty) is the ruler of Libra. This is one reason why a Libran son or daughter has a friendly, affectionate, appealing nature which is popular with most people. Libra is the hallmark of peace, harmony, tranquility and equilibrium, so for the child to be happy it is absolutely essential that the home environment reflects these qualities. There is nothing which will upset a Libran more than arguments, aggression, tension and conflicts, especially when this involves the family and loved ones.

Artistry of all kinds has an affinity with Libra, so your child may have a talent for music, painting, dancing, dress-making or other creative activities. Make the child's room attractive and elegant because anything ugly or discordant will have a disturbing effect on his or her senses – which appreciate refinement in all its forms.

Libra is the sign of partnership, so make sure your child has plenty of special playmates because he or she will not feel happy being alone for too long. It will not be difficult to teach your child to be polite and well-mannered because a courteous, gentle approach to others comes naturally. A Libran will often go out of his or her way to please people. Later in life he/she will discover that it is impossible to please everyone all the time.

Scorpio child

Because Scorpio is one of the water signs, this child is intensely emotional. However, like many facets of the Scorpio nature, these emotions are often concealed because there is a strong desire to keep things secret. Don't be surprised if your child hides some of his or her treasures in places which you don't know about; anything secret or mysterious holds a special fascination. Therefore, parents should double check for danger spots in and around the house.

Mars (the mythological god of war) and Pluto (lord of the underworld and symbol of the two extremes – the greatest depths and the supreme heights) are the rulers of Scorpio, so there is nothing wishy-washy about your child who will sometimes be a perfect saint and at others a little devil. There are no half measures for this star sign – things are either black or white, with no shades of grey – so, in relationships with other children (and even with some adults), he or she can either love or hate with equal intensity.

When trying to overcome an obstacle or an opponent, Scorpio can be ruthless and invincible and since this star sign endows your child with great will-power and determination, he or she will never give up until the goal or battle is won. In adult life this inner strength will be a great asset for achieving success. One of the negative aspects of Scorpio is a tendency to be somewhat cruel and destructive. This star sign gives an intuitive, perceptive and even psychic awareness so your child will always sense the reality behind the facade.

Sagittarius child

Sagittarius is one of the active, outgoing fire signs and it is ruled by Jupiter (the planet of expansion, success, joy and good fortune). Your child will be energetic, optimistic and fun loving. This is not a moody, depressing star sign, so it takes a lot to get a Sagittarian down and even then he or she soon bounces back. Even in times of trouble, Jupiter's lucky influence means that the person somehow manages to land on his or her feet.

Sagittarius is the hallmark of freedom and independence, so your child will not feel happy in confined areas or in cramped, restrictive conditions. A Sagittarian needs a taste of the wide open spaces. In some ways Sagittarians, at any age, want to be free spirits so a child will not take kindly to parental control and discipline which comes in the form of "you must not do .....". Tactfully educate your child to accept the limitations and responsibilities which life, society and the law demands, otherwise he or she may resent restrictions in adulthood.

This star sign will make your child generous, warm-hearted, friendly and straightforward – even to the point of being abrupt, but always with a good sense of humour.

Capricorn child

Being one of the earth signs, Capricorn is very cautious, realistic, practical and conservative. A Capricorn likes to get down to basics and, since Saturn (the ruler of Capricorn) is the symbol of maturity, responsibility, austerity and wisdom, your child is a serious-minded person who is likely to have an old head on young shoulders. He or she is reserved and somewhat modest rather than effervescent and demonstrative. There is not a great deal of interest in things which are superficial or frivolous because Capricorn is equipped to deal with fundamental matters. This child seems to have an affinity for older people and even at an early age can enjoy adult companionship. Capricorn is the hallmark of duty and responsibility.

This star sign strives for stability and security. "Slow but sure" is the motto and since there is a real capacity for perseverance, once this child decides that he/she wants to do or have something, there will be no giving up.

Capricorn does not often act spontaneously but prefers to plan well ahead so that everything can be done carefully and properly. Here is a thrifty person who cannot tolerate waste or extravagance.

Aquarius child

Aquarius is one of the most unusual, unpredictable, independent and enigmatic signs of the zodiac. Uranus, its ruling planet, is the symbol of all that is original, unique, unorthodox, surprising, erratic and rebellious, so don't expect your child to always fit into the traditional mould! Uranus is outside the orbit of conventional Saturn and in some ways Aquarians are outsiders because they are free spirits – untamable and uncatchable. Many are non-conformists who like to "do their own thing". The paradox is that they are happy to conform when they are not forced to do so, therefore parents will have to be extremely diplomatic in the way they administer discipline and guidance.

The child of Aquarius has a high degree of intelligence. However, in some things he/she will have very fixed ideas and the more you try to change those opinions the more inflexible the mind will become. This star sign gives a broadminded outlook and a wide range of interests which may include social issues, community affairs, outer space, astrology, electronics, inventions, computers and other aspects of science and technology.

Aquarians are friendly and sociable, often more at ease when mixing with large numbers of people rather than being restricted to one person, but sometimes an Aquarian will decide to go it solo. In other words, you never quite know what an Aquarian will do!

Pisces child

Whether developed and active or latent but dormant, the intuitive and psychic faculties are stronger in Pisces than in any other star sign. Therefore, parents of this child should be aware that he/she will often have hunches, "know" things without a word being spoken, have meaningful or even prophetic dreams, experience telepathy and ESP or become clairvoyant. Because of these and other unfathomable qualities, it is almost impossible to completely know and understand a true Piscean, young or old. One of the reasons is that Neptune which reigns over this star sign is as deep, mysterious and unplumbed as its kingdom – the sea.

A Piscean child is extremely sensitive, so if upset, he/she will withdraw into a private world; some Piscean children find it difficult to differentiate between fact and fantasy and quite frequently this star sign lives in a world of vivid imagination.

Pisces is guided by instinct and intuition rather than by logic and fact, so don't expect your child (even in adulthood) to have a practical or rational reason for many of the things he/she does. Pisces is super-sensitive and highly impressionable, making your child very responsive and receptive to external influences. Therefore parents should realise that it is of paramount importance that this child should mix with people whose ideas, interests, motives and way of life are of an exemplary nature. Your child will unconsciously imitate the people he/she likes, so if the company is of a high calibre the behaviour will be copied. However, the same rule will apply to bad company.

"...in some ways Aquarians are outsiders because they are free spirits – untamable and uncatchable."

Colour in the Stars

Colour plays a vital role in our lives. It can affect the way we feel: crisp white or icy blue can make us feel cool on a hot summer's day, while rich, dark colours have warm, wintery connotations. Advertising agencies place great importance on colour to sell all sorts of products, because they realise that particular colours are more appealing and eye-catching to consumers. This chapter explains why we are drawn to, or repelled by, certain colours.

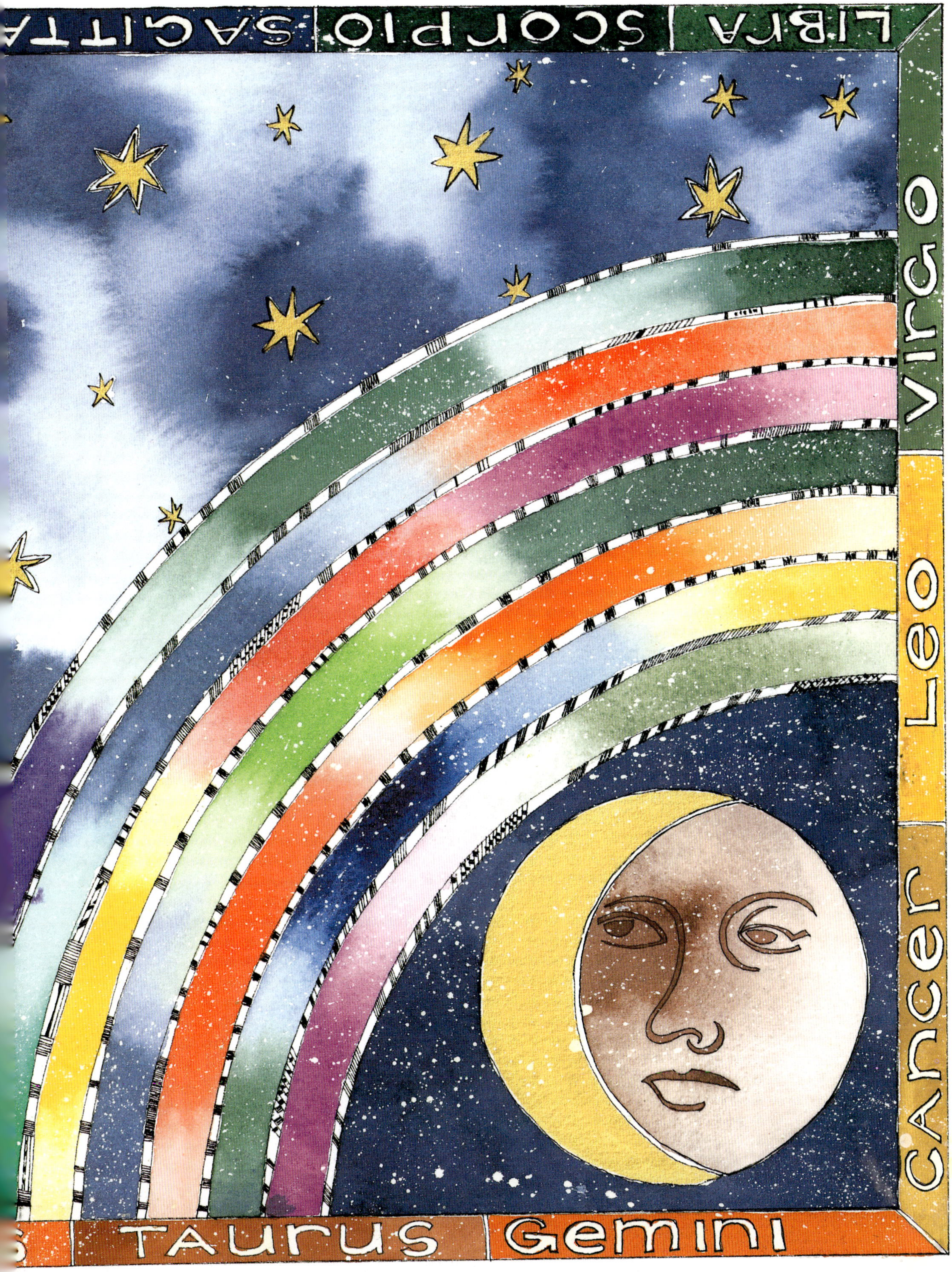

LIBRA
SCORPIO
SAGITTA
Virgo
Leo
Cancer
Gemini
TAURUS

"The sun controls and gives life to all the planets. It rules authority, celebrities, crowns, diamonds, fame, fathers and gold..."

Many industries, businesses and employers consult colour specialists to ascertain the most appropriate use of colour in the work place, the colour scheme which will make staff feel comfortable and will help maximise their productivity. Notice how some of the best restaurants and hotels make you feel welcome and put you immediately at ease by employing a subtle, unobtrusive use of colour in their decor and fittings. Who has not had the experience of eating steak and eggs in some small outback town cafe where the laminex tables are yellow, the chrome chairs are red and the lino is green with purple and orange circles! Even if the steak and eggs were great you would probably never want to go there again because the colours are overpowering and completely unappetising. That's the effect wrong colour combinations can have. A doctor's or dentist's surgery is generally painted in subdued tones, so that it's reassuring, even soothing to a patient. Dark-coloured or blood red walls convey a sense of impending doom – quite the wrong message!

Do you have a favourite colour? If so, have you ever wondered why you prefer that one? There is something in our mental, emotional and psychological make-up which attracts us to a particular colour which is not only in harmony with our nature but which is "in tune" with many of the things which correspond with a particular planet or star sign.

Maybe you are one of those people who do not have one special colour which is permanently your favourite. I have heard some people say "I'm going through my pink stage" or, "this is my purple phase" and so on. I remember there was one period in my own life when all I would ever wear was a combination of fawn and brown because I felt so good in it. Now, it no longer attracts me.

When interpreting the influence of colour and its relationship to the planets and star signs, try to assess which shade appeals to you permanently or during a temporary period – at present or in the past. Don't only think of it in terms of what colour you like in clothes or furnishings, just let pure, abstract colour signal its message to you. When you have found your favourite one you can then think about the colour (or colours) you really dislike. Then, by relating them to the zodiac, you can discover what qualities and characteristics in people, things, occupations or situations either attract or repel you.

Consider also whether you like (or dislike): light, bright or pale shades, dull, darker tones or a particular mixture of colours because these factors are significant. In this exercise, don't apply the interpretation exclusively to birthdates – either your own or those of other people – because it applies to a much wider field of "ingredients" in your life.

Before I give you a list of all the colours and their zodiacal co-ordinates I want you to make your clear-cut decision about your colourful likes and dislikes because, as you read through all the possibilities it is likely that some people will change their minds and end up becoming totally confused.

So now, think about it for a few minutes and while doing so, don't forget that, apart from the seven basic colours in the spectrum: red, orange, yellow, green, blue, indigo, and violet, there is a whole host of other colours to consider: brown, black, white, cream, olive green, grey, pink, burgundy, mauve, purple, ochre, turquoise, aqua, silver, gold, fawn, navy blue, apricot, powder blue, lime green, "dirty" sulphur, magenta, electric blue, shocking pink or ethereal, misty shades which only give a faint hint of a particular colour.

Under separate headings for the sun, the moon and each of the planets you will find a list of the things which are most commonly associated with them. Then the colours for each sphere are given.

Note. You will find a much more comprehensive collection of solar, lunar and planetary correspondences in the **Dictionary of Keywords** beginning on page 114, so once having chosen your colours and their corresponding spheres you may like to check those additional lists of items to see whether you are "in tune" or "out of tune" with them.

The sun

The sun controls and gives life to all the planets. It rules authority, celebrities, crowns, diamonds, fame, fathers, gala affairs, gold, glory, the heart, influential people, kings, light (as opposed to darkness), nobility, ostentation, pomp and ceremony, power, pride, royalty, splendour, superiors, theatrical work, vanity and VIPs.

The sun's colours

The sun rules **gold, orange, yellow,** and all the bright "sunny" colours. The sun also adds its supplementary influence to the colours of other spheres or signs wherever you see those "poster" colours which are brilliant, almost dazzling, in their brightness, for example, pink is ruled by Venus, but poster pink is a combination of Venus and the sun.

The moon

The moon has a great influence on us, governing birth and motherhood. The moon rules babies, beverages (non-alcoholic), breasts, boating, boat houses, cafes, cheese, cows, dew, digestion, family, fruitfulness, housewives, housework and domestic affairs, the home, irrigation, instinct, kitchens, moods, mushrooms, moon-stones, milk, sailors, the stomach, streams, silver (the metal), tides, washing and water.

The moon's colours

The moon rules *silver, white, cream,* and very pale, nondescript colours. Remember that one of grandma's old rules was to leave any white washing hanging on the line when the moon was bright because its rays would bleach the clothes and make them whiter. The moon also adds its supplementary influence to colours of the other spheres or signs when *white* is added to make them lighter and paler. For example, blue is ruled by Sagittarius (as will be explained later), but pale blue or powder blue is a mixture of blue and white, so it is a combination of Sagittarius and the moon.

Pink is ruled by Venus, but pale pink is a blend of white and pink – the moon and Venus – which are the two most feminine spheres, making pale pink the most ultra feminine of all colours.

The earth

Planet earth is related to all that is centred, down-to-earth (naturally!), fixed, materialistic, practical, reliable, realistic, stable, and worldly. At certain times and in certain places it can be lush, fruitful and generous, while at others it can be barren, lean, unproductive, mean and hard. Earth represents endurance, conservatism, caution, perseverance, persistence and punctuality.

The earth's colours

As you would probably already realise, earth rules *brown*. There are many different shades of this colour, all of them are ruled by planet earth. The lighter ones such as fawn and beige are a mixture of brown with white, so they are a combination of earth plus the moon. Very dark brown is a blend of brown with Saturn's colour – *black* – so dark brown relates to the earth and Saturn, a most resolute, materialistic combination.

Mercury

Mercury, the celestial "messenger" rules advertising, agents, arms (limbs), agility, books, buying and selling, cartography, commerce, cars, catalogues, correspondence and most forms of communication, couriers, carriers, debating, dexterity, deliveries, editors, gossip, the hands, interpreters, journalists, keys, lectures, labels, languages, libraries and librarians, literature, the media, the mind, news, names, orators, publishers, pens, pencils, study, secretaries, stamps, statistics, sleight of hand, speed, thought, trade, typewriters, transport, travel, teachers, talking, translation, trains, writers and youth.

Mercury's colours

Being the closest planet to the sun it is strongly illuminated by the sun's light. Its colour is *yellow*, the most luminous of all the colours. Being the planet of names and information shows just how appropriate the names of the telephone directory's "Yellow Pages" and "Yellow Express" deliveries are!

Venus

Venus rules affection, art, artists, adornment, beauty, beauticians, cosmetics, comfort, charm, clothes, concerts, copper, culture, decorators, dressmakers, elegance, embroidery, femininity, flowers, florists, furnishings, glamour, gift shops, harmony, hairdressers, jewellery, luxuries, love, love songs, lace, music, ornaments, parties, peace, pleasure, romantic atmospheres, social clubs, symmetry, sugar, women and weddings.

Venus' colours

Venus, the planet of love and beauty, is the hallmark of femininity, so what better colour could there be than *pink* to reflect these qualities? Pink is its principal colour, but because of this planet's gentle softness, it also has some connection with pastel shades, especially pastel pink which is a mixture of pink with white, a combination of Venus with the moon. The metal copper is ruled by Venus, so another of its colours is copper.

"Venus, the planet of love and beauty, is the hallmark of femininity, so what better colour could there be than pink..."

Mars

Mars is a most forceful, aggressive planet, the hallmark of masculinity, fire and passion. It also rules accidents, action, athletes, adventure, anger, barbers, boldness, boxing, bullets, butchers, burns, courage, cutlery, conflict, conquests, cuts, carpenters, combat, competition, danger, dentists, effort, energy, firearms, fire, fevers, firemen, furnaces, heat, hot or sharp utensils, hardware, impatience, iron and steel, mechanics, machinery, muscles, ovens, police, pioneers, soldiers, strength, stamina, surgeons, temper, virility and vitality, the will to win and war.

Mars' colours

Mars rules *red*, especially *vivid red, scarlet* and *flame*, which have always been associated with Martian characteristics such as anger ("he made me see red"); a red rag to a bull. When fire or heat is applied to steel it can become red hot. Someone can get into a flaming rage. Even the planet itself is the only one which appears to give off a reddish-orange glow when visible up in the heavens.

Jupiter

Jupiter is the most beneficial planet of all because it is the bringer of joy, laughter, happiness, success and good fortune. It also rules abundance, aldermen, archery, banking, bishops, bonuses, capital assets, cathedrals, charities, the church, endowments, ethics, excesses, expansion, foreign people and places, financiers, fun, honesty, holiday resorts, improvement, increase and growth, judges, lawyers and the law, the liver, luck, long journeys, large sums of money, missionaries, optimism, philosophy, profit, prizes, professional people, riches, religion, race horses, spirituality, ships, sincerity, tin, titles, truth, universities and winnings.

Jupiter's colours

As you progress up through the colour spectrum of red, orange, yellow, green, blue, indigo and violet, the vibratory rates increase from the lowest to the highest. Therefore, the last colour violet represents the most spiritual rays, and because Jupiter is definitely related to religion, spirituality and religious leaders, it is appropriate that Jupiter is associated with *violet* and *purple*. However, it is very difficult to reproduce violet in its true colour, so the more commonly seen shade purple is assigned to Jupiter.

Saturn

Saturn is the most austere taskmaster; it is the planet of wisdom and stability, bestowing reward for hard effort. Saturn rules age, archaeology, ancestors, architecture, agriculture, astringents, bones, barriers, boundaries, builders, brakes, burdens, cemeteries, ceramics, coal-miners and coal, clocks, cold, concrete, conservation, discipline, decrease, depression, endurance, farming, fences, fatigue, fear, foundations, handicaps, history, ice, inhibitions, insulation, lead (the metal), maturity, memories, materialism, obstacles, orthodoxy, perseverance, pessimism, patience, preservatives, pottery, rocks, responsibility, time, restriction, refrigeration, sculpture, security, seriousness, thinness, tradition and wisdom acquired through experience.

Saturn's colours

From the name Saturn we have the adjective "saturnine" which means grave, gloomy, sombre and dark. Therefore, it is fitting that Saturn rules *black*. This planet also has a supplementary influence on many of the other colours when they are made darker or duller than they would normally be. For example, when black is added to the moon's colour white, the result is *grey*, which is neither black nor white but a combination of both. So, grey is a blend of the moon and Saturn.

Vivid red is ruled by Mars (and also by Aries, as you will discover a little further on). Therefore, *dark red* (black mixed with red) is a combination of Saturn with either Mars or Aries.

Uranus

Uranus, the rebel or black sheep of the solar system, the planet associated with change; it represents all that is abnormal, avant-garde, erratic, nonconformist, odd, shocking, surprising, unusual, unorthodox, unpredictable and unconventional. It also rules aircraft, airports, aliens, ankles, astrology, brotherhood, bohemians, batteries, computers, cranks, discovery, disruptions, divorce, electricity, electricians, electronics, earthquakes, experiments, freedom, hippies, hiccups, homosexuals, impromptu, informality, inventions, inventors, radio, radio-

> "Jupiter is the most beneficial planet of all because it is the bringer of joy, laughter, happiness, success and good fortune."

activity, radar, radium, radicals, space age technology, science fiction, spasms, separations, sonar, sudden events, spontaneity, strangers, television, uranium and X-rays.

Uranus' colours

Uranus rules electricity, uranium and other radio-active substances such as cobalt, so maybe it is not just a coincidence that the unique colours *electric blue* and *cobalt blue* are ruled by Uranus. This planet often acts in a way which shocks people, so that other stunning colour *shocking pink* is a combination of Uranus and Venus.

Neptune

Neptune is the key to all that is intangible, ethereal, psychic, mysterious, inexplicable, and abstract. It also rules alcohol, anaesthetics, apparitions, aquariums, breweries, clairvoyance, camouflage, confusion, counterfeit, deception, drugs, dreams, delusions, disguise, ESP, enigmas, fables, films, fishing, fantasy, fakes, flying, fountains, ghosts, hydrotherapy, hallucinations, hospitals, hypnotism, idealism, imagination, inspiration, intuition, mariners, mediums (psychic), music, mist, oil, photography, puzzles, pilots, petroleum, poison, rubber, seclusion, the sea, sleep, spies, submarines, synthetics, transcendentalism, visions and yachting.

Neptune's colours

Because of Neptune's intangible qualities, its relationship to colour is not always positive nor clear cut. It is certainly connected with *lilac, mauve, lavender* and that ethereal shade of *jacaranda* which is so difficult to photograph. It is also related to opalescent, iridescent, translucent colours which almost appear to be different from what they are. This is in keeping with Neptune's illusory influence. Words which describe Neptune's colours are: faint, indefinite, ethereal, shadowy, misty and ghostly. They are all pale colours with the faintest suggestion of green, blue, shadowy grey, misty pink, ethereal mauve, ghostly blue. In other words, you think there may be a colour there but you are not absolutely sure.

All of Neptune's colours are associated with idealism, a non-materialistic outlook, impracticality, the search for perfection, day dreaming, an inner longing for you-know-not-what, imagination, intuition, psychic "feelings", escape from reality and seclusion.

Pluto

Pluto, the mythological god of the underworld, is associated with such things as annihilation and transformation, atomic energy, atrocities, corruption, calamities, death, degradation, destruction, filth, fumigation, fiends, kidnapping, nuclear war, organised crime, plagues, ransoms and vermin.

Pluto's colours

If there are colours which belong to Pluto, they must surely be ugly ones. I suspect that the horrible stench of sulphurous fumes which are emitted from deep underground (the underworld!), in certain countries could be associated with Pluto. For this reason it may be associated with a colour which could be described as *dirty sulphur*.

Being such a violent planet, Pluto is considered to be the higher octave of Mars, the god of war. As such, it has an affinity with the deep shades of red, such as *cerise, burgundy, beetroot,* and *plum.*

The 12 zodiac signs
Their Characteristics and Colours

Aries

Here are some of the "correspondences" which go with Aries: adventure, abruptness, aggression, bluntness, boredom, bossiness, burns or cuts, courage, capability, enterprise, enthusiasm, forcefulness, fighting spirit, headaches, hot temper, impetuousness, impatience, innovation, insomnia or fevers, loyalty, leadership, pioneering, rashness, speed, strong-will, the need to win, thriving on new challenges or competition, the need to be active and vitality.

Aries rules the armed forces, dangerous conditions, explorers, fire, firemen, guns, heat, hot or sharp utensils, machinery, mechanics, occupations which are mentally or physically active or require initiative, spicy foods, surgery and surgeons and welders. Aries is ruled by Mars. The colour of Aries is *vivid red* and *scarlet*.

Taurus

Here are some of the "correspondences" which go with Taurus: affection, dependability, caution, fixed opinions, good food, inclination to put on weight, long lastingness, loving, luxury, possessiveness, providing, possession and ownership, stability, reliability, security, stubbornness, slowness and stodginess.

Taurus rules art, artists, beauty, banks, carpets, confectionery, copper, carpet layers, cashiers, financiers, gardening, horticulture, jewellery, jewellers, landscape gardeners, music, musicians, money, storerooms, storemen, the throat, treasurers and wheat fields.

Taurus is ruled by Venus. The colour of Taurus is *reddish orange*. When the "earthiness" of Taurus is combined with this colour, it can give a *warm, rich bronze*.

Gemini

Here are some of the "correspondences" which go with Gemini: alertness, advertising, accountants, arms, books, book shops and sellers, communication, correspondence, couriers, commuting, car dealers, clerks and clerical work, conversation, duality, dexterity, documents, enquiries, information, graphologists, the hands, intelligence agents, interviews, journalists, lectures, languages and linguists, libraries, merchandising, manicurists, manuscripts, messengers, the mind, nerve specialists, news, publications, publishers, the press, post offices and postal workers, printers, quicksilver, reporters, railways, restlessness, roads, runners (sporting), respiratory system, schools and teachers, secretaries, short journeys, trains, taxis, telephones, twins, transporting, translators, visitors, vehicles and writers.

Gemini is ruled by Mercury. The colour of Gemini is *orange*.

Cancer

Here are some of the "correspondences" which go with Cancer: bakers, bakeries, bathrooms, boats, boating, breasts, breeding, catering, collectors, cooks, cooking, crabs and other shellfish, creeks, domestic life, the digestive system, fruitfulness, the family unit, fluids, food, glassware, grocers, guesthouses, homes and homemakers, housekeepers, hotels, kitchens, lakes, mothers, motherhood, mushrooms, nourishment, obstetrics, plumbers, pearls, pearling, real estate, restaurants, the stomach, sailors, sentimentality, storekeepers, streams, swimming, tides, vegetable growers, water, washing and washing machines.

      Cancer is ruled by the moon. The colour of Cancer is *yellowish-orange* and *ochre*.

Leo

Here are some of the "correspondences" which go with Leo: places of amusement and entertainment, bosses, directors, courtship, creativity, crowns, casinos, fame, gambling, gold, government, games, the heart, limelight, leadership, monarchs, matchmaking, managers, oranges, organisers, power and influence, playgrounds, pleasure resorts, romance, royalty, social clubs, the stock exchange, sunrooms, superiors, sport, speculation, stage performers, the first child, theatres, theatrical life, VIPs and warmth.

      Leo is ruled by the sun. The colours of Leo are *yellow, gold* and bright *sunny* hues.

Virgo

Here are some of the "correspondences" which go with Virgo: accountants, agencies, small animals and pets, analysts, chemists, critics, criticism, civil service, clerks, craftsmen, cynics, doctors, dietitians, draftsmen, employees, efficiency, health care, hygiene, health services, healers, herbalists, the intestines, labour, masseurs, minutiae, nursing, naturopathy, nutrition, osteopathy, pattern makers, recipes, small details, servants, staff, sanitation, satire, statistics, veterinarians, waiters and waitresses.

      Virgo is ruled by Mercury. The colours of Virgo are *lime green* and *olive green*.

The 12 zodiac signs
Their Characteristics and Colours

Libra

Here are some of the "correspondences" which go with Libra: affection, arbitration, art, artists, balance, beauty, beauty parlours, beauticians, boutiques, contracts, cosmetics, compromise, decorators, dressmakers, diplomacy, diplomats, embroidery, equilibrium, fashion, florists, flowers, fancy goods, furnishings, harmony, intermediaries, jewellery, jewellers, justice, the kidneys, love alliances, music, milliners, partnerships in marriage, love or business, ornaments, peace, pleasure, social occasions, scales for weighing, symmetry, strategy, tact, weighing up the pros and cons.

Libra is ruled by Venus. The colour of Libra is *green*.

Scorpio

Here are some of the "correspondences" which go with Scorpio: autopsies, abbatoirs, butchers, the bladder, cemeteries, cesspools, cremation, dangerous work or activities, deceased estates, detectives, death, drains, embalming, espionage, executions, floods, funeral directors, inheritance, insurance companies and salesmen, laboratories, legacies, morticians, the meat industry and its workers, nuclear science, passion, psychic abilities, psychic people, plumbing, plumbers, private investigators, rubbish dumps, the reproductive organs, surgery, surgeons, scorpions, secret matters, sorcery, sewers, taxation and tax workers, tyranny, treachery, vice squads, wills and witchcraft.

Scorpio is ruled by Mars and Pluto. Scorpio's colours are *bluish-green, sea green*.

Sagittarius

Here are some of the "correspondences" which go with Sagittarius: airline hostesses and stewards, archery, cheerfulness, churches, cathedrals, comedians, customs department and officers, explorers, exporting, foreign ambassadors, freedom, foreign people and places, humour, hunting, horses, horsemen, higher education, hips and thighs, importing, independence, judges, long journeys, lawyers, the legal profession, the liver, optimism, philosophy, race horses, radio and television announcers, religion, religious practitioners, sciatica, sportsmen, sporting goods, tin, universities and wide open spaces.

Sagittarius is ruled by Jupiter. The colour of Sagittarius is *blue*.

Capricorn

Here are some of the "correspondences" which go with Capricorn: age, archaeology, architecture, air conditioning, bricks, bricklayers, builders, bones, concrete, caves, crystals, clocks, cold, coal, chiropractors, civil, industrial and mining engineers, contraction, dark places, decay, dryness, engineers, endurance, economists, excavators, falls, farms, farming, government and officials, granite, ice, knees, long-range projects, limitation, lead (the metal), leather work, mines, mining, masonry, monuments, osteopathy, old ruins, the past, perseverance, pessimists, plasterers, politics, pottery, quarries, refrigeration, responsibility, rocks, sculptors, the skeleton, time, and underground places, passages, vaults and activities.

Capricorn is ruled by Saturn. The colour of Capricorn is *indigo*.

Aquarius

Here are some of the "correspondences" which go with Aquarius: aeronautics, aeroplanes, airports, altruism, ankles, astrology, advanced thought, batteries, computers, cooperative societies, cramps, detached, electricians, electricity, electronics, electroplating, explorers, erratic, friends, friendship clubs, humanitarians, your hopes and wishes, inventors, lightning, modern, modern technology, nuclear physics, the new age, originality, radio and television broadcasting, rebels, reformers, researchers, radio, radar, sonar, spasms, the space age, your social circle and associated activities, scientists, socialism and X-ray technicians. Aquarius is also associated with things which are avant-garde, detached, erratic, unorthodox, unpredictable, nonconformist or paradoxical.

Aquarius is ruled by Uranus. Aquarian colours are *violet, purple and deep amethyst*.

Pisces

Here are some of the "correspondences" which go with Pisces: actors, actresses, alcohol, anaesthetics, aquariums, bartenders, boats, confusion, chiropodists, clairvoyance, convents, coral, drugs, dancing, divers, delusion, deception, fish, the fishing industry, films, the feet, footwear, fog, fantasy, fountains, falsehood, fakes, fictitious names, hospitals, hidden things and places, imagination, hydraulics, imitation, impracticality, mist, muddle, mediums, mysteries, mazes, mysticism, naval affairs, occupations connected with water, oil, privacy, psychics, poisons, pretenders, petrol, photography, prisons and other places of confinement, rivers, retreats, swimmers, secrecy, sanitariums, seances, spiritualism, the sea, sensitivity, service stations, shipping, sleep, spirituality, submarines and television.

Pisces is ruled by Neptune. The colours of Pisces are *magenta* and *reddish-purple*.

67

A Summary of Colours and their Corresponding Spheres and Signs

Apricot ....Venus plus the Sun
Aqua ....Libra plus the Moon
Beige ....Earth plus the Moon
Beetroot ....Pluto
Black ....Saturn
Blue ....Sagittarius
    Bluish green ....Scorpio
    Bluish violet ....Capricorn
    Cobalt blue ....Uranus
    Dark blue ....Sagittarius plus Saturn
    Electric blue ....Uranus
    Iridescent blue ....Sagittarius plus Neptune
    Navy blue ....Sagittarius plus Saturn
    Pale blue ....Sagittarius plus the Moon
    Powder blue ....Sagittarius plus the Moon
Bronze ....Taurus
Brown ....Earth
    Light brown ....Earth plus the Moon
Burgundy ....Pluto
Cerise ....Pluto
Cobalt blue ....Uranus
Copper ....Venus
Cream ....The Moon
Dark blue ....Sagittarius plus Saturn
Dark brown ....Earth plus Saturn
Dark green ....Libra plus Saturn
Dark red ....Mars plus Saturn
....Aries plus Saturn
Deep amethyst ....Jupiter, Aquarius
Dirty sulphur ....Pluto
Ethereal colours ....Neptune
Faint colours ....Neptune
Fawn ....Earth plus the Moon
Green ....Libra
    Dark green ....Libra plus Saturn
    Pale green ....Libra plus the Moon
    Iridescent green ....Libra plus Neptune
    Lime green ....Virgo
    Olive green ....Virgo
Ghostly colours ....Neptune
Gold ....The Sun
Grey ....Saturn plus the Moon
Indigo ....Capricorn
Iridescent blue ....Neptune plus Sagittarius
Iridescent gold ....Neptune plus the Sun
Iridescent green ....Neptune plus Libra
Iridescent red ....Neptune plus Mars
....Neptune plus Aries

Iridescent silver ....Neptune plus the Moon
Jacaranda ....Neptune
Lavender ....Neptune
Light brown ....Earth plus the Moon
Lilac ....Neptune
Lime green ....Virgo
Magenta ....Pisces
Mauve ....Neptune
Misty colours ....Neptune
Navy blue ....Sagittarius plus Saturn
Ochre ....Cancer
Olive green ....Virgo
Opalescent colours ....Neptune
Orange ....Gemini, The Sun
    Orange-yellow ....Cancer
Pink ....Venus
    Salmon pink ....Venus plus the Sun
    Shocking pink ....Uranus plus Venus
Plum ....Pluto
Powder blue ....Sagittarius plus the Moon
Purple ....Jupiter, Aquarius
Pale blue ....Sagittarius plus the Moon
Pale green ....Libra plus the Moon
Pale orange ....Gemini plus the Moon
....The Sun plus the Moon
Pale pink ....Venus plus the Moon
Pale yellow ....The Sun plus the Moon
....Leo plus the Moon
....Mercury plus the Moon
Red ....Mars, Aries
    Reddish-orange ....Taurus
    Reddish-purple ....Pisces
    Rose ....Venus
    Salmon pink ....Venus plus the Sun
    Scarlet ....Mars, Aries
Sea green ....Scorpio
Shadowy colours ....Neptune
Shocking pink ....Uranus plus Venus
Silver ....The Moon
Sunny colours ....The Sun
Translucent colours ....Neptune
Turquoise ....Scorpio plus the Moon
Violet ....Aquarius, Jupiter
White ....The Moon
Yellow ....The Sun, Leo, Mercury
    Yellowish-green ....Virgo
    Yellowish-orange ....Cancer

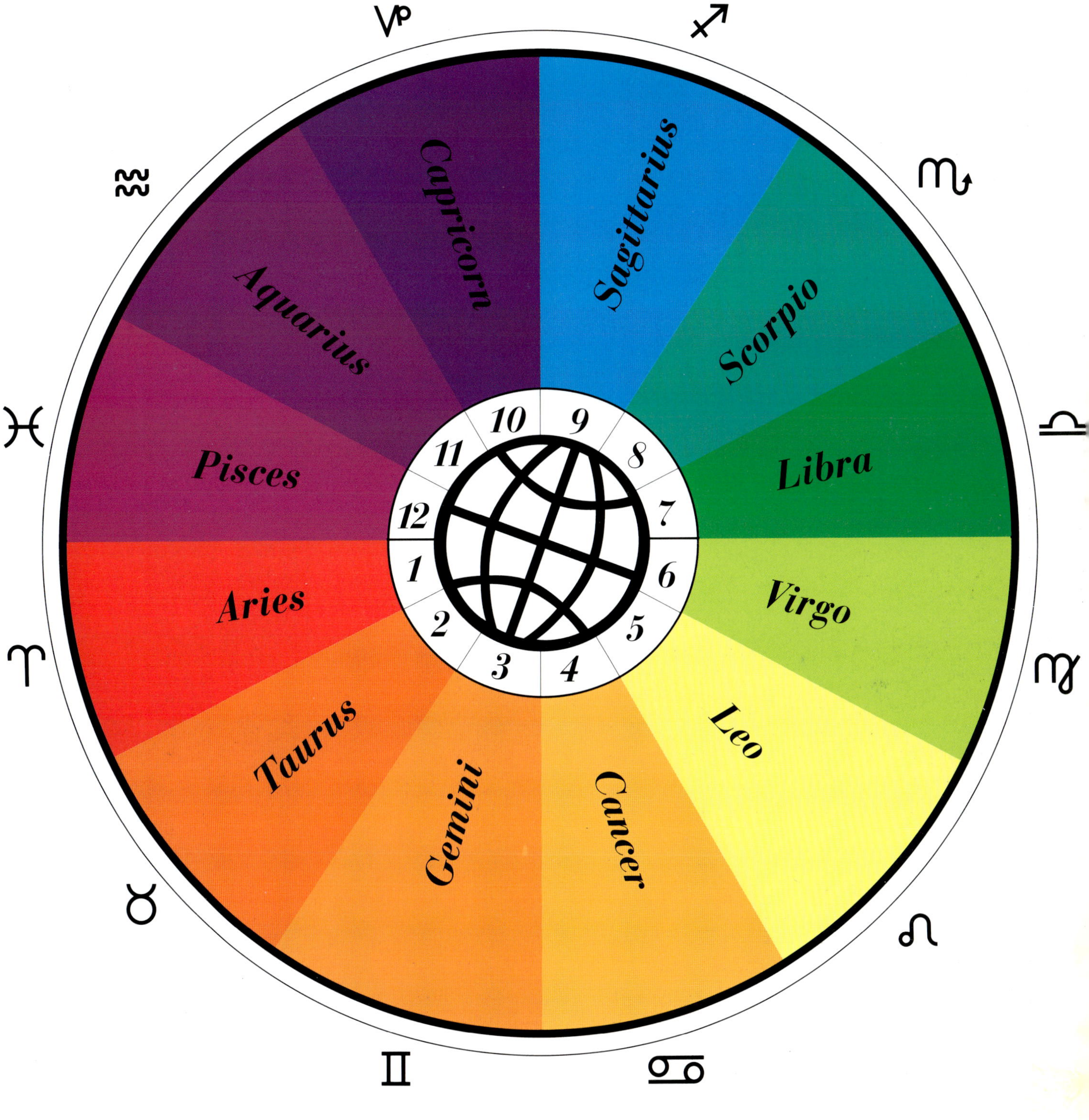

Capricorn
Sagittarius
Scorpio
Libra
Virgo
Leo
Cancer
Gemini
Taurus
Aries
Pisces
Aquarius
10
9
8
7
6
5
4
3
2
1
12
11

Planting by the Moon

Most people are aware that the moon influences tides, but did you know that it also affects the growth of plants? In this chapter, we explain how you can enlist the help of the moon to improve your gardening results – even if you weren't born with a green thumb! If you've never tried gardening, working with the cycles of the moon is the best way to start a most rewarding pastime.

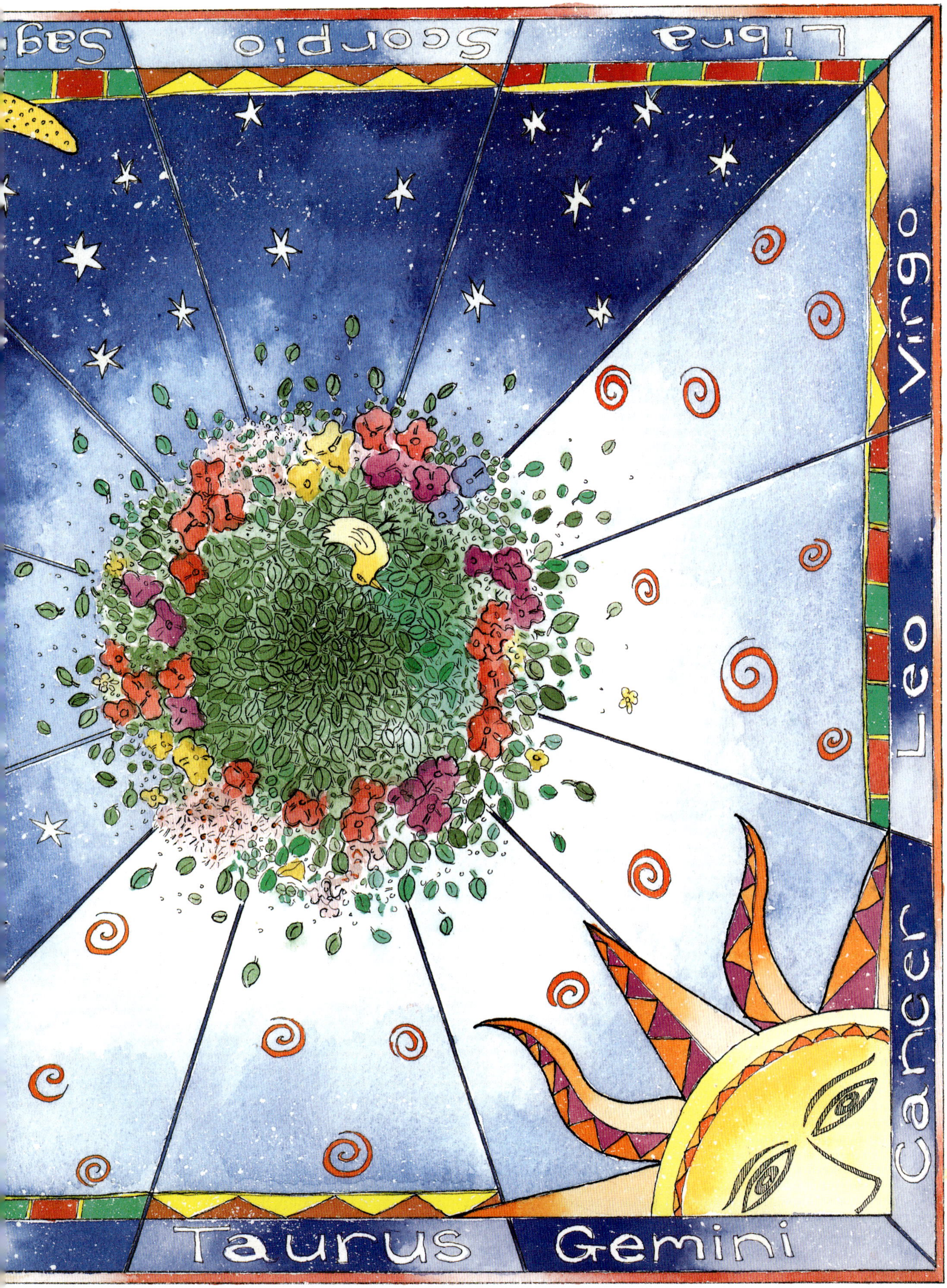
Sag
Scorpio
Libra
Virgo
Leo
Cancer
Gemini
Taurus

This wonderful, yet simple formula of gardening by the cycle of the moon will ensure success. It will bring you a great deal of pleasure and satisfaction, stimulate your tastebuds for home grown vegetables, give you a chance to enjoy some fresh air and gentle exercise, make your home look more attractive through the use of greenery and freshly-cut flowers and, it will save you money – always a bonus! Who could ask for more?

You don't need a big garden either; you'll be amazed at just how much you can grow in a small, well planned space – and if you live in a unit, don't give up because you can cultivate all sorts of plants in pots on the balcony, in a windowbox or even in a sunny room.

For many years *The Women's Weekly* has published my moon cycle charts and judging by all the letters I have received over a very long period I know there are already many people, including farmers and market gardeners, who work with the lunar cycle to get the best possible results. However, there are also many people who have never tried it. So why delay any longer, you may as well give it a go.

Anything which grows, whether it is a shrub, wheat, barley, oats, herbs, flowers, trees or vegetables, has an affinity with the two main cycles of nature. They are the solar cycle which determines the seasons and the lunar cycle which has an extremely important influence on all of the processes of germination, growth, development and productiveness – so important in a vigorous garden.

To plant a particular crop in the right season is definitely not good enough – you must choose the correct phase of the moon and, for the best results, plant when the moon is in a zodiac sign which is favourable for sowing, planting and even transplanting.

The 12 signs of the zodiac are divided into four groups of elements:

Fire: Aries, Leo, Sagittarius

Air: Libra, Aquarius, Gemini

Water: Cancer, Scorpio, Pisces

Earth: Capricorn, Taurus, Virgo

Each zodiac sign has a quality distinctly its own and, for gardening, they can also be divided into four groups:

❶ Cancer, Scorpio and Pisces are very fertile, therefore abundantly fruitful.

❷ Capricorn, Taurus and Libra are semi-fertile and reasonably productive.

❸ Sagittarius, Aquarius and Aries are all semi-barren.

❹ Gemini, Leo and Virgo are very barren.

It stands to reason that you would not plant any seeds while the moon is in Gemini, Leo or Virgo, if you wanted a high yield of strong, luxuriant, productive plants. Your results will be amazingly improved if you use the moon's power in one of the watery, fruitful signs: Cancer, Scorpio or Pisces.

It is equally important to choose the correct phase of the moon for various activities in your garden. The time of new moon is the start of its waxing cycle which continues for about 15 days during which the moon appears to grow bigger and brighter – culminating at the time of full moon. This waxing cycle of the moon is the only time you should plant anything (except all the root vegetables) – because the moon is growing and almost anything started then will have a much better chance to grow and increase in number.

This potential for success is considerably magnified if you plant and transplant when the moon is in Cancer, Scorpio or Pisces, while it is waxing. You also will have good results with the moon's position in Capricorn, Taurus or Libra. Avoid all the other signs – Sagittarius, Aquarius, Aries, Gemini, Leo and Virgo – because, for the purposes of gardening, they are just too barren and unproductive.

After the day of full moon the two-week waning cycle begins, during which the moon gradually appears to decrease in size and grow darker before finally vanishing into the dazzling rays of the sun. The first week of the moon's waning cycle is the best time for planting vegetables which produce their crops **below** the ground – such as carrots, potatoes, onions, beetroot, turnips, parsnips and radishes. The edible part of these vegetables, hidden beneath the earth, develops very well when the seeds are planted in the dark of the moon.

On the other hand, if they are sown during the waxing moon, they produce a lot of foliage above the ground, to the detriment of the edible tubers.

The moon completely fades during the last week of the waning cycle and this is not a favourable time for planting anything. However, the symbolism of this dying moon

"...the symbolism of the dying moon indicates the best time to destroy pests, weeds, fungus, noxious growth and prepare garden beds or farm paddocks for planting."

indicates the best time to destroy pests, weeds, fungus, noxious growth, to burn off rubbish and prepare garden beds or farm paddocks for planting. If you can find a time when this dying moon is in one of the barren signs – Gemini, Leo or Virgo – you have the best combination for ridding your garden of weeds and pests because their chances of survival and revival will be minimal.

During the lunar monthly cycle, the moon forms both favourable and adverse star patterns with the sun. For the purposes of gardening, you should avoid planting anything when these two spheres are in conflict. In most cases these adverse patterns occur on the day of new moon and on the 8th, 15th and 22nd days after that, corresponding to the times of first quarter, full moon and last quarter, which you will see marked in pale blue on the **Moon sign chart** on the following pages.

Some readers may like to try an experiment to test the validity of the moon's magical influence on gardening. You will need a packet of seeds of your choice, preferably flowers or a vegetable which produces its crop above the ground. Whichever you choose, make sure it is suitable for planting at the time you intend to carry out the experiment. After all, you should not sow seeds in January if they are meant to be planted in June!

You also will need four seed boxes which are filled with soil from the same source. Divide the packet of seeds into four equal parts and, using the **Moon sign chart**, plant them at the following staggered times:

❶ When the waxing moon is in either Pisces, Cancer or Scorpio.

❷ When the waxing moon is in either Gemini, Leo or Virgo.

❸ When the waning moon is in either Pisces, Cancer or Scorpio.

❹ When the waning moon is in either Gemini, Leo or Virgo.

You will find the time of day or night when the moon enters those signs in the **Moon sign chart**. The moon remains in each sign for approximately two and a half days.

Give the four boxes of seeds the same amount of water and sunlight and then compare each one for germination. When the seedlings are ready, transplant them into your garden, taking care that they all have equal advantage as far as soil composition, watering and sunlight are concerned.

As they grow, you will see a living example of the moon's magic. The difference between the strong, luxuriant plants from box number one and the weak, spindly ones from box number four will surprise you, especially when it is remembered that all the seeds came from the same packet and shared the same conditions.

Let the moon work a little of its magic for you!

☉ Sun	♆ Neptune	
Moon ☽	Pluto ♇	♎ Libra
☿ Mercury	♈ Aries	Scorpio ♏
Venus ♀	Taurus ♉	♐ Sagittarius
♂ Mars	♊ Gemini	Capricorn ♑
Jupiter ♃	Cancer ♋	♒ Aquarius
♄ Saturn	♌ Leo	Pisces ♓
Uranus ♅	Virgo ♍	

Phases of the moon

The following times tell you when each of the four phases of the moon begins. Each phase lasts approximately one week.

Eastern Standard Time is used throughout and also in the moon sign chart. In Australia, this applies to New South Wales, Victoria, Queensland and Tasmania (except when daylight saving is in force).

If you live in Western Australia, South Australia or the Northern Territory, adjust times accordingly.

July 1992

First quarter on July 7 at 12.44pm
Full moon on July 15 at 5.07am
Last quarter on July 23 at 8.13am
New moon on July 30 at 5.36am

August 1992

First quarter on August 5 at 9.00pm
Full moon on August 13 at 8.28pm
Last quarter on August 21 at 8.02pm
New moon on August 28 at 12.43pm

September 1992

First quarter on September 4 at 8.40am
Full moon on September 12 at 12.18pm
Last quarter on September 20 at 5.54am
New moon on September 26 at 8.41pm

October 1992

First quarter on October 4 at 12.13am
Full moon on October 12 at 4.04am
Last quarter on October 19 at 2.13pm
New moon on October 26 at 6.35am

November 1992

First quarter on November 2 at 7.12pm
Full moon on November 10 at 7.21pm
Last quarter on November 17 at 9.40pm
New moon on November 24 at 7.12pm

December 1992

First quarter on December 2 at 4.18pm
Full moon on December 10 at 9.42am
Last quarter on December 17 at 5.14am
New moon on December 24 at 10.44am

January 1993

First quarter on January 1 at 1.39pm
Full moon on January 8 at 10.38pm
Last quarter on January 15 at 2.02pm
New moon on January 23 at 4.28am
First quarter on January 31 at 9.21am

February 1993

Full moon on February 7 at 9.56am
Last quarter on February 14 at 12.58am
New moon on February 21 at 11.06pm

March 1993

First quarter on March 2 at 1.48am
Full moon on March 8 at 7.47pm
Last quarter on March 15 at 2.17pm
New moon on March 23 at 5.15pm
First quarter on March 31 at 2.11pm

April 1993

Full moon on April 7 at 4.44am
Last quarter on April 14 at 5.40am
New moon on April 22 at 9.50am
First quarter on April 29 at 10.41pm

May 1993

Full moon on May 6 at 1.35pm
Last quarter on May 13 at 10.21pm
New moon on May 22 at 12.07am
First quarter on May 29 at 4.22am

June 1993

Full moon on June 4 at 11.03pm
Last quarter on June 12 at 3.37pm
New moon on June 20 at 11.53am
First quarter on June 27 at 8.44am

July 1993

Full moon on July 4 at 9.46am
Last quarter on July 12 at 8.50am
New moon on July 19 at 9.25pm
First quarter on July 26 at 1.26pm

August 1993

Full moon on August 2 at 10.11pm
Last quarter on August 11 at 1.20am
New moon on August 18 at 5.29am
First quarter on August 24 at 7.58pm

September 1993

Full moon on September 1 at 12.34pm
Last quarter on September 9 at 4.27pm
New moon on September 16 at 1.11pm
First quarter on September 23 at 5.33am

October 1993

Full moon on October 1 at 4.55am
Last quarter on October 9 at 5.36am
New moon on October 15 at 9.37pm
First quarter on October 22 at 6.53pm
Full moon on October 30 at 10.39pm

November 1993

Last quarter on November 7 at 4.37pm
New moon on November 14 at 7.35am
First quarter on November 21 at 12.04pm
Full moon on November 29 at 4.32pm

December 1993

Last quarter on December 7 at 1.50am
New moon on December 13 at 7.28pm
First quarter on December 21 at 8.27am
Full moon on December 29 at 9.06am

Moon sign chart for 1992

Day	July	August	September	October	November	December
1	♋	♍	♏ 5.39am	♐	♒ 10.44pm	♓ 7.24pm
2	♌ 8.16am	♎ 6.18pm	♏	♐	♒ 1st quarter	♓ 1st quarter
3	♌	♎	♐ 10.51am	♑ 3.30am	♒	♓
4	♍ 8.38am	♏ 9.17pm	♐ 1st quarter	♑ 1st quarter	♓ 11.14am	♈ 7.50am
5	♍	♏ 1st quarter	♑ 8.07pm	♒ 2.54pm	♓	♈
6	♎ 10.28am	♏	♑	♒	♈ 11.20pm	♉ 6.17pm
7	♎ 1st quarter	♐ 3.58am	♑	♒	♈	♉
8	♏ 2.54pm	♐	♒ 8.09am	♓ 3.39am	♈	♉
9	♏	♑ 2.01pm	♒	♓	♉ 9.20am	♊ 1.38am
10	♐ 10.18pm	♑	♓ 8.57pm	♈ 3.37pm	♉ full moon	♊ full moon
11	♐	♑	♓	♈	♊ 4.50pm	♋ 6.06am
12	♐	♒ 2.07am	♓ full moon	♈ full moon	♊	♋
13	♑ 8.17am	♒ full moon	♈ 9.03am	♉ 1.49am	♋ 10.20pm	♌ 8.48am
14	♑	♓ 2.52pm	♈	♉	♋	♌
15	♒ full moon 8.04pm	♓	♉ 7.48pm	♊ 10.09am	♋	♍ 10.57am
16	♒	♓	♉	♊	♌ 2.24am	♍
17	♒	♈ 3.12am	♉	♋ 4.37pm	♌ last quarter	♎ last quarter 1.34pm
18	♓ 8.45am	♈	♊ 4.41am	♋	♍ 5.29am	♎
19	♓	♉ 2.11pm	♊	♌ last quarter 9.02pm	♍	♏ 5.21pm
20	♈ 9.08pm	♉	♋ last quarter 11.00am	♌	♎ 8.04am	♏
21	♈	♊ last quarter 10.37pm	♋	♍ 11.28pm	♎	♐ 10.43pm
22	♈	♊	♌ 2.20pm	♍	♏ 10.53am	♐
23	♉ last quarter 7.37am	♊	♌	♍	♏	♐
24	♉	♋ 3.37am	♍ 3.09pm	♎ 12.40am	♐ new moon 3.02pm	♑ new moon 6.05am
25	♊ 2.45pm	♋	♍	♎	♐	♑
26	♊	♌ 5.16am	♎ new moon 2.56pm	♏ new moon 2.05am	♑ 9.39pm	♒ 3.44pm
27	♋ 6.09pm	♌	♎	♏	♑	♒
28	♋	♍ new moon 4.47am	♏ 3.45pm	♐ 5.30am	♑	♒
29	♌ 6.40pm	♍	♏	♐	♒ 7.20am	♓ 3.29am
30	♌ new moon	♎ 4.11am	♐ 7.34pm	♑ 12.19pm	♒	♓
31	♍ 6.02pm	♎		♑		♈ 4.08pm

The key to the colour codes featured in the Moon sign chart appear on the following pages.
An astrological symbols key appears on page 73.
Times in the moon sign chart indicate when the moon enters the sign shown by the symbol.
1st quarter, full moon, new moon and last quarter indicate the phases of the moon.

Moon sign chart for 1993

Day	January	February	March	April	May	June
1	♈ *1st quarter*	♊ 9.16pm	♊ 4.53am	♋	♍ 10.01am	♏ 8.23pm
2	♈	♊	♊ *1st quarter*	♌ 12.22am	♍	♏
3	♉ 3.31am	♊	♋ 12.17pm	♌	♎ 11.21am	♐ 11.02pm
4	♉	♋ 2.57am	♋	♍ 2.11am	♎	♐ *full moon*
5	♊ 11.43am	♋	♌ 3.41pm	♍	♏ 11.58am	♐
6	♊	♌ 4.52am	♌	♎ 1.55am	♏ *full moon*	♑ 3.27am
7	♋ 4.11pm	♌ *full moon*	♍ 3.53pm	♎ *full moon*	♐ 1.35pm	♑
8	♋ *full moon*	♍ 4.30am	♍ *full moon*	♏ 1.33am	♐	♒ 10.40am
9	♌ 5.50pm	♍	♎ 2.47pm	♏	♑ 5.52pm	♒
10	♌	♎ 3.59am	♎	♐ 3.11am	♑	♓ 8.58pm
11	♍ 6.21pm	♎	♏ 2.41pm	♐	♑	♓
12	♍	♏ 5.24am	♏	♑ 8.25am	♒ 1.45am	♓ *last quarter*
13	♎ 7.31pm	♏	♐ 5.34pm	♑ *last quarter* 5.37pm	♒ *last quarter*	♈ 9.15am
14	♎	♐ *last quarter* 10.09am	♐	♒	♓ 12.51pm	♈
15	♏ *last quarter* 10.43pm	♐	♐ *last quarter*	♒	♓	♉ 9.20pm
16	♏	♑ 6.21pm	♑ 12.29am	♒	♓	♉
17	♏	♑	♑	♓ 5.34am	♈ 1.25am	♉
18	♐ 4.31am	♑	♒ 10.53am	♓	♈	♊ 7.13am
19	♐	♒ 5.06am	♒	♈ 6.15pm	♉ 1.17pm	♓
20	♑ 12.47pm	♒	♓ 11.12pm	♈	♉	♋ *new moon* 2.06pm
21	♑	♓ *new moon* 5.13pm	♓	♈	♊ 11.08pm	♋
22	♒ 11.01pm	♓	♓	♉ *new moon* 6.09am	♊ *new moon*	♌ 6.27pm
23	♒ *new moon*	♓	♈ *new moon* 11.52am	♉	♊	♌
24	♒	♈ 5.51am	♈	♊ 4.28pm	♋ 6.39am	♍ 9.19pm
25	♓ 10.48am	♈	♈	♊	♋	♍
26	♓	♉ 6.12pm	♉ 12.00am	♊	♌ 12.04pm	♎ 11.46pm
27	♈ 11.29pm	♉	♉	♋ 12.46am	♌	♎ *1st quarter*
28	♈	♉	♊ 10.49am	♋	♍ 3.47pm	♎
29	♈		♊	♌ *1st quarter* 6.40am	♍ *1st quarter*	♏ 2.38am
30	♉ 11.38am		♋ 7.15pm	♌	♎ 6.19pm	♏
31	♉ *1st quarter*		♋ *1st quarter*		♎	

Yellow: The very best time to plant all flowers, trees, shrubs, lawns, fruit trees and vegetables producing their crops above ground.

Red: A good time for planting trees, flowers, vegetables and fruit trees which produce their crops above ground.

Green: The very best time to plant all vegetables producing their crops below the ground, such as onions, carrots, potatoes, radishes and parsnips.

Day	July		August		September		October		November		December	
1	♐	6.29am	♑		♓ *full moon*		♈ *full moon*		♊	8.14pm	♋	12.18pm
2	♐		♒ *full moon*	2.37am	♓		♈		♊		♋	
3	♑	11.50am	♒		♈	7.22am	♉	2.14am	♊		♌	7.34pm
4	♑ *full moon*		♓	12.45pm	♈		♉		♋	6.26am	♌	
5	♒	7.15pm	♓		♉	8.10pm	♊	2.28pm	♋		♌	
6	♒		♓		♉		♊		♌	2.07pm	♍	12.44am
7	♒		♈	12.40am	♉		♊		♌ *last quarter*		♍ *last quarter*	
8	♓	5.11am	♈		♊	8.17am	♋	12.43am	♍	6.48pm	♎	4.04am
9	♓		♉	1.23pm	♊ *last quarter*		♋ *last quarter*		♍		♎	
10	♈	5.12pm	♉		♋	5.38pm	♌	7.35am	♎	8.43pm	♏	6.05am
11	♈		♉ *last quarter*		♋		♌		♎		♏	
12	♈ *last quarter*		♊	12.48am	♌	10.52pm	♍	10.37am	♏	9.01pm	♐	7.40am
13	♉	5.38am	♊		♌		♍		♏		♐ *new moon*	
14	♉		♋	8.47am	♌		♎	10.48am	♐ *new moon*	9.21pm	♑	10.07am
15	♊	4.08pm	♋		♍	12.21am	♎ *new moon*		♐		♑	
16	♊		♌	12.44pm	♎ *new moon*	11.45pm	♏	10.02am	♑	11.35pm	♒	2.52pm
17	♋	11.09pm	♌		♎		♏		♑		♒	
18	♋		♍ *new moon*	1.42pm	♏	11.15pm	♐	10.24am	♑		♓	11.00pm
19	♋ *new moon*		♍		♏		♐		♒	5.09am	♓	
20	♌	2.48am	♎	1.36pm	♏		♑	1.43pm	♒		♓	
21	♌		♎		♐	12.54am	♑		♓ *1st quarter*	2.28pm	♈ *1st quarter*	10.20am
22	♍	4.25am	♏	2.28pm	♐		♒ *1st quarter*	8.50pm	♓		♈	
23	♍		♏		♑ *1st quarter*	5.55pm	♒		♓		♉	11.06pm
24	♎	5.40am	♐ *1st quarter*	5.46pm	♑		♒		♈	2.31am	♉	
25	♎		♐		♒	2.20pm	♓	7.18am	♈		♉	
26	♏ *1st quarter*	8.01am	♑	11.59pm	♒		♓		♉	3.15pm	♊	10.47am
27	♏		♑		♒		♈	7.40pm	♉		♊	
28	♐	12.14pm	♑		♓	1.14am	♈		♉		♋	7.47pm
29	♐		♒	8.43am	♓		♈		♊ *full moon*	2.49am	♋ *full moon*	
30	♑	6.28pm	♒		♈	1.30pm	♉ *full moon*	8.21am	♊		♋	
31	♑		♓	7.20pm			♉				♌	2.00am

Brown: A good time for planting those vegetables that produce their crops below the ground, such as onions, carrots, potatoes, parsnips and radishes.

Pale blue: The periods affected by the four phases of the moon are not favourable for planting or transplanting. Instead, prepare the soil.

Purple: The best time for weeding, burning off and then preparing the garden beds for planting. Destroy pests and noxious weeds at this time.

Herbs of the Zodiac

Nicholas Culpeper, a famous astrologer and herbalist who lived in the 17th century, first discovered the link between herbs and the zodiac. He assigned each herb to its ruling planet, including the sun and moon and the 12 star signs. Since then, other astrologers who specialised in medical astrology, naturopathy and herbal remedies have expanded on his ideas.

Today, many people enjoy growing and using herbs, whether it is for the flavour they add to foods, for their medicinal value or for the aesthetic pleasure of a herb garden. Here, Richard Sterling lists the herbs he believes are in harmony with each of the signs of the zodiac.

Aries

Your ruling planet Mars rules the colour red and is associated with heat and fire. Although some foods and spices cannot be classified as herbs, they are in harmony with Aries, for example, red capsicums, ripe red tomatoes, red hot chillies, black or white pepper, cayenne pepper, curry and red cabbage.

Garlic: this is so well known and widely used that little needs to be said about it except that it supplies selenium, a trace element that is lacking in Australian soil. Peeled, chopped or minced bulbs complement almost all savoury food, particularly the foods of Asia and the Mediterranean countries. Garlic is thought to have strong medicinal powers.

Horseradish: is a relative of the mustard family. The white roots are grated and used as a condiment, high in Vitamin C and some essential minerals. It's hot, biting taste makes it ideal for use in creamy sauces, mixed with coleslaw and as a sauce with roast or corned beef.

Marjoram: there are three types of marjoram: pot marjoram, sweet marjoram and wild marjoram. Each variety is spicy and aromatic, but wild marjoram has the strongest flavour and is also known as **oregano**, which is ideal for adding to pizzas and pasta dishes. Marjoram is an ingredient in bouquet garni. It was a popular strewing herb in days gone by, when herbs were thrown about the house to give a pleasant scent.

Watercress: has a pungent, peppery flavour. It is rich in iron and vitamin C and can be used in salads, soups, casseroles and as a tasty garnish.

Taurus

Lemon verbena: has very strong lemon-flavoured leaves. It can be used in jellies, fruit salad and casseroles or infused to make a tea.

Lovage: the leaves have a strong yeast-like flavour with a hint of peppery celery; they are a tasty addition to salads, soups and casseroles. The stalks, which are hollow, are often crystallised and used as sweet decoration.

Mint: Taurus is in harmony with mint, probably one of the most popular of all herbs. There are three well known varieties, garden mint, spearmint and peppermint, which can be used in sauces, salads and desserts.

Tansy: tastes aromatic and somewhat bitter. Tansy pudding is strongly flavoured and was originally eaten during Lent in England.

Thyme: comes in many varieties but the most popular ones for culinary purposes are lemon thyme and garden thyme.

Gemini

Caraway: is a versatile herb because the leaves, dried seeds and the roots can all be used. Chopped leaves and seeds are delicious in breads, biscuits and cakes. In ancient times caraway seeds were used to freshen the breath.

Dill: has blue-green leaves and yellow flowers. The leaves can be used as a garnish for soups and salads and in cooked seafood, the seeds for making dill pickles, chutney or vinegar.

Lavender: seldom used in cooking nowadays; it is widely used in pot-pourris and lavender bags. Lavender oil, when added to the bath water, is fragrant and refreshing.

Parsley: probably the best known of all herbs. There are several varieties, but the most popular ones are curled parsley for garnishes and decoration, while Italian parsley has larger, flatter leaves and a mild celery flavour. It is one of the four essential ingredients in the "fine herbes" mixture (the others are tarragon, chervil and chives).

Cancer

Anise: often used in cooking and as a flavouring in drinks. The taste is quite strong, similar to licorice. The dried seeds are the most widely used part of the plant. It is widely believed that aniseed, whole or ground, assists digestion and aniseed tea keeps colds and flu at bay and freshens the breath.

Ginger: the hot, aromatic roots of the ginger plant should be peeled and grated or thinly sliced, often used in preserves, stir-fries and curries; it has a tenderising effect on meat. Powdered or crystallised ginger is used in sweets, biscuits (particularly gingerbread) and cakes.

Lemon balm: a fragrant, lemon-scented herb which can be used in salads and in cool drinks or as a herbal tea. Also used to flavour soups, stews, casseroles and dressings.

Leo

Bay leaves: can be used either fresh or dried in cooking many types of food. Bay leaves are an essential ingredient in a bouquet garni and add a tantalising flavour to fish, meat, stews, soups, vegetables and rice desserts.

Borage: a very useful herb because you can add both the leaves and the vivid blue flowers to garden salads, raw vegetables, coleslaw and soups. It has a flavour reminiscent of cucumber.

Chamomile: grown for the flowers which are used in salads or infused to make a tea.

Marigold: with its brilliant splash of bright orange and yellow flowers it is in harmony with the colours of Leo and the sun. The petals can be used as an inexpensive substitute for saffron. Fresh or dried petals can make a refreshing herbal tea and they can add a delicate flavour to rice, cheese, egg and savoury dishes. Add fresh marigold petals to garden salads.

Saffron: genuine saffron is a rare and very expensive herb, so it is seldom used in everyday cooking. It is appropriate that this brilliant golden yellow herb should be ruled by Leo and the sun. The herb comes from the orange stigmas of the saffron crocus.

Virgo

Fennel: has fine, feathery, green leaves with a delicious sweet flavour similar to aniseed. It is particularly suitable to use with fish, and the fresh green leaves and soft stems can be chopped up and eaten in salads or steamed as a vegetable served with butter. Also add it to an omelette or scrambled eggs. The seeds are used in bread, pastries, biscuits and pasta.

Salad burnet: is not so well-known today although it was well regarded in ancient times. It has a mild flavour, similar to cucumber. Add to garden salads, raw vegetables or use as a garnish. Whole sprays may be added to punches and fruit drinks.

Southernwood: a bitter herb, with fine grey-green leaves which are lemon-scented when crushed. Infuse it, sweeten it and enjoy its unusual flavour as a herbal tea. Southernwood has medicinal properties – it has been used in tonics, baths and as an antiseptic.

Summer savory: a Virgoan herb with long narrow leaves and small blue and white flowers. Its flavour is stronger than winter savory. It has a delicate spicy flavour which makes it suitable as a seasoning for fish, meat, egg dishes, poultry, vegetables and soup.

Libra

Angelica: a sweetly scented plant with large leaves and strong stems which can be crystallised and used as decorations for cakes and puddings. Stalks and stems give a sweet flavour to stewed fruits, jams and jellies while the roots can be eaten steamed as a vegetable.

Juniper: has an aromatic scent and the shrub produces blue-black berries with an unusual bitter-sweet flavour. These berries can be ground and infused to make a tea which is beneficial to the kidneys (ruled by Libra). The crushed berries can be added to rich meats and game and to stuffings. Small branches added to barbecue coals will give a pine scent to meat or fish.

Scorpio

Basil: the two best known varieties are bush basil and sweet basil. Sweet basil is a popular, versatile herb and can be added to soups, sauces, casseroles, tomato-based dishes, pasta dishes, green salads, dressing and is excellent with zucchini, squash and eggplant. In ancient times it was regarded as a sacred herb and there are many legends concerning it.

Chives: could be described as mild, miniature onions as far as flavour is concerned and they make a wonderful seasoning for soups, salads, egg dishes, mornays, sandwiches, dips, mayonnaise and as a garnish. It is one of the four essential ingredients in the "fine herbes" mixture (the others are tarragon, chervil and parsley).

Nettles: these are the common stinging nettles. I have a friend who swears by their nutritional and medicinal value, so much so that he grows a large patch of them in his vegetable garden. They can be steamed or boiled as vegetables and the liquid saved, mixed with honey and drank. Nettle juice is alleged to be extremely helpful for lowering high blood pressure.

Tarragon: with its tangy, sweet piquant flavour is much sought after. It is one of the four essential ingredients in the "fine herbes" mixture (the others are chives, chervil and parsley). The aromatic fragrance complements seafood, poultry, game and egg dishes.

Sagittarius

Chervil: a feathery, fern-like herb with a delicate, spicy flavour which is delicious in chervil soup, green salads and with vegetables. It is one of the four essential ingredients in the "fine herbes" mixture (the others are chives, tarragon and parsley). Also suitable as a garnish on steak, chops and pork.

Coriander: is grown for its sweet, spicy, highly aromatic flavour. The seeds are used in cakes and can be cooked with cauliflower and celery. They are an essential ingredient when mixing a curry blend. The leaves are used in Egyptian, Indian and Mediterranean cuisines.

Sage: there are several varieties, but the one with little purple flowers and silver-grey leaves is the most popular. For healthy living this is one of the most beneficial herbs as it is said to aid digestion and soothe nerves. It can be used with port, stews, casseroles, duck, garden salads, tomato dishes, stuffing, cream cheese spreads, fritters and hamburgers.

Capricorn

Comfrey: can be used to make a healing poultice for skin sores, ulcers, chapped hands and to help mend broken bones. The succulent young leaves (don't eat the outer, coarse leaves) have a cucumber taste. These can be battered or fried, or they can be steamed as spinach.

Cumin: has deep green leaves and small pink or white flowers. However, it is only grown for the seeds which are truly spicy and aromatic. They are liberally used in Mexican style dishes as well as in Indian and Middle Eastern cooking. Add to meat casseroles, soups, savoury rice, pickles and chutney, mashed potato and bread.

Sorrel (French): is considered by many people to be a nuisance because it spreads so quickly, so it is wise to grow it in a pot or trough to contain it. The leaves have a distinctly sour taste so it can be added to salads to give them a tangy "bite". Sorrel soup is also a popular dish.

Aquarius

Elder: Black elder shrubs produce highly perfumed creamy-white flowers; when these die the black elderberries begin to form. They taste much better when cooked rather than eaten raw and can be used for making wine, jam, jellies, producing a unique flavour when mixed with crab apples and rose hips. The elderflowers can also be used to make fritters.

Marshmallow: Has soft, velvety grey-green leaves with attractive pale pink flowers. It has been found to be efficacious in the relief of bronchial congestion. The sweet tasting white roots were dried, powdered and made into candies. Our modern fluffy marshmallow sweets were originally flavoured with the powdered roots.

Pisces

Purslane: a tender herb with moist, succulent leaves and small yellow flowers. It has a tangy, crisp flavour and goes well when mixed with other herbs. Mix some of the soft, young leaves in a garden salad or with cream cheese in a sandwich or dip. Cook the leaves as a vegetable with a little butter or add them to soups and broth.

Rose hips: have a high concentration of Vitamin C and they are also a good source of Vitamin E. They can be soaked in water overnight then brought to the boil and left to simmer for about half an hour. This makes a very healthy herbal tea. They are very good for the kidneys.

Sweet cicely: has a sweet, fragrant aniseed flavour. Use it liberally when cooking tart fruits and it will reduce the sugar needed. Add it to salads and dressings, omelettes and fruit salads.

Oriental Astrology

It is not unusual to hear people discussing the qualities of an "Aries personality" or a "typical Leo"; opinions based on the 12 familiar star signs in western astrology. However, we rarely hear of the 60 symbols of oriental astrology, which are associated with your birth year. In this chapter you will discover whether you were born in the Year of the Earth Pig, the Metal Dog or perhaps the Fire Tiger, and how this combination of ruling animal and element can influence your life.

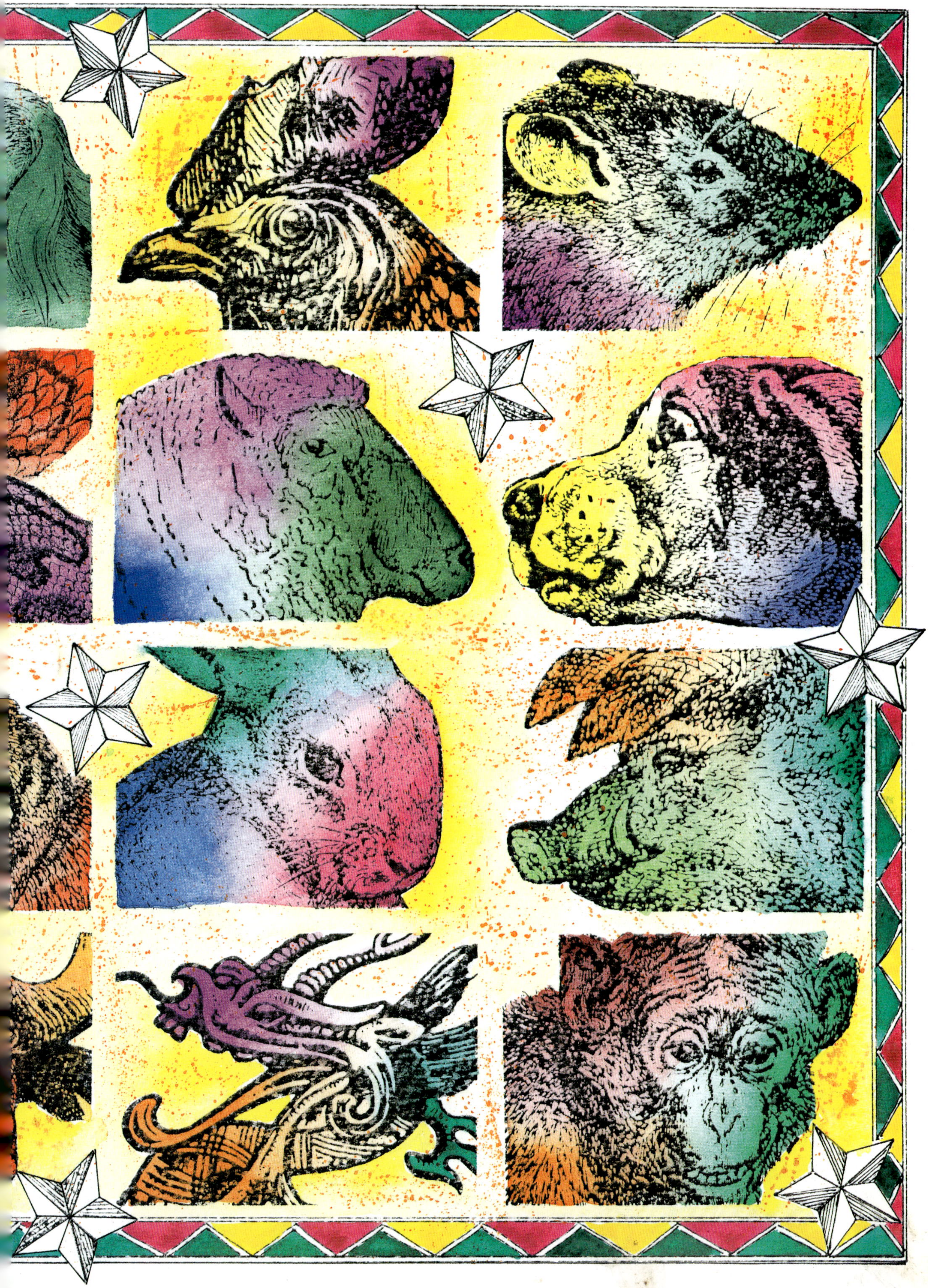

Every January or February the western world is witness to the colourful celebrations which mark the Chinese New Year. We hear that it is the start of the Year of the Dragon or the Year of the Rabbit and so on, but few people realise the significance of this ancient system of astrology. Even fewer people know whether it is the Year of the Metal Ox, the Water Ox, the Wood Ox, the Fire Ox or the Earth Ox, so you see, there are many fascinating discoveries to be made in the study of this ancient knowledge.

Oriental astrologers practised this art many thousands of years ago and today no-one is quite sure how the signs acquired their animal names. One legend suggests that it happened one Chinese New Year when Buddha requested that all the animals in his kingdom appear before him. It seems that only 12 animals turned up. The first to arrive was the Rat, followed by the Ox, the Tiger, the Rabbit, the Dragon, the Snake, the Horse, the Sheep, the Monkey, the Rooster, the Dog and finally the Pig.

As a thankyou to the animals who made the journey, Buddha decided to name a year after each of the animals and people born during that year would inherit some of the qualities of that animal. For example, those born in the Year of the Horse would possess stamina and strength, those born in the Year of the Pig would be very determined and down to earth and those born in the Year of the Dog would be loyal and fair-minded. You'll find that many people born in these years possess these qualities.

Our western zodiac is based on the fact that the sun appears to move through the 12 star signs in one complete year, spending approximately *one month* in each sign. Oriental astrology has a totally different foundation. It is based on the cycles of Saturn and Jupiter. The first is a 60 year period which is the time it takes for Saturn to travel around its orbit twice. Therefore, Jupiter will make five complete journeys during the time it takes Saturn to travel around the circle twice. This is the reason why there are five different "elements" used in oriental astrology: metal, water, wood, fire and earth.

The oriental zodiac does have 12 divisions, but they are based on the cycle of Jupiter which takes 12 years to complete one journey around the circle. Therefore, Jupiter remains for *one year* in each of these 12 divisions and each of these consecutive years is named after an animal whose nature, attributes and behaviour are supposed to express the qualities of that period and, therefore, of people born during that period.

The previous 60 year cycle began in 1924 and concluded in 1983; the current 60 year cycle began in 1984.

Each great cycle begins with the Year of the Wood Rat and the order of the animals which rule each consecutive year is: Rat, Ox, Tiger, Rabbit, Dragon, Snake, Horse, Sheep, Monkey, Rooster, Dog and Pig. Because Jupiter makes five complete journeys around the great circle in 60 years, there are five variations of each of the Animals, for instance, people can be born in the Year of the Metal Dog, the Water Dog, the Fire Dog or the Earth Dog.

Therefore the cycle of animals is completed every 12 years but the entire cycle of elements in combination with animals takes 60 years to run through. For example, the Year of the Metal Rat was 1900; 1912, was the Year of the Water Rat. Add another 12 years and that brings us to 1924, the Year of the Wood Rat. Then 1936 is the Year of the Fire Rat and finally 1948 is the Year of the Earth Rat. If we add another 12 years to 1948, it brings us to 1960, the start of another cycle. Consequently, 1960 is again the Year of the Metal Rat which last occurred in 1900 and will not occur again until the year 2020.

Before you race to find which animal ruled your year of birth, you must know this very important point: the Chinese year does **not** begin on January 1, but on the day of the New Moon in what we call the sign of Aquarius which, in oriental astrology is the Moon of the Tiger. Therefore, I have given you dates for each individual year when these important New Moons occurred so that the many people who were born in January or February (depending on the actual year of birth) will not make a mistake. Although January 1 is the beginning of the year for us in the modern western world, it has no special significance in oriental astrology.

Refer to the **Table of Astrological Elements and Animals** at the end of this chapter to find your ruling animal and element. Find the period in which your birthday occurred and make a note of your ruling animal and element. All you have to do then is turn to the pages with the corresponding description of your element and ruling animal and combine the two for an analysis. You may be surprised by what you discover!

Note: The names of the animals in the Chinese zodiac may differ in some books and journals although the characteristics remain the same. The Ox is sometimes called the Buffalo or Bull, the Rabbit: the Cat or Hare, the Sheep: the Goat and the Pig: the Boar.

"Because Jupiter makes five complete journeys around the great circle in 60 years, there are five variations of each of the animals..."

The five elements

According to tradition, the elements are all interrelated and they interact in two different fashions. One way is to conquer or control, while the other is to promote or produce. The first sequence is: Wood conquers Earth, Earth conquers Water, Water conquers Fire, Fire conquers Metal and Metal conquers Wood.

Applying this to human relationships, it means that your particular element will conquer (or control) and be conquered (or controlled) by other elements. This can be seen when person A feels superior to, or dominates person B, but, in turn, either feels inferior to or is dominated by person C.

The second sequence is: Metal produces Water, Water produces Wood, Wood produces Fire, Fire produces Earth and Earth produces Metal.

In human relationships, this means that your element both promotes (or encourages) and is promoted (or encouraged) by other elements. Again, in human relationships it means that person A promotes person B, while person A is benefited by person C.

The five elements are also known as *agents* or *energies* and they are not meant to be interpreted solely in a material sense as we know them. They represent various energies and forces of nature.

Metal

Metal can function in many different ways. At times it is cold, hard, tough and almost inflexible, refusing to bend. In its primitive state it can be dull and heavy. However, when given attention, it can be slowly moulded and polished to a high lustre. Metal can be sharpened to a point where it will cut, destroy or inflict pain and cruelty.

Some metals are common and easily found, but man must dig deep to find the rare precious metals. Many of the common metals will rust, corrode and decay, but this does not happen to the precious metals.

In the form of quicksilver, metal can be very flexible and is able to adapt itself to fit into any situation. But quicksilver is also hard to hold and will slip through your fingers.

Metal can be magnetised, so metal people have the ability to attract and accumulate money, luxuries, power and the good things in life.

Being rigid, inflexible and resolute can sometimes be an asset when pursuing a particular goal, but there are times when compromise or giving way to another person's wishes is necessary. This is not always easy for metal people to do because they prefer to follow their own pathway without interference or unsolicited advice. Their persistence, perseverance and tenacity will influence the qualities of their particular animal. Being so stubborn and fixed in their opinions means that they will sometimes sever a good relationship when the other person will not bend to their wishes.

Water

Nothing will grow without water, so it is one of nature's most essential elements. There will always be someone who needs it because it nourishes and sustains.

Water finds its own level which means it can achieve a state of equilibrium. However, unless it is contained or directed on a particular course, it will spread without direction and dissipate.

Water can be calm and serene or storm-lashed and furious, causing havoc wherever it goes. Because of this it is related to people's emotions which can be deep or shallow, peaceful and harmonious or turbulent, icy cold, moderate or boiling.

Water will slowly but relentlessly wear away even the hardest rocks, so water people will eventually get their way and achieve their goals often in a silent, subtle but inexorable way. Many water people are intuitive, so they can sense things about others and get "feelings" when something important arises, allowing them to assess any future potential.

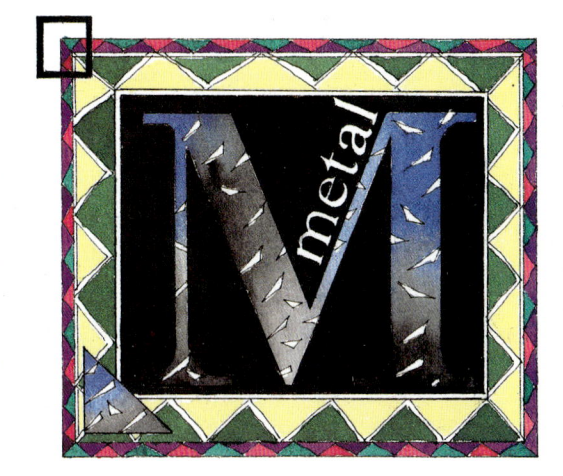

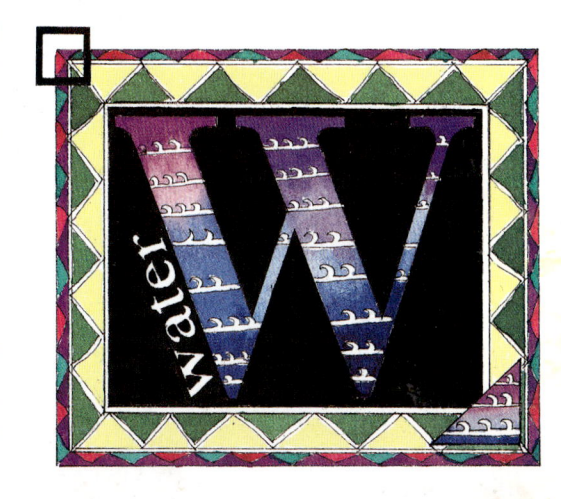

Somewhat like a true Libran, a water person is quietly tactful, diplomatic and very good at strategy, with the knack of persuading other people that what they want to do is exactly what the water person had already planned. If there is a weakness in the water type it is a tendency to be too conciliatory, to take the easy way out, or to rely too heavily on others for support.

Wood

While it is alive, wood in the form of trees and plants will keep on growing and producing things which people and other species in nature need, and when you look at what grows on this planet you cannot help but be amazed, even overwhelmed, by the incredible variety of ways in which wood can manifest.

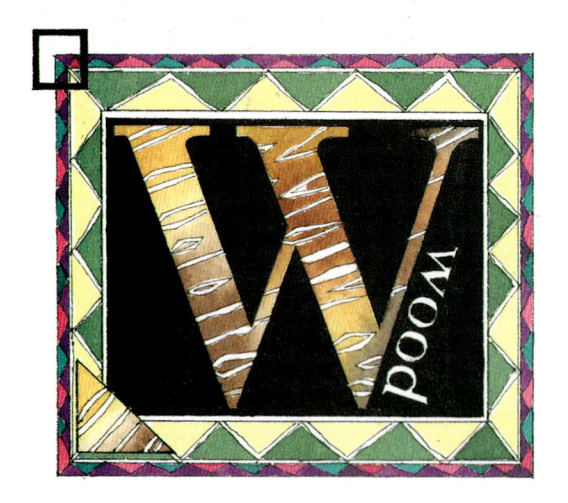

There is an instinctive urge to survive (plants form seeds to reproduce) and they follow regular, well ordered cycles which are dictated by the seasons. Some trees and plants can create the most beautiful things – as shown by their flowers. Beauty is an integral part of their nature and they willingly share it with those who can appreciate it.

Most trees and plants will bend against the force of wind without breaking, but they have little defence against the many creatures which will eat them. However, some types of vegetation have unsuspected forms of self-protection, and if a predator attacks them it is certainly in for a nasty shock.

Wood can be dry, hard and resilient or soft, tender and easily bruised, so wood people know how to differentiate and separate matters into their correct categories. They constantly like to keep on growing and expanding their interests, endeavours and lifestyles, so wood people have the potential to be very successful. They have faith in themselves and in their abilities. This attracts the confidence and support of others whenever it is needed, so in this sense they are fortunate.

Wood people are naturally willing to share things with others. They also have the knack of drawing people into their circle or even joining forces with them in some type of project or business. It is then that they genuinely enjoy sharing whatever rewards result from the joint effort. In other words, they are generous people and, like the trees in the wind, they are willing to bend and to "give a little" when necessary. They like to be productive.

Fire

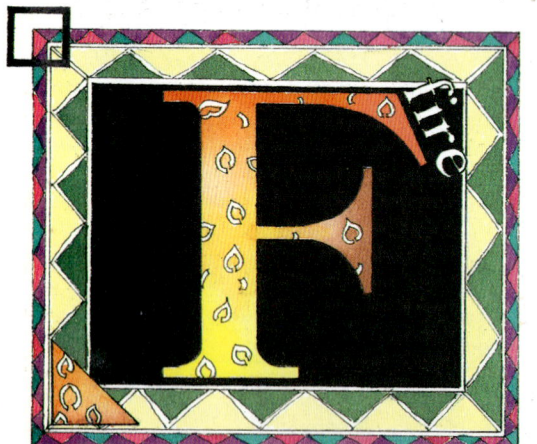

Fire is the symbol of the spirit because it has the ability to warm, energise and vitalise. Without the Sun's fire, which gives us heat and light, nothing on earth would grow or flourish. Therefore, like water, it is indispensable, so there will always be those who cannot do without the fire people.

This element is restless and driven by a natural urge to climb higher and higher. Unless it is confined or subdued by water it will spread out in all directions.

Fire in the form of lightning can be unpredictable and act with a will of its own. When out of control, nothing can be more destructive than this element because it will burn anything in its path. But a fire out of control also eventually burns itself out. Nothing can give more comfort than a fire when it is gentle and moderate. Fire brings light where there is darkness and gives warmth where there is cold, so people in this category can attract others into their aura and radiate a beneficial influence upon those who seek their company.

Fire is dynamic and active, so these people are the doers and achievers, loving adventure, innovation, creativity, experimentation, originality and challenge. When they come up against an opponent they can be too aggressive, abrupt, impulsive and outspoken for their own good.

Fire people are capable, positive, decisive and usually sure of themselves. These are the ones who do things that others would not even contemplate, so you will often find them exploring new horizons. If they fail to control and direct their energies into constructive channels, fire people can become destructive and do a lot of harm.

Earth

Earth is the most basic of all the elements because to everyone and everything on this planet it is our centre, our home. Earth does not readily change, therefore it symbolises stability which, if carried too far, can produce stubbornness and fixed ideas. Although earth is basically stable, it can erupt with the terrifying fury of earthquakes and volcanoes. At such times earth becomes primitive, even brutal and no-one has any hope of controlling it.

Most of earth's treasures are hidden below the surface, so, many of its qualities are not immediately obvious; it can take a long time for the best to be found. The same applies to earth people because they are not overly demonstrative, flamboyant, ostentatious or the least bit likely to blow their own trumpets.

Earth is constantly producing, supplying and sustaining, so it is a very good provider. However, when people abuse this and keep on taking without giving anything back to the earth, it will become desolate and barren.

Earth's cycles which produce the seasons, never vary, so this element represents reliability and punctuality. When we say that someone is "down-to-earth", it means that the person is practical, realistic, and needs to have a good commonsense reason for doing something. Earth people are just like that. Even though they move slowly and cautiously, they eventually achieve their goals because they have qualities of endurance and perseverance and the necessary tenacity to "stick it out".

If prudence and self-discipline are carried too far, they can become mean and selfish. Because earth people are practical and realistic they often lack imagination and flights of fancy. Being conservative by nature, there is seldom any outrageous exaggeration and they try to keep a sensible perspective about most things.

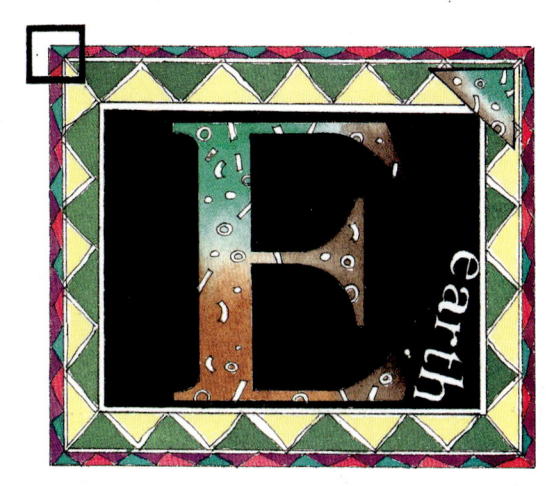

The 12 animals

The Rat

The rat is very versatile as shown by the fact that it can dig, swim and climb. It is also very brave because it is not afraid to defend itself against a larger animal. The old saying about rats deserting a sinking ship shows that they are intuitive and can often sense things before they happen. Rats have a fascination for things which are in the dark – mysteries and secrets – and they have the ability to ferret things out.

Rats enjoy exploring unfamiliar territory and places far away from their base. They like plenty of room to move and if confined within narrow limits they will become frustrated, dejected and unhappy.

Rats will often retrace their steps to double check that they have done the correct thing and to some extent they like to do things alone because they are independent. Rats are naturally restless so they always need to be doing something or going somewhere.

A Rat person can appear to be quiet and serene, but when aroused by opposition or conflict he/she can become very aggressive. These people are lively, high spirited and thorough in whatever they do. There is a tendency to be impulsive and extravagant. The Rat anticipates what the future holds and takes a wide angled view of what that could be.

The Rat is very compatible with the Dragon, the Monkey or another Rat. It is incompatible with the Horse and there can be problems with the Rabbit and the Rooster. It is reasonably compatible with the other animals.

Some famous Rats: William Shakespeare, Marlon Brando, Lord Louis Mountbatten, Prince Charles, Vanessa Redgrave, Dave Allen, Gary MacDonald, Maggie Tabberer, Nastassja Kinski, Ivan Lendl, Ben Elton, Yves St Laurent, Leo Tolstoy, Richard Nixon, Doris Day, George Bush, Kenneth Branagh, the Queen Mother.

The Ox

Being the beast of burden, the ox often ends up carrying someone else's load, However, they are very patient and seldom raise objections, but when they do so they can become the proverbial bull in a china shop. However, an ox is usually calm and quiet which is one reason why people feel they can trust this animal.

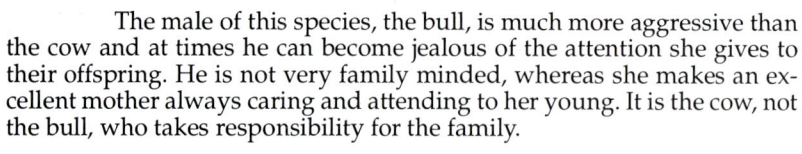

The male of this species, the bull, is much more aggressive than the cow and at times he can become jealous of the attention she gives to their offspring. He is not very family minded, whereas she makes an excellent mother always caring and attending to her young. It is the cow, not the bull, who takes responsibility for the family.

The ox enjoys leisure and you will seldom see them rushing around unless an emergency arises. Just as this animal "chews the cud", most people born in the Year of the Ox like to chew things over before making a move.

Ox people have plenty of patience and fortitude to cope with the hard work they will choose to do or which will be thrust upon them. Most Oxen are comfortable when in solitude or living a quiet, well-ordered existence; they are not given to a gay, frivolous social life. These people are intelligent, but not overly talkative nor demonstrative, and although they can be the reliable salt of the earth types, they can also be obstinate and narrow-minded.

Being conservative and conventional, these people need to know that they have the respect of others. The Ox is very compatible with the Snake, the Rooster or another Ox. It is incompatible with the Sheep and there can be problems with the Dragon and the Dog. It is reasonably compatible with the other animals.

Some famous Oxen: Warren Beatty, Richard Burton, Peter Sellers, Adolf Hitler, Walt Disney, Tony Curtis, Charlie Chaplin, Vincent Van Gogh, Rudyard Kipling, Jessica Lange, Nelson Eddy, Rock Hudson, Kerry Packer, Bruce Springsteen, the Princess of Wales, Bill Cosby, Dustin Hoffman, Anthony Hopkins, Jack Nicholson, Paul Newman, W.B. Yeats, Handel, Bach, Napoleon Bonaparte, Monica Seles.

The Tiger

Although the tiger has a reputation which arouses fear in animals and humans, it will only attack to kill when it is hungry or when its cubs are threatened. Therefore, it is not a malicious animal and it does not take delight in destroying anything just for the thrill of it. However, heaven help anyone who annoys or provokes a tiger because it will tear its tormentors to pieces. In the orient, many people believe that a girl born in the Year of the Tiger will cause trouble especially for her husband, particularly if he is born in the Year of the Snake.

The male tiger is somewhat lazy compared with the tigress because she is the one who is expected to supply the food and look after the cubs. He is a bit of a loner and likes to go wandering off. When the need arises a tiger is capable of incredible bursts of energy and can accomplish a great deal in a brief period but these sudden displays of hectic activity are usually short lived.

Don't forget that the much loved domesticated cat also belongs in this group and members of it can be real favourites for many people.

Tiger people have great courage and they enjoy the thrill of taking risks. They have a very generous nature and, like the tigress with her cubs, they are willing to make sacrifices for others, especially those they love.

At times they can be hot tempered and likely to unleash their fury on some poor victim. They will certainly not brook any interference in what they wish to do. There can be a tendency to show off or play the superior role. This can make others feel in awe of Tiger people, so that unwittingly, they are in danger of alienating some of their friends.

The Tiger is very compatible with the Horse, the Dog, or another Tiger. It is incompatible with the Monkey and there can be problems with the Snake and the Pig. It is reasonably compatible with the other animals.

Some famous Tigers: Charles de Gaulle, Princess Anne, Beethoven, Queen Elizabeth II, Tom Cruise, Rudolf Nureyev, H.G. Wells, Karl Marx, Sir Ralph Richardson, Betty Cuthbert, Bert Newton, Don Dunstan, Dame Joan Sutherland, Stevie Wonder, Goya, Marilyn Monroe, Sir David Attenborough, Agatha Christie, William Hurt, Marco Polo.

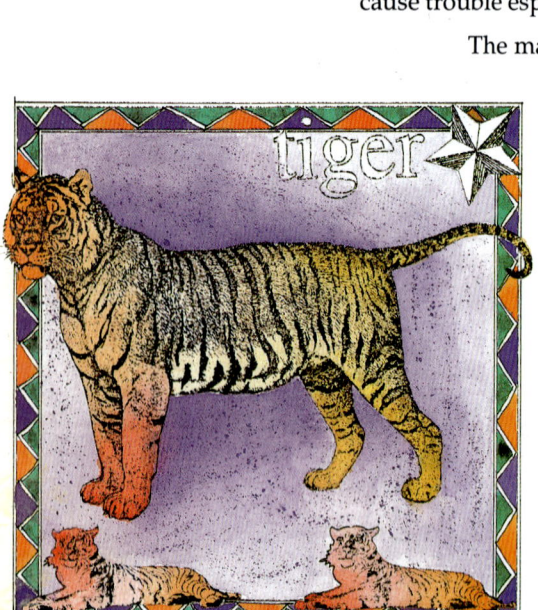

The Rabbit

According to Chinese tradition the rabbit sits quietly in its burrow beneath the earth and listens to the secrets that Mother Nature has to tell.

A rabbit in its natural state can be very timid, extremely sensitive and afraid of stronger more aggressive animals because it knows they can hurt it. However, rabbits can also become domestic pets and when given care, attention, affection and protection they are very friendly, companionable and loving. Any extreme form of noise, violence, cruelty or harshness is absolutely intolerable to this little creature.

A rabbit will usually find a way of avoiding trouble because it will have more than one exit to its burrow. When danger threatens the front entrance it will slip out the back door! Unlike some of the other animals who have a touch of wanderlust, rabbits prefer familiar territory where they have a feeling of safety and security. Their food supply is never far from home and many humans born in the Year of the Rabbit like to earn their living at or near their home base.

Rabbits are not aggressive and when cornered they try to avoid trouble by running here, there and everywhere. There is a soft, gentle, even timid quality about Rabbit people which often goes hand in hand with some degree of artistic or creative ability. They like to enjoy life and will often overspend to entertain friends. They can be emotional and sentimental, with a deep love of nature and a desire to protect, help and care for other people.

Rabbit people dislike too much change and feel uneasy in unfamiliar territory. They prefer the past and when they form friendships they want them to be long-lasting. Rabbit people often search for some impossible dream. They should try not to take things so personally and avoid being too possessive.

The Rabbit is very compatible with the Sheep and the Pig or another Rabbit. It is incompatible with the Rooster and there can be problems with the Horse and the Rat. It is reasonably compatible with the other animals.

Some famous Rabbits: Cecil Beaton, Jodie Foster, Clive James, Edith Piaf, Neil Simon, J.R Tolkien, Orson Welles, the Duke of Argyle, Queen Victoria, Walt Whitman, John Galsworthy, Barbara Eden, Bart Cummings, Frank Sinatra, Harry Belafonte, Ingrid Bergman, Fidel Castro, George Michael, Whitney Houston.

The Dragon

The dragon is unique because of all the 12 animals, it is the only one which is a mythical creature; it symbolises the phoenix, the bird which has the ability to rise again from its own ashes. Therefore, the dragon is the personification of man's immortal soul and people who are born under its influence have the ability to draw upon their inner resources. Dragons are in tune with the infinite and they are able to transform the lowest into the highest not only in their own lives but in the lives of those with whom they come into close contact.

A dragon will not accept limitations because it realises that all things are possible and the only limitations are those which are self-imposed. A dragon is not particularly interested in the narrow-minded world where earthly creatures have to experience the opposites of good-bad, happy-unhappy, love-hate, ups and downs etc. Therefore, a dragon can often appear to be impersonal and detached because it knows that lasting satisfaction is rarely found in material things alone. A dragon also needs food for the soul.

These dynamic, independent creatures will fly away if someone tries to dominate them because dragons refuse to be pushed around. There is something aloof, detached and independent about dragon people; they do not like to be tied down, restricted or dominated. They are "free spirits" with a touch of wizardry and plenty of resourcefulness, intelligence and inventiveness. They love to be active either mentally or physically and usually do most things in a hurry.

Dragon people are capable of great concentration and their minds probe the mysteries of life, why we are here, where are we going? Their agile minds give them a tendency to leap from one thought to another. They are powerful, determined, full of life and can be real fighters.

The Dragon is very compatible with the Monkey, the Rat or another Dragon. It is incompatible with the Dog and there can be problems with the Sheep and the Ox. It is reasonably compatible with the other animals.

Some famous Dragons: Abraham Lincoln, Charles Darwin, George Bernard Shaw, Oscar Wilde, Sigmund Freud, James Cagney, Bing Crosby, Marlene Dietrich, Princess Grace Kelly (Rainer), Rex Mossop, Gough Whitlam, Salvador Dali, Francois Mitterand, Joan of Arc, Placido Domingo, Matt Dillon, Faye Dunaway, Michael Gambon, Sir John Gielgud, John Lennon, Yehudi Menuhin, Florence Nightingale.

The Snake

There are many different types of snakes ranging from the very small to the very large pythons and there are also venomous and non-venomous varieties. Therefore, all sorts of people can be born in the Year of the Snake.

With a few exceptions, most snakes will not attack unless provoked or hungry, but when aroused into anger this reptile is an extremely dangerous adversary and it will strike with lightning speed. Most creatures instinctively know the deadly risks involved in provoking a snake and they wisely leave it alone.

The fact that a snake regularly sheds its skin shows that it has the ability to transform and renew itself. In other words, it outgrows old conditions and takes on new ones. A snake is an expert at disappearing when it does not wish to be seen, so while others are looking for it in one place it has quickly and quietly slipped away. Its actions are superbly streamlined and it never wastes time nor effort in awkward manoeuvres.

A snake must have periods of peace and solitude as shown by the fact that it goes into hibernation when external conditions are unsuitable for its particular needs and activities. Snake people like to find a real purpose or mission in life and until they find it they will not be able to enjoy peace, contentment and satisfaction. They are fairly deep, serious and profound by nature, not really interested in trivia or small talk. Consequently, they are selective about the people with whom they mix. Snakes will definitely not suffer fools gladly. Because they are stable and tenacious there is good organisational ability.

Snakes have very good taste, dislike fussy, untidy conditions, usually look well groomed and appreciate beautiful things.

The Snake is very compatible with the Rooster, the Ox or another Snake. It is incompatible with the Pig and there can be problems with the Tiger and the Monkey. It is reasonably compatible with the other animals.

Some famous Snakes: John F. Kennedy, Mao Tse-Tung, Pablo Picasso, Audrey Hepburn, Sarah Bernhardt, Bob Hawke, Alan Wilkie, Johnny Tapp, Jacqueline Onassis, Fats Domino, Nigel Mansell, Jean-Paul Satre, Brooke Shields, Oprah Winfrey, Mahatma Ghandi, Stefan Edberg, Ann-Margaret, Henri Matisse, Paul Simon.

The Horse

"Eager for action but in need of restraint" is a Chinese saying which applies to the horse. This refers to the fact that it has a tendency to race headlong into a situation without giving enough consideration to the consequences.

At times, every horse is high spirited and enjoys kicking up its heels. A horse loves its freedom, enjoys the wide open spaces and is much happier when it has plenty of room to move. Cramped conditions and "narrow limits" breed discontentment.

Horses usually have plenty of stamina, strength and speed, all of which are necessary because they lead busy, active lives and are continually on the go. The more highly bred a horse is, the more sensitive, highly strung and restless it will be. These thoroughbreds are extremely intelligent animals.

A horse is not naturally aggressive, but if you annoy them you will probably receive a very swift kick; treat a horse well and it will always be your friend.

Horse people are lively, cheerful, outgoing, restless, energetic and demonstrative. This can all be too overwhelming for quieter, more reserved people who will see you as a loud-mouthed, boastful show off! This animal thoroughly enjoys fun and games.

You take an element of fun and happiness with you wherever you go, but like the frolicsome horse, you do it in a happy-go-lucky manner.

Horse people are very sociable and make friends easily, but many of these acquaintances do not endure; they become bored with routine and distant pastures always appear to be greener.

It takes a long time for Horse people to feel settled because their enthusiasm for new adventures, experiences, people and places keeps them darting this way and that.

The Horse is very compatible with the Dog, the Tiger or another Horse. It is incompatible with the Rat and there can be problems with the Rooster and the Rabbit. It is reasonably compatible with the other animals.

Some famous Horses: Samuel Beckett, Lord Snowdon, Princess Margaret, Sean Connery, Leonard Bernstein, Elvis Costello, Kirk Douglas, Igor Stravinsky, Rolf Harris, Sir Robert Menzies, Mike Willesee, Malcolm Fraser, Lady Sonia McMahon, Barbara Streisand, Harrison Ford, Annie Lennox, Vivaldi, Harold Pinter, Boris Yeltsin, Tammy Wynette, Nelson Mandela, Spike Milligan, Aretha Franklin.

The Sheep

Some rams can be cantankerous and belligerent, but the females of the species are generally placid, good natured and mild mannered. These animals are very devoted to their offspring and they make very good parents. The family unit is very important to them and the little lambs hate to become separated from mother.

Sheep are not loners like some of the other animals but prefer to have the company of familiar friends – they will often be seen in herds. This is particularly noticeable in times of trouble when they will race together to form a closely knit group. They are not averse to letting strangers lend a helping hand when necessary.

Even though a sheep loses its wool when it is "fleeced", it grows it again, so the Chinese believe that people born in the Year of the Sheep will not want for the important things in life for too long.

Sheep people have traditional tastes and flexible, easy going natures. They are not innovators or pioneers and are not inclined to take the initiative nor to engage in controversial or unorthodox behaviour.

They are dependent people and being community minded they work best and are happiest when cooperating with other people.

They are gentle, compassionate, emotional, sensitive and easily hurt. Working under pressure will cause them great stress. The Sheep is the eighth animal, and to the Chinese, number 8 symbolises prosperity and comfort, thus ensuring that Sheep people will always have the three essentials: food, shelter and clothing. And yet, strangely enough they are usually worriers, tending to be pessimistic, expecting the worst.

The Sheep is very compatible with the Pig, the Rabbit or another Sheep. It is incompatible with the Ox and there can be problems with the Dog and the Dragon. It is reasonably compatible with the other animals.

Some famous Sheep: Robert de Niro, Dame Margot Fonteyn, Sir Laurence Olivier, Leslie Caron, Brian Henderson, Liberace, Rupert Murdoch, Rudolf Valentino, Vangelis, Bruce Willis, Boris Becker, Catherine Deneuve, Mick Jagger, Doris Lessing, Michelango, Keith Richards, Lech Walesa, Margaret Whitlam, Mikhail Gorbachev.

The Monkey

A monkey is a very intelligent animal, but there are many different ways of using this intelligence. The wise monkey who sees no evil, hears no evil and speaks no evil is symbolic of the best qualities, but unfortunately there are other types who love to show off because they constantly need to be the centre of attention.

Monkeys can seldom remain calm and serene for long because they are highly strung, restless. Some get up to all sorts of mischief including practical jokes, taking things which belong to other monkeys and butting in where they are not welcome. Some monkeys can be disorderly, selfish, quarrelsome, cunning and fickle, and when they are not able to get what they want they become petulant. Monkeys have a natural sense of humour and love to play. For this reason many monkeys waste a great deal of time on unimportant trifles.

When they feel like it, monkeys can be very friendly, affectionate and charming. Monkey people are lively, fun loving, restless and excitable; they can be the life of a party.

They are very clever with a good sense of humour and a quick, alert mind which is always one step ahead of everyone else. They are opportunists, and will sometimes use their talents to manipulate other people to get what they want. Some will even resort to lying or cheating.

Monkey people are inquisitive, inclined to waste time finding out about other people's business. They have good dexterity or nimble fingers and are often doing things with their hands. With their intelligence and proficiency they generally become successful, even winners. Being adroit at self-preservation, they know how and when to escape trouble.

The Monkey is very compatible with the Dragon, the Rat or another Monkey. It is incompatible with the Tiger and there can be problems with the Pig and the Snake. It is reasonably compatible with the other animals.

Some famous Monkeys: Leonardo da Vinci, Elizabeth Taylor, Bobby Womack, Leo McKern, Nelson Rockerfeller, Damon Runyon, Rex Harrison, Arthur Caldwell, Harold Holt, Julius Caesar, Sir William McMahon, John Newcombe, Kylie Minogue, Jerry Hall, Edward Kennedy, Martina Navratilova, Rod Stewart, Diana Ross, Paul Gauguin.

The Rooster

"It is the early bird that catches the worm" and since the rooster is awake and crowing in the early hours of dawn it is the symbol of capability, progress and achievement. The hen, which also belongs in this group, is very productive as shown by the many eggs she will lay.

The rooster can be aggressive and will fight to the death when threatened by another rooster. To others, the rooster can appear to be vain, haughty and full of self-confidence as shown by the way he struts around the barnyard. However, this display of bravado is his means of self-protection and does not reflect his true nature. It is impossible for this species to fly for any great distance, so although people born in the Year of the Rooster have high aspirations, they are constantly being brought back down to earth. For this reason they often suffer from feelings of frustration.

The rooster who crows the loudest is not necessarily the best nor the strongest in the group. Both the males and females of this group are inclined to be bossy, outspoken and to pick things to pieces. Rooster men are often very handsome. Alternatively, they will dress impeccably.

Most Rooster people are basically extroverts, self-assured and friendly; they shine when they are the centre of attention. As you watch a rooster strut around the yard, it is obvious that he is neat, self-controlled, positive, alert, precise and direct with an imposing personality.

If they display their worst qualities they can be boastful bullies with a hot temper and a sarcastic tongue. They have good leadership and organisational abilities and are well equipped to handle anything requiring courage, initiative and a practical approach.

The Rooster is very compatible with the Ox, the Snake or another Rooster. It is incompatible with the Rabbit and there can be problems with the Rat and the Horse. It is reasonably compatible with the other animals.

Some famous Roosters: Michael Caine, Prince Phillip, Joan Collins, Errol Flynn, Douglas Fairbanks junior, D.H. Lawrence, Sir Robert Helpmann, Katherine Hepburn, Harry Secombe, Yoko Ono, Van Morrison, Sir Peter Ustinov, Lang Hancock, Harry M. Miller, Diane Keaton, Roman Polanski, Dirk Bogarde, Bryan Ferry, Steffi Graff, Nancy Reagan.

The Dog

Appropriately enough, the Chinese consider the dog to be the emblem of fidelity and guardian of the home. Certainly both the males and females of this species are renowned for being faithful to those they love and they will do almost anything to protect them. However, some of them are "one man dogs" and they can be extremely jealous of anyone who shares the owner's affection. Sometimes, for no apparent reason, a dog will turn against someone he loves, causing the victim to wonder what on earth he or she has done.

The continual barking of a dog can be very irritating, but it is usually meant to be helpful in warning of intruders or dangers. Therefore, if someone born in the Year of the Dog keeps telling you what you should do, he probably means well even though this annoys you.

Dogs are very unselfish and they will often put the interests of the ones they love before themselves; they certainly try to give of their best even when it is not appreciated.

Many a dog's bark is worse than his bite! They become very happy and extremely enthusiastic when doing things they enjoy.

Some of the most praiseworthy qualities in Dog people are a deep sense of loyalty and an insistence on justice and fair play. With them, everything is either black or white, there is nothing in between, so you will always know where you stand. They have high ideals and moral values, prefer plain talk and make very faithful friends. The Chinese hold this sign in high esteem because these people are straightforward, sincere, honest, always willing to listen to reason and ready to help someone in trouble.

Dog people are not usually malicious or jealous and they only get angry when provoked. It is then that these normally placid, peace-loving people will really take a piece out of you! Behind that bright, cheerful appearance there is someone who worries about lots of things.

The Dog is very compatible with the Horse, the Tiger or another Dog. It is incompatible with the Dragon and there can be problems with the Ox and the Sheep. It is reasonably compatible with the other animals.

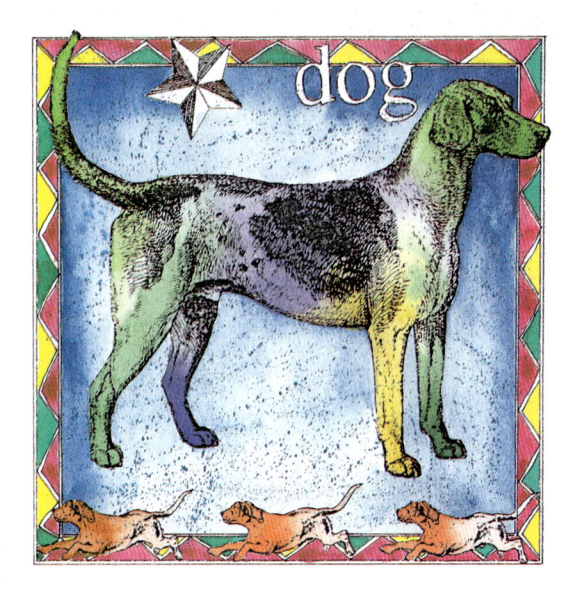

Some famous Dogs: Brigitte Bardot, Sophia Loren, Ava Gardner, Winston Churchill, Liza Minnelli, Elvis Presley, Mother Teresa, Paul Schofield, Graham Kennedy, Joh Bjelke Peterson, Barry Humphries, Cher, David Bowie, Norman Mailer, Donald Sutherland, Gabriella Sabatini, Kate Bush, Madonna, Michelle Pfeiffer, Prince William.

The Pig

There are many Chinese legends about the boar and the pig but none of them have any connection with what we in the west associate with these animals.

The pig does not have its head in the clouds, but nearly always looks to the earth, so it is a very earthy animal with strong passions and determination but naturally it can also be very pig-headed. When angry it can go into a furious rage and even become quite violent.

A pig is very fond of its food, but it is inclined to be wasteful and extravagant with what it has. Thrift is certainly not one of this animal's virtues. A pig is a very sensuous animal and it thoroughly enjoys periods of laziness and self-indulgence, but when it is time for action, that is when you see just what a pig is capable of. This animal is fairly self-sufficient and it does not feel the need for company all the time.

Many people born in the Year of the Pig have strong feelings about water – they may either love it or hate it.

Those who are fortunate enough to be born in the Year of the Pig are some of the nicest people you could hope to meet. On the surface some of them may appear to be a little rough cast, but underneath is a heart of gold combined with great strength, courage, endurance, sincerity, faith in others and a desire for universal harmony.

Pig people are kind, understanding and always ready to lend a helping hand. They don't go in for devious methods; what you see is what you get. They are tough and resilient; they work hard and play hard.

These people are deeply emotional; they love with all their heart and they don't try to hide their feelings.

The Pig is very compatible with the Rabbit, the Sheep or another Pig. It is incompatible with the Snake and there can be problems with the Tiger and the Monkey. It is reasonably compatible with the other animals.

Some famous Pigs: Woody Allen, Tennessee Williams, Duke Ellington, Sir Richard Attenborough, Henry VIII, Elton John, L. Ron Hubbard, Salman Rushdie, Steven Spielberg, the Dalai Lama, William Randolf Hearst, John Laws, Ernest Hemingway, Maria Callas, Humphrey Bogart, Helen Morse, Alfred Hitchcock, John Mortimer, the Duchess of York.

Table of astrological
From 1880-2000

February 10, 1880, to January 29, 1881:
.........Metal Dragon

January 30, 1881, to February 17, 1882:
.........Metal Snake

February 18, 1882, to February 7, 1883:
.........Water Horse

February 8, 1883, to January 27, 1884:
.........Water Sheep

January 28, 1884, to February 14, 1885:
.........Wood Monkey

February 15, 1885, to February 3, 1886:
.........Wood Rooster

February 4, 1886, to January 23, 1887:
.........Fire Dog

January 24, 1887, to February 11, 1888:
.........Fire Pig

February 12, 1888, to January 30, 1889:
.........Earth Rat

January 31, 1889, to January 20, 1890:
.........Earth Ox

January 21, 1890, to February 8, 1891:
.........Metal Tiger

February 9, 1891, to January 29, 1892:
.........Metal Rabbit

January 30, 1892, to February 16, 1893:
.........Water Dragon

February 17, 1893, to February 5, 1894:
.........Water Snake

February 6, 1894, to January 25, 1895:
.........Wood Horse

January 26, 1895, to February 13, 1896:
.........Wood Sheep

February 14, 1896, to February 1, 1897:
.........Fire Monkey

February 2, 1897, to January 21, 1898:
.........Fire Rooster

January 22, 1898, to February 9, 1899:
.........Earth Dog

February 10, 1899, to January 30, 1900:
.........Earth Pig

January 31, 1900, to February 18, 1901:
.........Metal Rat

February 19, 1901, to February 7, 1902:
.........Metal Ox

February 8, 1902, to January 28, 1903:
.... Water Tiger

January 29, 1903, to February 15, 1904:
.... Water Rabbit

February 16, 1904, to February 3, 1905:
.... Wood Dragon

February 4, 1905, to January 24, 1906:
.... Wood Snake

January 25, 1906, to February 12, 1907:
.... Fire Horse

February 13, 1907, to February 1, 1908:
.... Fire Sheep

February 2, 1908, to January 21, 1909:
.... Earth Monkey

January 22, 1909, to February 9, 1910:
.... Earth Rooster

February 10, 1910, to January 29, 1911:
.... Metal Dog

January 30, 1911, to February 17, 1912:
.... Metal Pig

February 18, 1912, to February 5, 1913:
.... Water Rat

February 6, 1913, to January 25, 1914:
.... Water Ox

January 26, 1914, to February 13, 1915:
.... Wood Tiger

February 14, 1915, to February 2, 1916:
.... Wood Rabbit

February 3, 1916, to January 22, 1917:
.... Fire Dragon

January 23, 1917, to February 10, 1918:
.... Fire Snake

February 11, 1918, to January 31, 1919:
.... Earth Horse

February 1, 1919, to February 18, 1920:
.... Earth Sheep

February 19, 1920, to February 7, 1921:
.... Metal Monkey

February 8, 1921, to January 27, 1922:
.... Metal Rooster

January 28, 1922, to February 15, 1923:
.... Water Dog

February 16, 1923, to February 4, 1924:
.... Water Pig

94

elements and animals

February 5, 1924, to January 23, 1925:
.... Wood Rat

January 24, 1925, to February 11, 1926:
.... Wood Ox

February 12, 1926, to February 1, 1927:
.... Fire Tiger

February 2, 1927, to January 21, 1928:
.... Fire Rabbit

January 22, 1928, to February 8, 1929:
.... Earth Dragon

February 9, 1929, to January 28, 1930:
.... Earth Snake

January 29, 1930, to February 16, 1931:
.... Metal Horse

February 17, 1931, to February 5, 1932:
.... Metal Sheep

February 6, 1932, to January 24, 1933:
.... Water Monkey

January 25, 1933, to February 13, 1934:
.... Water Rooster

February 14, 1934, to February 2, 1935:
.... Wood Dog

February 3, 1935, to January 23, 1936:
.... Wood Pig

January 24, 1936, to February 10, 1937:
.... Fire Rat

February 11, 1937, to January 30, 1938:
.... Fire Ox

January 31, 1938, to February 18, 1939:
.... Earth Tiger

February 19, 1939, to February 7, 1940:
.... Earth Rabbit

February 8, 1940, to January 26, 1941:
.... Metal Dragon

January 27, 1941, to February 14, 1942:
.... Metal Snake

February 15, 1942, to February 3, 1943:
.... Water Horse

February 4, 1943, to January 24, 1944:
.... Water Sheep

January 25, 1944, to February 11, 1945:
.... Wood Monkey

February 12, 1945, to February 1, 1946:
.... Wood Rooster

February 2, 1946, to January 21, 1947:
.... Fire Dog

January 22, 1947, to February 9, 1948:
.... Fire Pig

February 10, 1948, to January 28, 1949:
.... Earth Rat

January 29, 1949, to February 15, 1950:
.... Earth Ox

February 16, 1950, to February 5, 1951:
.... Metal Tiger

February 6, 1951, to January 25, 1952:
.... Metal Rabbit

January 26, 1952, to February 13, 1953:
.... Water Dragon

February 14, 1953, to February 2, 1954:
.... Water Snake

February 3, 1954, to January 23, 1955:
.... Wood Horse

January 24, 1955, to February 10, 1956:
.... Wood Sheep

February 11, 1956 to January 29, 1957:
.... Fire Monkey

January 30, 1957, to February 17, 1958:
.... Fire Rooster

February 18, 1958, to February 6, 1959:
.... Earth Dog

February 7, 1959, to January 27, 1960:
.... Earth Pig

January 28, 1960, to February 14, 1961:
.... Metal Rat

February 15, 1961, to February 4, 1962:
.... Metal Ox

February 5, 1962, to January 24, 1963:
.... Water Tiger

January 25, 1963, to February 12, 1964:
.... Water Rabbit

February 13, 1964, to January 31, 1965:
.... Wood Dragon

February 1, 1965, to January 20, 1966:
.... Wood Snake

January 21, 1966, to February 8, 1967:
.... Fire Horse

February 9, 1967, to January 28, 1968:
.... Fire Sheep

Table of astrological elements and animals
From 1880-2000

January 29, 1968, to February 15, 1969:
........*Earth Monkey*

February 16, 1969, to February 5, 1970:
........*Earth Rooster*

February 6, 1970, to January 25, 1971:
........*Metal Dog*

January 26, 1971, to February 14, 1972:
........*Metal Pig*

February 15, 1972, to February 2, 1973:
........*Water Rat*

February 3, 1973, to January 23, 1974:
........*Water Ox*

January 24, 1974, to February 10, 1975:
........*Wood Tiger*

February 11, 1975, to January 30, 1976:
........*Wood Rabbit*

January 31, 1976, to February 17, 1977:
........*Fire Dragon*

February 18, 1977, to February 6, 1978:
........*Fire Snake*

February 7, 1978, to January 27, 1979:
........*Earth Horse*

January 28, 1979, to February 15, 1980:
........*Earth Sheep*

February 16, 1980, to February 4, 1981:
........*Metal Monkey*

February 5, 1981, to January 24, 1982:
........*Metal Rooster*

January 25, 1982, to February 12, 1983:
........*Water Dog*

February 13, 1983 to February 1, 1984:
........*Water Pig*

February 2, 1984, to January 20, 1985:
........*Wood Rat*

January 21, 1985, to February 8, 1986:
........*Wood Ox*

February 9, 1986, to January 28, 1987:
........*Fire Tiger*

January 29, 1987, to February 16, 1988:
........*Fire Rabbit*

February 17, 1988, to February 5, 1989:
........*Earth Dragon*

February 6, 1989, to January 25, 1990:
........*Earth Snake*

January 26, 1990, to February 13, 1991:
........*Metal Horse*

February 14, 1991, to February 2, 1992:
........*Metal Sheep*

February 3, 1992, to January 21, 1993:
........*Water Monkey*

January 22, 1993; to February 9, 1994:
........*Water Rooster*

February 10, 1994, to January 30, 1995:
........*Wood Dog*

January 31, 1995, to February 18, 1996:
........*Wood Pig*

February 19, 1996, to February 6, 1997:
........*Fire Rat*

February 7, 1997, to January 27, 1998:
........*Fire Ox*

January 28, 1998, to February 15, 1999:
........*Earth Tiger*

February 16, 1999, to February 4, 2000:
........*Earth Rabbit*

Living with Numbers

Did you know that your home, through its street number,

has its own zodiac sign? Learn the star sign of your home and

discover whether it is more likely to give a quiet and restful

atmosphere or an active and busy aura. The stars can even give

you tips on the best style of decor and furnishings for your home!

The importance of numbers has been recognised by scholars for centuries. In one way or another, almost everything can be weighed, measured, analysed and catalogued by the use of numbers. You can certainly do this with your home by relating its address number to one of the signs of the zodiac. The formula for doing so is a simple one.

Beginning with Aries and following the natural sequence of the signs, count your address number as follows:

1. Aries; 2. Taurus; 3. Gemini; 4. Cancer; 5. Leo; 6. Virgo; 7. Libra; 8. Scorpio; 9. Sagittarius; 10. Capricorn; 11. Aquarius; 12. Pisces.

Follow the same procedure for numbers higher than 12. Therefore: 13. Aries; 14. Taurus; 15. Gemini; 16. Cancer; 17. Leo; 18. Virgo; 19. Libra; 20. Scorpio; 21. Sagittarius; 22. Capricorn; 23. Aquarius; 24. Pisces. The next round begins with: 25. Aries; 26. Taurus; 27. Gemini etc. For high numbers, it will be much quicker if you divide them by 12. If this can be done evenly with no fraction left over, the number belongs to Pisces. For example, 12, 24, 36, 48, 60, 72, 84, 96, 108, 120, 132, 144, 156, 168 can all be divided evenly by 12, making them Piscean numbers.

If there is a fraction left over, that fraction will lead you to the correct sign. For example, 61 divided by 12 gives 5 and $1/12$; the 1 in $1/12$ belongs in Aries. Therefore, 61 is an Aries number.

To make it as easy for you, here is a list of the fractions with their signs:

$1/12$ = Aries, $2/12$ = Taurus, $3/12$ = Gemini, $4/12$ = Cancer, $5/12$ = Leo, $6/12$ = Virgo, $7/12$ = Libra, $8/12$ = Scorpio, $9/12$ = Sagittarius, $10/12$ = Capricorn, $11/12$ = Aquarius.

Having found the zodiac sign which corresponds with your home address number, read on to see how the residence and the people who live there respond to the influences of that particular star sign.

The Aries home

Some of these home address numbers are: 1, 13, 25, 37, 49, 61, 73, 85, 97, 109, 121, 133, 145, 157, 169, 181, 193, 205, 217, 229, 241, 253, 265, 277, 289, 301, 313, 325.

First and foremost, it is a very busy place. There is a strong field of energy and vitality about this home which, when transferred to the occupants, means that one or more members of the household are always on the go and able to accomplish a great deal in a short period of time.

Depending on the amount of available space, there will probably be a tool box or a tool shed, a workshop or a room for do-it-yourself activities. Part or whole of the house will be very hot in summer. The kitchen will contain a good assortment of cutlery (especially knives), scissors, cutting and heating utensils. Some of the interior and/or exterior colours will be strong and decisive and because this house is made to be used in practical, efficient ways, it is unlikely to be a soft, pretty, highly ornamented place.

This house can sometimes be accident prone. Because there is often a lot of rushing around, there is the likelihood that some things will be damaged, broken, scorched, cut or burnt. Life is seldom dull or boring in an Aries home.

The Taurus home

Some of the Taurean home address numbers are: 2, 14, 26, 38, 50, 62, 74, 86, 98, 110, 122, 134, 146, 158, 170, 182, 194, 206, 218, 230, 242, 254, 266, 278, 290, 302, 314, 326.

This home gives the impression of being solid, well built and made to last. In most cases it will be just that, with good foundations and quality materials used in its construction. Either the building, the contents and decor or some of the members of the household will be conservative and traditional rather than pretentious and ostentatious.

Your Taurus home is ruled by Venus, the mythological goddess of love and beauty, so, part, or all, of this residence will be very attractive, even beautiful, but understated.

The aura of a Taurus home is very much in tune with a beautiful garden, so if you haven't yet experienced the pleasure of helping nature grow flowers, ferns, herbs, shrubs, trees, lawns and delicious vegetables, you should do so while in your Taurus home. Even if you live in a unit, you can grow many of these beautiful things in pots on your balcony, on a windowsill or in a sunny room.

Taurus is a sign of deep, enduring affection, so don't settle in this home unless you intend to make a lasting, loving commitment to someone – either as a friend, a companion, a partner or a lover.

If space permits, every Gemini residence should have a study or library to house the great variety of interesting books..."

The Gemini home

Some of the Gemini home address numbers are: 3, 15, 27, 39, 51, 63, 75, 87, 99, 111, 123, 135, 147, 159, 171, 183, 195, 207, 219, 231, 243, 255, 267, 279, 291, 303, 315, 327, 339, 351, 363.

It will always be interesting to live in a Gemini home. If you want peace, quiet and relaxation, this is not the place for you because it is the centre of communication, a meeting place where all sorts of people forever seem to be coming and going. The phone is always busy, bikes and cars will be parked in the yard, there are papers, magazines, books and documents spread all over the place and there are endless discussions going on. The radios or TV sets will be overworked and, although this house seems to be a breeding ground for pens, pencils, memo pads and note books, they are never around when you want them!

Gemini symbolises the twins, so if the house happens to be a two storey one, it will be even more likely to express the busy, restless and changeable qualities of this sign. There will often be two or more of the same or similar things in this home; gadgets, vacuum cleaners, vehicles, musical instruments, TV sets, radios, utensils, tools and telephones seem to exist in pairs!

If space permits, every Gemini residence should have a study or a library to house the great variety of interesting books, papers, magazines, letters and documents which are accumulated here.

The Cancer home

Some of the Cancerian home address numbers are: 4, 16, 28, 40, 52, 64, 76, 88, 100, 112, 124, 136, 148, 160, 172, 184, 196, 208, 220, 232, 244, 256, 268, 280, 292, 304, 316, 328, 340, 352, 364.

This is a home which says welcome, not only to the family who lives here but also to the people who come to visit. It is not likely to be ostentatious; in fact, some of the furnishings and paintwork may be slightly worn or faded, but the atmosphere will always be warm and cosy. This home is a place to be lived in and enjoyed.

Cancer and its ruler the moon are both specifically related to food, nourishment and, of course, to the kitchen, so, the cupboards will usually be well stocked. Whenever friends drop in they will always be given a welcoming cuppa and probably some homemade goodies. It is no wonder people enjoy visiting!

There is also a strong maternal, protective influence associated with Cancer and the moon, so there is no doubt that either the home itself or some of the people who live there will exhibit these qualities. Although I have never seen one, it would be very fitting if you could find a front door mat inscribed with the words: "I want to take care of you".

The Leo home

Some of the Leo home address numbers are: 5, 17, 29, 41, 53, 65, 77, 89, 101, 113, 125, 137, 149, 161, 173, 185, 197, 209, 221, 233, 245, 257, 269, 281, 293, 305, 317, 329, 341, 353, 365, 377.

Because Leo is ruled by the brilliant sun, part or all of this house will be very well lit; it is the ideal place to incorporate a big, beautiful sunroom. If this is not possible, try to utilise some of the sun's vital colours such as yellow, gold and orange in one area of the house to give it strength, energy and brightness. It will lift your spirits.

A Leo home is a happy, vibrant place and some of the people who live there for any length of time will be strong, positive, decisive and confident.

There will be some feature about this residence which is impressive and creates an impact on people who come there. It could be the building, the decor, the lifestyle, the location, the garden, the view or someone who lives there. In some cases it could be the fact that everything is overdone to the point of being pretentious or gaudy.

If you are the type of person who derives pleasure from such things as crystal chandeliers or other beautiful light fittings, rich brocades and velvets, tapestries, paintings, elaborate ornaments, mirrored walls or gilded furniture, then you would be in your element in a Leo home.

The Virgo home

Some of the Virgo home address numbers are: 6, 18, 30, 42, 54, 66, 78, 90, 102, 114, 126, 138, 150, 162, 174, 186, 198, 210, 222, 234, 246, 258, 270, 282, 294, 306, 318, 330, 342, 354, 366, 378.

From my own observations, the majority of Virgo homes are unpretentious and it is fair to say that this type of residence (or some of the people who live there) is neat, clean and tidy. It is a functional home and, in general, there is a place for everything and everything is usually in its place. There are lots of useful gadgets around the house.

One or more of the residents is likely to be particularly conscious of health, diet, fitness and hygiene or may even work in a medical occupation.

Quite a few people who are settled in a Virgo house bake their own bread or cultivate herbs and organic vegetables because they have an instinctive antipathy towards contamination, pollution or artificial ingredients.

Nature's colours, lime green and olive green, are in harmony with this sign and address number. Obviously they will be found in your garden, but you may also like to feature them in the interior decor in some way.

Lots of small things and detailed work are some of the hallmarks of a Virgo home.

The Libra home

Some of the Libra home address numbers are: 7, 19, 31, 43, 55, 67, 79, 91, 103, 115, 127, 139, 151, 163, 175 187, 199, 211, 223, 235, 247, 259, 271, 283, 295, 307, 319, 331, 343, 355, 367, 379.

Libra is the sign of partnership and it is ruled by Venus, the planet of love, affection and beauty. Therefore, this home is meant to be shared by one or more people who need and care for one another.

Part or all of this residence and/or garden will be very attractive, featuring beautifully harmonious colour combinations, elegance and style in the furnishings and decor, symmetry of design plus a peaceful atmosphere in which residents and visitors can enjoy themselves. One or more people who live here will probably be musical or artistic in some way; there will always be beautiful things to listen to and to look at in the Libra home.

Most parts of this property will usually give the appearance of being kept in a state of near perfection because Libra, lover of well-balanced things, has a deep aversion to anything that is harsh, ugly, dirty or discordant.

Although Libra and Venus are related to beautiful combinations of colour, their predominant ones are soft shades of green and pink. Apart from seeing these colours in the garden you could use them as part of the interior colour scheme, especially in the bedroom where love and partnership are most intimately expressed.

The Scorpio home

Some of the Scorpio home address numbers are: 8, 20, 32, 44, 56, 68, 80, 92, 104, 116, 128, 140, 152, 164, 176, 188, 200, 212, 224, 236, 248, 260, 272, 284, 296, 308, 320, 332, 344, 356, 368, 380.

A Scorpio home is not for the faint-hearted because there will be strong physical, emotional, mental or financial demands made on one or more of the people who live there for any length of time. This home is the focus of its occupants' activities, including work, play, entertaining, planning, exercising and even loving. If ever there was a place where work is brought home from the office, this is it.

On occasions certain things may be hard to find, they may get lost, misplaced or damaged. Drainage, dampness, sewer pipes, the hot water system or peculiar odours which are difficult to trace could sometimes be a problem in a Scorpio home.

There is likely to be a place in the house or garden which is hidden or not easily accessible. Many Scorpio properties have a basement, a cellar, a well, an underground stream, a spring or a cave-like feature.

There could be stories attached to the house, tales about how someone died or disappeared while living there. These are just some of the mysterious things associated with a Scorpio house, but, of course, there could be others!

This is a very sexy place for lovers, but don't let jealousy spoil the relationship.

The Sagittarius home

Some of the Sagittarian home address numbers are: 9, 21, 33, 45, 56, 69, 81, 93, 105, 117, 129, 141, 153, 165, 177, 189, 201, 213, 225, 237, 249, 261, 273, 285, 297, 309, 321, 33, 345, 357, 369, 381.

One or more features of a Sagittarian property will give the impression of spaciousness and freedom. This can happen in one of several different ways. For example, the house, garden or block of land may be large or it may provide an expansive view, a broad uninterrupted vista. Alternatively, one or more rooms in the house may be larger than normally expected for a building of its size.

For people with a free spirit, a zest for life and who are not inhibited or tied to formality, traditions or restrictions, a Sagittarian house can be a happy place because it generates a sense of optimism, independence, good humor and a happy-go-lucky outlook.

Some of the people who are attracted to this house are busy, excitable, restless and active. There will be times when a twosome can become like ships that pass in the night.

People who love sport and other outdoor activities or the wide open spaces often gravitate to a Sagittarian house and feel good in it. Overseas visitors are likely to be invited to this place which often contains a wide selection of imported goods.

The Capricorn home

Some of the Capricorn home address numbers are: 10, 22, 34, 46, 58, 70, 82, 94, 106, 118, 130, 142, 154, 166, 178, 190, 202, 214, 226, 238, 250, 262, 274, 286, 298, 310, 322, 334, 346, 358, 370.

Capricorn and its ruling planet Saturn are two of the most stable, solid, enduring and down-to-earth astrological influences, so this type of home is usually built to last, with the result that there are some very old Capricorn houses to be found. This star sign goes well with old-fashioned styles rather than with a modern, contemporary look, but even if your house is a relatively new place you can still decorate to add a touch of old world charm.

People who have a practical, responsible or mature nature will feel at home in this place. However, unless you deliberately put some fun into life you can slowly get into a rut and begin to take things too seriously in a Capricorn house.

Part of the residence could be very cold in winter, so, unless this problem can be overcome with efficient central heating or a bevy of heating appliances, it is not a suitable place for people who suffer from rheumatic or arthritic pains.

Anything to do with gardens, rural activities or nature and the earth is compatible with a Capricorn house; it's excellent for people who have a long-term ambition to achieve success in their chosen career. Like a good wine, this place seems to improve with age.

The Aquarius home

Some of the Aquarius home address number are: 11, 23, 35, 47, 59, 71, 83, 95, 107, 119, 131, 143, 155, 167, 179, 191, 203, 215, 227, 239, 251, 263, 275, 287, 299, 311, 323, 335, 347, 359, 371, 383.

Something about the property will be unusual or distinctive – whether it is the

> "A Sagittarian house can be a happy place because it generates a sense of optimism, independence, good humour..."

design of the house, the colour, the decor, the block of land, the view, the position or some of the people who live there.

The aura and atmosphere of this place and/or one of the residents is different from what is considered normal, so it is not in tune with people who wish to live a traditional, conventional lifestyle. If you are an independent thinker, a free spirit who likes to go your own way and carve out an original niche in life, this is the place for you.

Often, there is something significant involving electricity. It may be near a power station or high voltage wires or an electronics expert lives there. There may be many electrical appliances, or some appliances or electrical circuits frequently cause trouble. The residents could be interested in computers, scientific or hi-fi equipment, inventions, gadgets, space age technology, astronomy, astrology, antiques and off-the-beaten-track pursuits which other people would not think about.

Sometimes a part of the house which has been changed by alterations, or an extension, looks different from the original building.

The Pisces home

Some of the Pisces home address numbers are: 12, 24, 36, 48, 60, 72, 84, 96, 108, 120, 132, 144, 156, 168, 180, 192, 204, 216, 228, 240, 252, 264, 276, 288, 300, 312, 324, 336, 348, 360, 372, 384.

There are many different ways in which the Piscean influence will manifest in this home or in the lives of some of the residents.

The house and/or the block of land is in a secluded area or it may be almost totally obscured from view. There could be a room or part of the house which no-one would suspect was there because it is so well hidden away. Alternatively, other people are not allowed in a particular area or some type of secret work or activity is carried out there.

On the positive side, the property is often beautifully situated near water, either by the sea, a river or a lake. On the negative side, there could be problems with dampness, drainage, waterpipes, leaking gutters or roof or the house could be subject to flooding.

In this house, mysterious things can sometimes happen for which there are no logical explanations, perhaps there are strange noises, voices, odours, perfumes, apparitions or things being moved from one place to another. The interior is often dimly lit or the curtains and blinds are constantly drawn.

One or more of the people who live in a Pisces home could be interested in such things as photography, films, music, psychic matters, meditation, fantasy, spiritualism, nursing, working in a hospital or an institution where people are confined, chiropody, boats, fishing, aquatics, hypnotism or mysteries.

Which Day Was It?

The day of the week on which a particular event occurred is important when exploring the astrological calendar. It could be the day you were born, married, started a business or moved house. In this chapter you'll find a formula for working out which day it was, and a fascinating explanation of the role your day of birth plays in determining the qualities you display.

If you know the date, month and year, but you do not have access to a calender for that period, here is a relatively simple but infallible formula for you to use in order to discover which day of the week a special event occured. This method applies to any period between the years 1752 and 2099. I shall give you an example to show you step by step exactly what to do. The example will be 17 September, 1927.

❶ First of all you must know whether the event occurred in a **leap year**, or an **ordinary year**. To find out, simply divide the year by 4. If it will divide evenly, with nothing left over, it is a leap year. The one exception is 1900 which was an ordinary year. If the year will not divide evenly by 4, but has a fraction left over, it is an ordinary year.

Here are some examples:

1903 divided by 4 = 475 with 3 (ie ¾) left over. Therefore, it was an ordinary year.
1928 divided by 4 = 482 with no fraction left over. Therefore, it was a leap year.

Having ascertained what type of year it was when the event took place, simply follow the next seven steps and you will discover the day of the week. Remember, we are using 17 September, 1927 as our example. 1927 divided by 4 = 481 with ¾ left over, so it was an ordinary year.

❷ Take the last two figures of the year, 1927, in this case, 27.

❸ Divide that number by 4, ignore any fraction left over and only use the whole number. In this case, 27 divided by 4 = 6 ¾. Therefore, the number you need to work with is 6.

❹ Add the result of step 3 to that of step 2. In this case, 6 plus 27 = 33.

❺ Add the day's date in the month to the result of step 4. In this case it is the 17th of the month, so 17 plus 33 = 50.

❻ To the result obtained in step 5, add the following number which coincides with the month when the event took place:

January:
(a) Add 1 for an ordinary year;
(b) Don't add anything for a leap year.

February:
(a) Add 4 for an ordinary year;
(b) Add 3 for a leap year.

March:
Add 4.

April:
Don't add anything.

May:
Add 2.

June:
Add 5.

July:
Don't add anything.

August:
Add 3.

September:
Add 6.

October:
Add 1.

November:
Add 4.

December:
Add 6.

Therefore, in our example for 17 September 1927, add 6 (for September) to the result obtained in step 5. In this case, 6 plus 50 = 56.

❼ (a) Add 4 for any event in the 18th century; (b) Add 2 for any event in the 19th century; (c) Don't add anything for any event in the present century, the 20th; (d) Add 6 for any event which will occur in the 21st century.

In our example, 1927 belongs in the 20th century, so don't add anything. The total remains at 56.

❽ Divide the total by 7. If there is any fraction of 7 left over, that fraction will give the day of the week as follows: $1/7$ = Sunday; $2/7$ = Monday; $3/7$ = Tuesday; $4/7$ = Wednesday; $5/7$ = Thursday; $6/7$ = Friday.

If the number can be divided evenly by 7 with no fraction left over, the day was a Saturday. In our present example, 56 divided by 7 = 8 with no fraction left over, so 17 September 1927 was a Saturday. This is confirmed in a 1927 almanac.

Which is your day?

Are you guided by the planet Venus, which rules love? Or influenced by the gloom and doom of Saturn? Each day of the week is ruled by the sun, the moon or a particular planet, so the day of the week on which you were born has special significance. Just as your star sign gives rise to certain qualities, so does the planet that rules your day. Richard Sterling explains his ideas about the qualities of your day of birth.

There is an old rhyme which says:

Monday's child is fair of face,

Tuesday's child is full of grace,

Wednesday's child is full of woe,

Thursday's child has far to go,

Friday's child is loving and giving,

Saturday's child works hard for its living,

But the child that is born on the Sabbath day

Is happy, bonny, blithe and gay.

I have never been able to track down the origin of this old saying, but I am sure it has astrological connections and somewhere down the line it has become distorted, so that the true meaning it was meant to convey has been lost.

The ancients named the seven days of the week after the seven visible spheres – the sun, the moon, Mercury, Venus, Mars, Jupiter and Saturn. By referring to the English and French languages it is very easy to see the connection between those spheres and our days of the week.

Sunday is the sun's day.
Monday is the moon's day.

It does not take much stretch of the imagination to think of Monday as Moonday. Luna is another name for the moon and in the French language, Lunedi is the name for Monday.

Tuesday is ruled by Mars.

In French, it is easy to see the connection between their name for Tuesday – Mardi – and the planet Mars.

Wednesday is ruled by Mercury.

Again, in French, the name for Wednesday is Mercredi, showing a clear link with the planet Mercury.

Thursday is ruled by Jupiter.

Thursday is a corruption of Thor's Day. Thor was the mythological god of thunder, also known as Jupiter, so it is obvious that Thursday (or Thor's Day) is related to the planet Jupiter.

Friday is ruled by Venus.

In French, Friday is known as Vendredi, which shows a link with the name Venus.

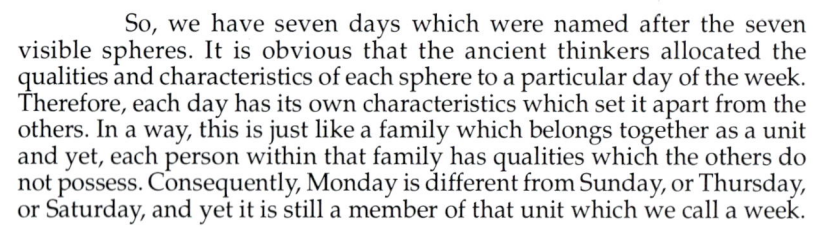

Saturday is Saturn's day.

So, we have seven days which were named after the seven visible spheres. It is obvious that the ancient thinkers allocated the qualities and characteristics of each sphere to a particular day of the week. Therefore, each day has its own characteristics which set it apart from the others. In a way, this is just like a family which belongs together as a unit and yet, each person within that family has qualities which the others do not possess. Consequently, Monday is different from Sunday, or Thursday, or Saturday, and yet it is still a member of that unit which we call a week.

In the past, say in great-grandma's time – before high technology and automatic washing machines – Monday was always "washing day". Although great-grandma didn't realise it, she was washing in tune with the moon, the ruler of Monday and the sphere which is directly associated with water and washing!

When we look at the ancient symbolism of the sun, moon and five visible planets, after which our days of the week were named, it becomes obvious that the old saying beginning *Monday's child is fair of face*, was interpreted incorrectly in the first place or, alternatively and more likely it has been distorted during a long passage of time.

The first phrase, *Monday's child is fair of face*, fits perfectly with the moon as ruler of Monday. For example, when the moon is strongly placed in a horoscope such as near the ascendant (ie the eastern horizon), that person's face will be soft, rounded and usually fair-skinned. Therefore, I have no argument with the first description in that old legend.

However, such is not the case when it comes to *Tuesday's child is full of grace*. Tuesday is ruled by Mars, the planet of effort, initiative, drive, action, stress and the competitive spirit. In no way is it the symbol of grace. On the other hand, Jupiter (the ruler of Thursday) is associated with religion, spirituality, the church, religious leaders and therefore, with grace, a spiritual quality. Consequently, it would be much more appropriate if the second phrase in this old saying was *Thursday's child is full of grace*, which rhymes with the first phrase, *Monday's child is fair of face*.

The third phrase is *Wednesday's child is full of woe*. Wednesday (or Mercredi in French) is ruled by Mercury, the winged messenger of the gods. There is absolutely no connection whatsoever between this planet and the meaning of woe. However, this word can certainly be related to Saturn, the ruler of Saturday and the key to worry, pessimism, negativity, depression, gloom and doom. Therefore, I feel sure that the third phrase should read *Saturday's child is full of woe*.

Following this, in this commonly accepted version, we have the fourth phrase which reads *Thursday's child has far to go*. As already explained, I think that *Thursday's child is full of grace* is more appropriate for Jupiter, the ruler of Thursday.

So, who is the person who has *far to go*? The answer is not hard to find. Mercury, the ruler of Wednesday, is the key to the mind, the planet of intelligence, alertness, keenness, mental prowess and the ability to think, plan, communicate, analyse, rationalise and to progress in life. Consequently, it is far more appropriate to say that *Wednesday's child has far to go*, rather than *Wednesday's child is full of woe*.

Venus is the planet of love, the symbol of caring, giving and sharing. It rules Friday, so there is no need to question the phrase *Friday's child is loving and giving*.

Next comes the child who *works hard for its living*. Effort, action and hard work are the hallmarks of Mars, the ruler of Tuesday. Therefore, it seems much more appropriate to say that *Tuesday's child works hard for its living*, instead of *Tuesday's child is full of grace*. After all, the planet Mars has no connection whatsoever with spiritual grace or any religious matters.

Finally, we come to Sunday, ruled by the radiant, outgoing sun. There is no question about the symbolic validity of the phrase: *But the child that is born on the Sabbath day is happy, bonny, blithe and gay*. Those descriptions, although old-fashioned, reveal a wonderful harmony with the nature of the sun.

Here is my amended version, based on the natures of the seven spheres which rule the seven days of the week:

Monday's child is fair of face,

Thursday's child is full of grace,

Saturday's child is full of woe,

Wednesday's child has far to go,

Friday's child is loving and giving,

Tuesday's child works hard for its living,

But the child that is born on the Sabbath day

Is happy, bonny, blithe and gay.

By now, you probably realise that your birthday star sign is ruled by a particular heavenly sphere but the day of the week has a ruling planet which can influence your character. If you don't know the day of the week on which you were born, refer to our formula under **Which is your day**, at the beginning of this chapter. Although a star sign such as Aries, Pisces, Sagittarius, Gemini, is a sign of the zodiac, *not a planet*, there is a strong similarity between the nature, qualities and characteristics of any one particular star sign and the planet (including the sun and moon) which happens to rule it. For example, Aries is positive, dynamic, enterprising, courageous and aggressive. Its ruling planet is Mars, the mythological "God of War", which symbolises a fighting spirit, the will-to-win, a desire to lead the way, to show initiative, to be active, to get up and go, to achieve success and to progress through effort, drive, enthusiasm and energy.

Regardless of your birthday star sign, if you were born on a Tuesday, you can consider Mars (the ruler of Tuesday) as a supplementary ruler of your horoscope. This is just one reason why no two people born in the same star sign are exactly alike. There are many other reasons, such as those described in the chapter entitled **Your Rising Star**.

People who were born on a Wednesday will inherit some of the restless and questioning qualities associated with Mercury, the ruler of

Wednesday. Therefore, if your birthday star sign belongs to one of the placid categories such as Taurus, Cancer, Virgo, Libra, Capricorn or Pisces, and yet you are anything but placid, maybe you were born on a Wednesday (ruled by Mercury), a Tuesday (ruled by Mars), or a Sunday (ruled by the sun).

If you were born on a Thursday, one of the supplementary rulers of your horoscope is Jupiter, the most beneficial of all the planets, the symbol of expansion, happiness, optimism, good humour, room to move – either mentally or physically, spaciousness, freedom and independence. Regardless of your date of birth, if you were born on a Thursday you will need and appreciate these types of things. Thursday could often be your lucky day.

Were you born on a Friday? If so, your supplementary ruler is Venus, the planet of beauty, love, affection, sharing, artistry, pleasure, colour, elegance, refinement and romance. If you were born on a Friday, try to fill your life with these beautiful things, especially on Fridays.

If you were born in the star sign Capricorn, your ruling planet is Saturn. This combination makes you serious-minded, ambitious, responsible, mature, cautious, down-to-earth, practical and realistic. Your plans or projects will usually be long-range and well thought out rather than done on impulse.

Regardless of your date of birth and star sign, if you were born on a Saturday, you inherit some of these qualities of Saturn and Capricorn. With Saturn's influence, you may not be the quite so dreamy, idealistic Piscean; the restless, frivolous Geminian; the impulsive, happy-go-lucky Sagittarian or the domineering, bombastic Leo. Saturn both subdues and consolidates the qualities of each star sign.

Sunday's child has the majestic, radiant sun as a supplementary ruler in the horoscope, regardless of the date of birth. You will never be satisfied with anything dull or ordinary in your life and wherever you go you will always be like a ray of sunshine with your aura of lightness and brightness. You will often be at your best on Sundays. Orange, gold, yellow and the bright sunny colours will be good for you.

If you were born on a Monday, the moon will play a role in your life. This orb, with its waxing and waning cycles, is changeable, so you may find that your moods and feelings fluctuate between ups and downs. The moon is the key to your home, family ties and the familiar, ordinary, things in life. Because these are the basic fundamentals in most peoples' lives, you are very fortunate because you can derive much satisfaction and contentment from what they have to offer.

As you can now see, it is very important to know on which day of the week you were born because each day has its own special planetary "vibration" which puts you in tune with certain things, but not with others.

When you take into account your star sign plus the other influences of your rising sign, the ruler of the day on which you were born, the Chinese animal and element which was in control at the time of birth, as well as the characteristics of the numbers which apply to your birthday and your home address, it is not surprising that humans are such complex beings. And, it is no wonder that two people born under the same sign can be quite different.

If you think that sounds complicated, just try to imagine what is revealed when the birth positions of the moon, Mercury, Venus, Mars, Jupiter, Saturn, Uranus, Neptune and Pluto are added to your star sign. But, that's another story!

And They're Racing

Almost everyone is attracted to winning whether it be the lottery, the local church raffle or a horse race. Although it's not failsafe, the stars do offer a little insight into how to pick that elusive winner; a combination of good sense and knowing how to interpret the special language of the stars may be your key to success at the track.

Over the years a great number of different systems for picking winners have come and gone. Methods have been based on all sorts of things such as form, colours, weights, numbers and even the magic pin! There is no infallible method which will enable you to pick a winner in every race, but if you learn to interpret the language of the stars you may frequently have the pleasure of seeing your horse first past the post.

This method of using astrology can be applied with equal success to dog races because starters in all racing events have a name which, in many cases, suggests certain characteristics which can then be matched up with the keywords of the stars.

The secret of this system depends entirely on the symbolism of the sun, moon and the planets. Each one of these heavenly spheres has a distinctive character and function and when these qualities and characteristics are applied to racing, they manifest in the actual *meaning of the words* which are used in the names of horses and dogs.

Many people are familiar with the way in which certain characteristics have come to be associated with the sun, moon and planets in mythology, such as Venus, the goddess of love and beauty; Mars, the god of war, and Mercury, the winged messenger. Down through the ages, the sun has always been associated with royalty and leaders; Saturn has been thought of as old father time, and it is recognised that Neptune rules the oceans and the seas.

These are just a few of the popular, well known correspondences which exist between earthly matters and the heavenly orbs. However, there are literally thousands of other items which can be correlated with the sun, moon and planets because every single thing you can think of which exists on earth corresponds with one or more of the other members of our solar system, and although it is impossible to tabulate every one of them in this book, you will find comprehensive lists in this chapter, in the **Dictionary of Keywords**.

Star patterns

Because the sun, moon and planets are all moving at different speeds in their journeys through the zodiac, they are constantly forming all sorts of star patterns seen from earth. These patterns are combinations which one sphere can form with another and they can be divided into three main categories: ❶ harmonious and favourable, ❷ discordant and unfavourable, ❸ neutral. It is the actual angular distance between any two spheres, measured in degrees of longitude, which determines to which of those three categories the star pattern will belong. However, it is important to remember that almost any pair of heavenly spheres can form these major star patterns. When you realise that several different combinations can occur simultaneously, it becomes obvious that the solar system is like a gigantic computer capable of creating an almost infinite number of possible *circuits*; these star patterns are the keys to winning opportunities.

The **Calendar of Star Patterns** beginning on page 122, lists varying combinations of the sun, moon and eight planets. When one or more favourable star patterns happen to be operating on the days when races are to be run, I have named each combination. For example, the calendar shows that on 1 December 1992, the sun and Jupiter are combined in a favourable star pattern.

Races of one variety or another are held almost every day of the week. However, not every race day or night coincides with a good link between two or more spheres, in which case no indications are given for those dates.

Frequently an adverse star pattern overshadows a day on which races are run and naturally, these discordant planetary combinations will seldom indicate successful winners.

However, I have included them in the **Calendar of Star Patterns** for two reasons. Firstly, they can warn you that certain names will be affected by adverse influences and secondly, you can use these discordant star patterns to help you avoid other problems.

Next look at the names of the two or more spheres which form favourable star patterns on a particular race day and then study the names of all the horses or dogs (especially those which have ability or which are favourably handicapped) to see if you can find one whose name matches the type of keywords which belong to those spheres. The **Dictionary of Keywords** begins on page 114.

If a star pattern involves the sun and Mars, you would look for a runner whose name suggests a combination of things related to the sun and to Mars. Check the list of keywords under the headings of **The Sun** and **Mars** to see if you can find any words which have an affinity with a particular starter's name. For example, the sun is related to royalty, while Mars is associated with soldiers, so a horse called *Royal Warrior* would have an excellent chance of winning because its name is a perfect reflection of the star pattern which happens to take priority at that time.

For example, if Mercury and Venus formed a good combination, a name such as *Love Letter* would be a good match because Venus rules love and affection, while Mercury is related to mail and correspondence.

Venus is feminine and related to beauty and women; Uranus rules radar and sonar. Therefore, on a day when Venus and Uranus formed a favourable star pattern, *Sonar Belle* would be a good choice.

When several star patterns are operating, things can become complicated, but if you assess the complete picture very carefully you will often be able to select several winners or place getters. A case in point occurred when four star patterns were in force. These were Mercury-Saturn; sun-Saturn; sun-Mercury; Neptune-Pluto. The star keywords of these spheres which manifested in the winners' names were: **the sun** – princes, vanity; **Mercury** – roads, chatter; **Saturn** — memories, the past, recollections, bridges; **Neptune** – secrets, dreams. Some of the winners on that particular day were *Quaint Prince, You're So Vain, Chocolate Bridge, Recollect, Ludwig Road, Star Chat, Secret Dream.*

There will be many occasions when you cannot find a name which has a clear-cut link with the reigning star pattern. When this happens, do not attempt to make it fit because if you do you will fail. This astrological system will only work when the name of a horse or dog is an authentic reflection of its corresponding star pattern.

Sometimes a starter will win if one or both of its parents have names which match the star pattern at the time of the race, even though the actual starter's name has no connection with any of the heavenly spheres. This can be a helpful pointer to a possible winner or place getter, particularly if there are other reasons to consider it, such as good form, a favourable barrier position etc. Occasionally two runners will share the power of a star pattern, in which case it is almost impossible to decide which will run first and which will come in second.

A classic example of this phenomena occurred when the sun and Mars formed a favourable combination. Remembering that the sun rules royalty and Mars is related to war, the results were as follows: second place getter was *Red Invader* which has a direct link with Mars. The winner was called *Edward* but because his father (ie the sire) was named *Abdicating*, there is a clear reference to King Edward VII, the royal who abdicated the throne and this gives *Edward* a link with the sun. Therefore, the sun-Mars star pattern was shared by *Edward* and *Red Invader*.

"...if Mercury and Venus formed a good combination, a name such as 'Love Letter' would be a good match..."

Hot Talk   *Lord Lieutenant*   *Mr Pen*   *Visions Splendid*
Dancing Away   *Sir Sovereign*   *Count Zulu*

The secret of success, using this system, depends entirely on the relationship between the meanings of words and their correspondence with the symbolism of the sun, moon and planets, so to help you gain a better understanding of just how it all fits together, here are some more examples of races run in Australia in 1990 and early 1991.

8 September 1990, Sydney

★ *The sun was in conjunction with Mercury.*

★ *The sun and Mercury both formed a favourable star pattern with Pluto.*

In Race 3 the first three place getters had a correspondence with those combinations.

❶ The winner was **Bequeath** whose sire was **Vice Regal**. Pluto is related to deceased estates and death. **Bequeath** suggests something inherited after death. **Vice Regal** is related to the sun which rules aristocrats, VIPs, nobility and prominent or powerful positions.

❷ The second place getter was **Big Wraps**. This name suggests such things as references, publicity or being talked about, all of which relate to Mercury. Pluto rules anything mammoth, gigantic or very big, so **Big Wraps** relates to Pluto and Mercury.

❸ The third place getter was **Raise a Million** whose sire was **Raise a Crown**. This name implies the influence of Pluto, which rules large things, and the sire's crown is ruled by the sun, which rules royalty.

8 September 1990, Flemington

★ *The same sun-Mercury-Pluto star patterns apply as in the previous example.*

The winner in Race 3 was **Kilki** whose sire was **Voodoo Rhythm** where Pluto rules voodoo and other forms of black magic. Mercury rules tags, labels, names. **Kilki** is simply a made-up name and the sire brings in the influence of Pluto.

15 September 1990, Moonee Valley

★ *Mercury was in conjunction with Venus, that is, in line with Venus.*

In Race 4, the winner was **Darling**. This name is a word or a description involving love. Mercury rules descriptions and words in general while Venus is the goddess of love. That's an easy one!

6 October 1990, Sydney

★ *The sun formed a favourable star pattern with Mars.*

★ *The sun was in conflict with Neptune.*

★ *Venus was in conflict with Uranus.*

The winner was **Takeover Battle** whose sire was **Battle**. Both of these names are related to Mars, the god of war, the planet of fighting and battles. No other starters had appropriate names, so, although the symbolism of the sun is absent in the name **Takeover Battle**, the Martian influence was particularly strong, making it the winner.

5 January 1991, Sydney and Melbourne

★ *The sun was in conjunction with Neptune.*

In Race 2 in Sydney, the second place getter was **King's Secret** where the sun is related to rulers, royalty and kings, while Neptune rules secrets. The winner, **Siegfried** was not nearly so obvious unless you realised that the composer, Wagner wrote a famous opera called Siegfried. The sun rules fame and Neptune rules operas.

In Race 1 in Melbourne on the same day, the winner was **Grey Legend**. As you will discover, Neptune rules such things as myths and legends.

Unfortunately, many horses and dogs have made-up names which are meaningless, in which case it is impossible to apply this system. Naturally, some of these runners can and do win races, so you should play safe whenever good form suggests that one of these could win, even though you have found another horse or dog with an appropriate name.

Providing you think very carefully about every facet of each star pattern, you should have a fairly high degree of success in your selections. However, do not expect to find a positive indication in every race, and do not try to apply this system to any event unless there is a very definite link between a name and a star pattern.

The qualities associated with each of the 10 heavenly spheres are all quite different and since you have to learn to read their "language", it would be a very good idea to start by reading through the list of the keywords several times so that you begin to get a "feel" for them and for the type of things they signify, because in the final analysis this is the basis of the whole system. It is like an astrological jigsaw puzzle and you have to learn how to fit the pieces together.

The moon's star patterns

Because the moon moves very quickly, its star patterns are short-lived and they are only effective for a period of approximately two hours. Therefore, whenever you see a moon star pattern listed in the **Calendar of Star Patterns**, don't forget that it only operates during the stated time period. All our times are quoted in Eastern Standard Time, so people living in the states not operating on this time will have to make adjustments.

Be aware that during Daylight Saving periods the times I have listed will need to be adjusted; the beginning of Daylight Saving means that clocks are turned forward by 1 hour, at the end of Daylight Saving clocks are turned back by 1 hour.

On the following pages you will find an exhaustive list of keywords which have a correspondence or affinity with the sun, the moon and all the known planets.

Dictionary of keywords
Star keywords

In the following lists you will find many of the things which have a correspondence to or an affinity with the sun, moon and all the known plants. I make no apology for the large number of words I have included, nor that some are definitely of the weird and wonderful variety. After all, many horses and dogs have extraordinary names and, if you wish to use this astrological system, you need a comprehensive dictionary of keywords.

Even so, there will be times when you cannot find a precise word used in a runner's name. However, it is the actual meaning which is important. So, if you are looking for the word "hot" and cannot find it, bear in mind that "heat" is listed under Mars.

The sun

Achievement
Aggrandisement
Ambitious
Apollo
Approbation
Ardour
Aristocrats
Arrogance
Authority
Ballrooms
Boastful
Bombastic
Bosses
Bright
Brilliant
Candour
Cardiac
Celebration
Celebrities
Centre
Chief
Circles
Circumference
Commanding
Conceit
Confidence
Coronation
Creativity
Crowns
Dawn
Daylight
Despotic
Diamonds
Dignity
Egotism
Elevate
Emblems
Eminence
Emperor
Energy
Encourage
Exaltation
Eyes
Fame
Famous
Father
Gala affairs
Games
Gaudy
Gilt
Glare
Glory
Glow
Gold, metal and colour
Government
Greatness
Halo
Haughty
Healing
Health
Heart
Heat
Honour
Hope
Hot
Illumination
Illustrious
Imperious
Imperialistic
Importance
Individuality
Influential
Joyous
Kind
Kings
Kingdom
Lavish
Leader
Leo (the zodiac sign)
Life
Light
Limelight
Lion
Living
Lordly
Loyalty
Luminary
Luminous
Lustrous
Magnaminous
Magnificence
Majestic
Males
Managers
Manfully
Monarchs
Nobility
Notorious
Notable
Nucleus
Officials
Omnipotent
Orange
Ornate
Ostentation
Palaces
Palatial
Parks
Pinnacle
Playgrounds
Pomp and ceremony
Pompous
Power
President
Pride
Prince
Prominence
Quality
Queen
Quintessence
Radiant
Rank
Regal
Renown
Respect
Resplendent
Royalty
Rulers
Sabbath
Salamander
Show-offs
Solariums
Sovereign
Splendour
Spotlight
Stately
Status
Sumptuous
Sunday
Sunburn
Sunflowers
Sunny
Sunshine
Superiors
Supreme
Theatres
Thrones
Valuables
Vanity
Vigour
VIPs
Vitality
Virile
Vivifying
Warmth
Wasteful
Willpower
Yellow
Zeal

The moon

Abdomen
Adaptable
Affable
Aquatic matters
Babies
Bakers
Barmaid
Barges
Baths
Bathing
Beverages
Boathouses
Boating
Bottles
Breasts
Brewing
Brooding
Butter
Cafes
Canals
Cancer (the zodiac sign)
Caterers
Changeable
Cheese
Chickens
Childhood
Children
Cisterns
Clams
Cleaning
Collecting
Common
Conception
Cooking
Cooks
Cows
Crabs
Crescent
Crops
Crying
Cupboards
Dairies
Damp
Dew
Digestion
Dilution
Dining
Docks
Domestic front
Domicile
Dough (cooking)
Drains
Dreamy
Drinks
Dropsy
Drowsy
Dyspepsia
Ebb and flow
Eggs
Emotional
Evening
Eyes
Family
Familiar
Fecundity
Feelings
Female
Feminine
Fermentation
Ferries
Fertility
Fickle
Fish
Fishing
Flabby
Fluids
Foam
Food
Fountains
Fowls
Fruitful
Gardens
Gastric
Generative
Germinate'
Gestation
Glands
Glass
Groceries
Habits
Habitation
Harbours
Hatch
Hens
Herbs
Home
Hotels
House
Houseboats
Housewife
Housework
Humid
Hydrant
Hydro
Immerse
Impressionable
Inconsistent
Indigestion
Infants
Inns
Instincts
Irrigation
Jam (food)
Janitors
Juice
Kitchens
Kitchenware
Lactic
Lady
Lakes
Laundry
Lighthouse
Lillies
Linen
Liquids
Luna
Lunatic
Lunch
Mammals
Marine
Maritime
Markets
Marshes
Masses, the
Maternal
Meals
Melons
Menstruation
Midwives
Milk
Milkman
Moats
Moist
Monday
Moods

114

Moony
Moonstones
Mother
Mushrooms
Mutation
Naval
Navigation
Night
Nocturnal
Nourishment
Nursery
Nursing
Nurseries
Nutrition
Obstetrics
Opticians
Ordinary
Owls
Oysters
Pale
Pans
Pantries
Pearls
Personality
Phase
Pipes, water
Planting
Plebeian
Plumbing
Ponds
Pools
Ports
Poultry
Public, the
Pumps
Quail
Queen
Quiet
Rain
Rambling
Recepticals
Receptive
Reflector
Removing
Reproductive
Residences
Restaurants
Restless
Rivers
Rooms
Roving
Sailing
Sailors
Saloons
Sap
Scrubbing
Seafood
Seamen
Silver, metal and colour
Sleep
Soft
Smooth
Snails
Stomach
Streams
Subconscious, the
Swimming
Taverns
Tear drops
Tender
Tides
Timid
Umbilical
Underwear
Unrest
Vacillating
Variable
Voyage, water

Vulnerable
Waiters
Waitresses
Waning
Washing
Washerwomen
Water
Waxing moon
Wells
Wet
White
Wife
Women
Young

Mercury

Accountants
Accounts
Advertisements
Advice
Agents
Agreements
Alert
Ambassadors
Analytical
Announcement
Announcers
Apprentices
Aptitude
Arms, body
Artful
Atlases
Attentive
Auditors
Authors
Autographs
Automobiles
Bicycles
Billboards
Bills
Biographies
Bookings
Books
Bookkeeping
Boys, youthful
Brainy
Broadcasting
Bronchial
Brothers
Buses
Business matters
Busy
Busybodies
Buying
Cabs
Calculate, to
Cars
Catalogues
Certificates
Changeable
Charts
Chatter
Cheating
Checking
Clerks
Clever
Columnists
Commentators
Communication
Comprehension
Concentration
Conferences
Contacts
Conversation
Copy
Correspondence
Coupons

Couriers
Credentials
Criticism
Debate
Deeds, legal
Deceiving
Delineate
Deliveries
Descriptions
Desks, writing
Details
Dexterity
Diaries
Dictation
Dictionaries
Diction
Diets
Discussion
Distribution
Double
Drafts
Dual
Edict
Editors
Education
Effervescent
Elocution
Eloquence
Employees
Encyclopaedias
Envelopes
Errands
Essays
Explanation
Fable
Facile
Facts
Falsity
Fanciful
Filing, clerk or cabinet
Fiction
Fingers
Fluent
Forgery
Forgetfulness
Fidgeting
Fraud
Gemini
Garrulous
Gibes
Glib
Gossip
Grammar
Graphology
Grumble
Hands
Handwriting
Handy
Herald, to
Hygiene
Ideas
Illegible
Illiterate
Imagination
Imbecile
Imitate
Information
Ingenious
Inquiries
Inquisitive
Inspectors
Instructions
Intellect
Interceptors
Interviews
Investigation
Invoices
Jargon
Journals

Journalists
Journeys, short
Juggle
Juvenile
Keys
Kin (brothers, sisters)
Knack
Knave
Knowledge
Labels
Language
Learning
Lectures
Letters
Libel
Libraries
Linguists
Literature
Lively
Logic
Loquacious
Luggage
Lungs
Magazines
Mail
Manicures
Manuscripts
Maps
Meddling
Mediator
Memorising
Mentality
Mentor
Merchants
Messages
Messengers
Mimicry
Mind, the
Mouth, the
Names
Narrators
Neighbours
Nerves
Nervous system
Neurotic
News
Newspapers
Nimble
Nonsense
Notary
Notes
Notify
Novels
Numbers
Observation
Opinions
Orators
Oscillation
Pairs
Pamphlets
Papers
Patterns
Papyrus
Pencils
Pens
People, young
Perception
Periodicals
Perjury
Persuasive
Petitions
Pickpockets
Pilfering
Porters
Postal
Post offices
Posters
Prattle
Press, the

Printing
Prose
Proverbs
Psychiatry
Publications
Publishers
Puns
Pupils, school
Quacks
Quandary
Query
Questions
Quickly
Questions
Quotations
Reaction
Reading
Reason
Receipts
Recipes
Reckoning
Records
Registers
Relate, to
Relatives, close
Repartee
Reply
Reports
Research
Respiration
Restless
Rhymes
Roads
Rumours
Salesmen
Saleswomen
Satire
Scholars
Schools
Scripts
Secretaries
Seeing
Selling
Servants
Shifting
Shorthand
Shoulders
Shrewd
Signals
Signatures
Signposts
Sisters
Skill
Sleight of hand
Small
Speaking
Speech
Speed
Spokesperson
Stammering
Stamps
Statements
Stationery
Statistics
Stenographers
Stoolpigeon
Storekeeper
Stories
Streets
Students
Study
Suggest
Swift
Tales
Talking
Talkative
Teachers
Telegrams
Telephones

115

Tellers
Testimony
Textbooks
Theft
Theories
Thinking
Thought
Tickets
Tittle-tattle
Tongue
Topics
Trade
Traffic
Trains
Translation
Transport
Transposing
Transient
Transmit
Travel, short
Treaties
Trembling
Tricks
Trifling
Tutors
Twins
Typewriter
Typists
Understanding
Utterance
Variable
Vehicles
Verbal
Versatile
Vibrating
Visitors
Vocabulary
Voice
Voluble
Vouchers
Walking
Wednesday
Whispering
Wit
Witnesses
Words
Writers
Writing
Youth
Youthful people

Venus

Accessories, dress
Admire
Adornment
Adulterous
Affection
Agreeable
Alliances
Amorous
Amusement
Appease
Arbitration
Art
Artists
Attachments, emotional
Attractive
Ballet
Balmy
Banquets
Beauticians
Beauty
Beauty parlours
Bedroom
Beneficent
Blossoms
Bonnets
Boudoir
Bouquets
Boutiques
Bracelets
Brooches
Cabarets
Cakes
Calm
Cameos
Candy
Caresses
Cash
Celebrations
Charm
Clothes
Coalition
Coins
Colour
Comforts
Companions
Compatible
Comrades
Concerts
Confectionery
Conjugal
Connubial
Co-operation
Consort
Copper
Cosmetics
Costumes
Courtesy
Courtship
Culture
Dancing
Decor
Decoration
Decorum
Delectable
Delicacies
Delicious
Delightful
Diplomacy
Dissolute
Dolls
Donations
Drapes
Dresses
Dressmakers
Duets
Ease
Effeminate
Elegance
Embellishment
Embroidery
Emeralds
Endearment
Engagements, romantic
Enjoyment
Entertainment
Equally
Erotic
Escorts
Etiquette
Fair
Fair play
Fancy goods
Favours
Feminine
Festivals
Festivities
Fiancee
Finance
Fine arts
Finery
Flattery
Flirting
Floral
Florists
Flowers
Fondle
Fraternities
Friday
Friendship
Fun
Furnishings
Gaiety
Gain
Gallant
Garlands
Garments
Garnishes
Gatherings, social
Gems
Genial
Genteel
Gentility
Gentle
Gifts
Girls
Glamorous
Gloves
Good taste
Gowns
Graceful
Gratitude
Greetings
Haberdashery
Hairdressers
Hairstyles
Handsome
Happiness
Harmony
Hats
Holidays
Honey
Honeymoon
Horticulture
Hospitality
Hostelry
Immaculate
Immodest
Immoral
Income
Indolent
Indulgent
Interior decorators
Intimate
Invitations, social
Jewellery
Jocular
Joyous
Just
Kidneys
Kindness
Lace
Ladies
Lass
Laughing
Lazy
Lecherous
Leisure
Lenient
Lewd
Licentious
Likeable
Lingerie
Lockets
Love
Lovely
Loving
Luxurious
Maiden
Makeup
Manners, good
Marriage
Mate
Matrimony
Melody
Millinery
Mirthful
Models, fashion
Modest
Money
Music
Neat
Neck
Necklaces
Nectar
Negotiation
Normal
Nosegay
Nourishing
Nurturing
Obliging
Orchestras
Ornaments
Pacifists
Pacts
Paintings
Parties
Partners
Pastels
Pastime
Peace
Perfume
Picnics
Pictures
Picturesque
Pink
Pleasing
Pleasure
Poetical
Poise
Popular
Possessions
Posy
Presents
Profits
Proposals of marriage
Qualify
Receptions
Reconciliations
Recreation
Refinement
Rejoicing
Relaxation
Ribbons
Rings
Romance
Rouge
Salons
Scarves
Sensual
Serenades
Sex appeal
Singing
Smooth
Sociable
Social affairs
Society
Sofa
Soft
Songs
Soothing
Style
Sugar
Suitors
Sweethearts
Sweets
Symmetrical
Sympathetic
Tact
Tactile
Tailors
Tapestries
Throat
Toiletries
Tonsils
Touch
Trousseau
Truces
Tunes
Underwear
United
Unity
Untidy
Upholstery
Vacations
Vases
Vocalist
Voluptuous
Wages
Wallets
Wanton
Warm
Wedlock
Weddings
Wigs
Women
Yielding

Mars

Abrasive
Abusive
Accidents
Acrobatics
Action
Acute
Adventure
Aggravate
Aggression
Agitators
Agony
Ammunition
Amputation
Anger
Antagonism
Ardent
Arguments
Armaments
Armed forces
Armour-plate
Army, the
Arrows
Arsenals
Arson
Artillery
Assailant
Assassins
Assault
Athletic
Attack
Audacious
Axes
Barbarous
Barbers
Battles
Battleships
Bayonets
Bellicose
Belligerent
Bites
Blacksmiths
Blazing
Blisters
Boilermakers
Boldness
Boxing
Brave
Brawls
Brazen
Breakages
Brutal

Bullets
Bullfights
Bullies
Burns
Butchers
Cannons
Carpenters
Carving
Caustic
Cayenne
Challenges
Chimney
Chisels
Choleric
Cleaver
Coarse
Combat
Combustion
Conflict
Conquests
Construction
Contests
Cooking utensils
Courage
Crimes of violence
Cruelty
Cutlass
Cutlery
Cuts
Daggers
Damaging
Danger
Daring
Darts
Defend
Defiant
Dentists
Destructive
Discord
Disturbance
Dreadful
Effort
Emergencies
Energy
Engineers
Engraving
Enmity
Excitement
Exercise, physical
Explosives
Feats
Ferocious
Feuds
Fevers
Fiery
Fighting
Fire
Firearms
Firebugs
Firecrackers
Firemen
Force
Forge
Forks
Foundaries
Friction
Frightful
Furious
Furnaces
Gall
Gash
Gauntlet
Gladiators
Guards
Gunner
Guns
Gun-powder
Gymnastics
Hardware

Haste
Hawks
Headaches
Headstrong
Heat
Hectic
Helmets
Hoodlums
Hostility
Hurly-burly
Impatience
Impetuous
Implements
Impudence
Impulsive
Incinerators
Incisions
Industrious
Inflammation
Initiative
Injury
Instruments, hot or sharp
Intense
Intrepid
Invaders
Invincible
Iron
Irritation
Jack-knife
Jailer
Javelin
Jolt
Jostle
Junk
Keen
Kick
Kindle
Knaves
Knives
Lancer
Locksmith
Loud
Lumberjack
Lusty
Machinery
Manufacturers
Marauders
Masculine
Mechanical
Mechanics
Military
Missiles
Muscles
Muscular
Murder
Mustard
Mutilation
Nails
Needles
Nettles
Noisy
Notch
Obscene
Obstinate
Operations
Opponents
Oppressive
Ovens
Pain
Peril
Perjurer
Perpetrate
Pestilent
Pins
Pioneers
Pistols
Pointed
Police

Prize-fighters
Provoke
Prowess
Pugilist
Pugnacious
Punctures
Quarrels
Quick
Radiators
Rage
Rams
Rambunctious
Rampage
Ramrod
Rape
Rascals
Rash
Rasps
Ravish
Razors
Rebellion
Reckless
Red
Regiments
Resentment
Resourceful
Rifles
Ribald
Rivals
Rough
Rowdy
Ruddy
Ruffians
Rugged
Sabres
Sandpaper
Savagery
Saws
Scalds
Scalpels
Scarlet
Scars
Scissors
Scorching
Scorpions
Scratches
Sensual
Sexual
Sharp
Shooting
Singeing
Sinewy
Slaughter
Smelting
Soldiers
Spears
Spikes
Sport, competitive
Stabs
Stakes
Stamina
Steam engines
Steel
Stimulate
Stings
Stoves
Strength
Strenuous
Strife
Strong
Surgery
Surgeons
Swords
Temper
Terrifying
Thistles
Threats
Thugs
Tigers

Toasted
Tools
Torment
Torpedoes
Torture
Tournaments
Tuesday
Turbulent
Uncouth
Uproar
Urgent
Vanguards
Vaunt
Venturesome
Veterans, war
Vexation
Victorious
Vigour
Vile
Violation
Violence
Virility
Vivisection
Vixen
War
Warships
Weapons
Welding
Whips
Whittle
Wilful
Wounds
Wreck, to
Wrench, to
Wrestling

Jupiter

Abscesses
Absconding
Abundance
Academic
Accumulation
Adjudicate
Advantages
Adviser
Affluence
Aldermen
Alderwomen
Altars
Ambassadors
Ample
Amplify, to
Animals, large
Apoplexy
Appraise
Arbitration, legal
Archdukes
Archery
Aristocrats
Attorneys
Auspicious
Awards
Bailiffs
Banking
Banks
Banquets
Barons
Barristers
Benediction
Benefactors
Beneficial
Benevolent
Big
Bilious
Bishops
Blessings
Bonds
Bonuses

Books, legal, religious or philosophical
Bounty
Budgets
Capital assets
Capitalist
Carbuncles
Cardinals, church
Carnivals
Cashiers
Cathedrals
Ceremonies, religious or legal
Charity
Cheerful
Church, the
Clergymen
Colleges
Comfortable
Commerce
Communication, far distant or overseas
Complacency
Convents
Convivial
Copyright
Corporate law
Corpulent
Correct
Counsellors, legal or religious
Countries, foreign
Counts
Countesses
Courts of law
Credentials
Customs department
Deacons
Decamp
Default
Defray
Deputies
Development
Devotion
Diplomats
Disburse
Disorders of liver and blood
Doctors
Donations
Dukes, duchesses
Education, higher
Embassies
Embezzle
Endowments
Enlargement
Erroneous
Ethics
Exaggeration
Excellence
Excesses
Exchequer
Executives
Expansion
Expensive
Faith
Faraway places
Fat
Festering
Finance, large
Financiers
Fines, legal
Flourish, to
Foreign affairs, places and people
Formal
Fortunate
Fortune
Fruitful

117

Fun
Gains
Gallantry
Gambling
Generous
Gluttonous
Good fortune
Goodwill
Grandiose
Growth
Hams
Happiness
Hearty
Hair
Hips
Holidays
Holy matters
Honesty
Honorary
Hope
Hospitable
Huge
Humour
Illegal
Illicit
Immense
Important
Imports
Improvement
Income
Increase
Indemnity
Indolent
Indulgent
Inflated
Inquests
Insurance
International affairs
Jaundice
Jocose
Journeys, long
Joviality
Jubilant
Judicious
Judges
Judicial matters
Juries
Jurors
Justice
Knowledge
Large
Lavish
Law, the
Lawsuits
Lawyers
Leases
Legacies
Legal affairs
Leisure
Lending
Licences
Literature
Litigation
Liver, the
Loans
Lucky
Lucrative
Luxury
Magistrates
Magnate
Magnificent
Maximum
Medals
Mercy
Millionaires
Ministers
Mirth
Misjudgement
Missionaries

Monasteries
Money, large amounts
Morals
Noble
Nourishing
Official
Opportune
Optimism
Opulent
Ordainment
Orderly
Ordinances
Pageant
Palatial
Parole
Parsons
Passports
Patrons
Philanthropists
Philosophy
Physicians
Pilgrims
Plenty
Policies
Popes
Praise
Prayer
Preachers
Premiums
Prestige
Priests
Principles
Prizes
Productive
Professional people
Profligate
Profitable
Prosperity
Pulpits
Quality
Quantity
Rabbis
Racehorses
Rain
Ransom
Reckless
Recompense
Rectors
Redemption
Redundance
Refunds
Regain
Regalia
Regulations
Religion
Replete
Respectable
Reverence
Riches
Rosaries
Rotund
Satiate
Scholarly
Science
Scripture
Search warrants
Serene
Sermons
Shares
Sheriffs
Ships
Sincerity
Speculating
Spendthrift
Sporting
Stocks
Stoutness
Success
Summons

Supply
Suppurate
Surfeit
Surplus
Swelling
Temperate
Theology
Thighs
Thrive
Thunder
Thursday
Tin
Titles
Tours
Travel, far distant
Treasury
Tremendous
Trials, law
Tributes
True
Trust
Truth
Unadulterated
Unharmed
Unimpeachable
Universities
Valuers
Venerable
Veracity
Viscounts
Vows
Wagers
Wealth
Wholesome
Winnings
Worship

Saturn

Abbreviations
Aches
Acoustics
Acquire
Adhesives
Afflictions
Afraid
Aged people
Aggrieve
Agriculture
Ailing
Apprehensive
Ancestors
Anchors
Anxiety
Apathy
Archaeology
Architecture
Asbestos
Ascetic
Ash
Asphalt
Astringents
Atrophy
Austerity
Ballast
Bankrupt
Barriers
Basements
Basics
Beggars
Begrudge
Belittle
Belts
Bemoan
Bereavement
Binding
Bitter
Black
Blindfolds

Blockages
Bones
Boredom
Boulders
Boundaries
Brakes
Bricks
Bridges
Brief
Builders
Building
Bruises
Burdens
Calamities
Calculating, attitude
Calendars
Callous
Calm
Carbon
Castles
Caution
Caves
Cell
Cement
Cemeteries
Censors
Ceramics
Chalk
Chills
Chronic
Chronometers
Clamps
Clay
Clocks
Coagulate
Coal
Coalminer
Cohere
Cold
Compression
Congeal
Concrete
Condensed
Conscientious
Conservation
Conservative
Continuity
Contraction
Cowards
Cynical
Dark
Deaf
Debility
Debt
Decay
Decripitude
Deficient
Delay
Denial
Depression
Despair
Destitute
Destroy
Detain
Deteriorate
Devitalise
Difficulties
Diminishing
Dirty
Disaster
Discipline
Discontent
Discounts
Discretion
Disintegration
Dissatisfaction
Doleful
Doom
Doubt

Drudgery
Dryness
Dull
Dumps, rubbish
Duty
Earthy
Economical
Elderly
Emaciation
Embargoes
Endings
Enduring
Equipoise
Estates
Excavations
Failure
Faithful
Falls, bodily
Famine
Farms
Fasting
Fatality
Fate
Fatigue
Fear
Fences
Fidelity
Fields
Finality
Firm
Fixture
Flint
Foreclosure
Formation
Fortitude
Fossils
Foundations
Fractures
Framework
Freezing
Frigid
Frost
Frowning
Frugal
Frustration
Fundamental
Funerals
Goals
Garbage
Garters
Gaskets
Gates
Gather
Glaciers
Gloom
Glue
Glum
Granite
Graphite
Grasping
Grave
Gravel
Greed
Grievous
Grindstone
Ground
Grounded
Haggard
Handcuffs
Hard
Hardship
Harness
Hatred
Heap
Hearing, sense of
Hearse
Heavy
Hermits
Hesitation

Hibernation
Hide
Hindrances
Hireling
History
Hold, to
Holes
Hostages
Hour-glass
Houses
Humility
Hunchbacks
Ice
Immobility
Immovable
Impede
Impossibilities
Indomitable
Inertia
Inferiority
Inflexible
Inhibitions
Inscrutable
Inside
Insulation
Integrity
Introspective
Introverted
Invalids
Irksome
Isolated
Jackass
Jeering
Join
Junk
Keep, to
Kill
Killjoy
Kink
Knees
Knell
Knocks
Knot
Laborious
Lack
Laggard
Lament
Land
Languor
Last
Latches
Late
Lead, the metal
Leanness
Leather
Lime
Limitation
Limits
Loads
Lonely
Loss
Malevolent
Malformation
Malice
Malign
Masonry
Materialism
Meager
Meditation
Melancholy
Memories
Methodical
Mines
Minimum
Misers
Misery
Misfortune
Mistrust
Monument

Morgues
Morose
Mortar
Mortgage
Mortification
Mortuary
Mourning
Mud
Mummy, Egyptian
Nanny
Narrow
Necessities
Needy
Negation
Neglect
Negro
No
Nonchalant
Nunnery
Obedience
Obituaries
Obnoxious
Obsolete
Obstruction
Old
Onyx
Opaque
Ordeal
Orthodox
Pains
Paint, protective
Paralysis
Parsimonious
Past, the
Patience
Paupers
Pavements
Peevish
Penury
Permanent
Pernicious
Perpetual
Perseverance
Pessimism
Petrify
Plaster
Plebeian
Politics
Poor people
Postponement
Pottery
Poverty
Practical
Precaution
Predecessors
Prejudice
Problems
Profound
Prohibit
Property
Prudent
Prudery
Punctual
Qualm
Quarantine
Quarries
Quash
Querulous
Quiet
Quill
Quit
Ranch
Real estate
Realistic
Recession
Recluse
Recollections
Reduction
Refrigeration

Regrets
Regular
Relics
Remains
Remorse
Repentance
Repose
Reservoirs
Resistance
Responsibility
Restriction
Retaining
Retard, to
Retirement
Retrenchment
Rheumatism
Rickets
Rocks
Routine
Rubbish
Ruination
Ruin, to
Ruins, ancient
Sadness
Safety
Sand
Saturday
Saturnalia
Scant
Scapegoat
Scarce
Scavengers
Sceptics
Scrupulous
Sculpture
Secondhand
Secretive
Security
Sedative
Sediment
Selfishness
Senile
Sepulchre
Seriousness
Set
Sexton
Shabby
Shade
Shale
Shortage
Shrinkage
Sickening
Silence
Sinking
Skeleton
Skin
Skinflint
Slate
Slavery
Slow
Slums
Snow
Sober
Solitude
Soot
Sordid
Sorrow
Sour
Spleen
Spoil
Stability
Stale
Starvation
Statues
Stiff
Stoics
Stones
Stop
Strict

Subdued
Subjective
Substantial
Subways
Suppression
Surveyors
Suspicion
Synopsis
Taciturn
Taint
Tale
Tank
Tanners
Tar
Tardy
Tasks
Tedious
Teeth
Tenacity
Tenements
Tense
Terminations
Terminus
Terror
Thickening
Thin
Thorough
Threadbare
Thrift
Thwart
Tightness
Tiles
Time
Timekeeper
Tired
Toil
Tombs
Traditions
Tragedies
Tragic
Trench
Tranquil
Ugly
Underneath
Undertakers
Unhappy
Unity
Unlucky
Uphold
Urn
Valley
Vaults
Vested
Vicissitudes
Vows
Vulcanise
Walls
Watches
Weary
Wedges
Weights and measures
Wintry
Woe
Worry
Wrapping
Wrinkles
Yesterday
Yoke
Yore

Uranus

Abnormal
Abortion
Abrupt
Acute
Advanced ideas
Adventurous
Aerial

Aeronautics
Aeroplanes
Agitators
Air
Airports
Alarmist
Aliens
Alteration
Altruism
Amazement
Anarchy
Ankles
Antiquarians
Antiques
Appliances, electrical
Astrology
Astronomy
Aura
Auto-electricians
Avant garde
Aversion
Aviation
Batteries
Bizarre
Bohemian
Bombs
Boycotts
Broadcasting
Brotherhood
Brusque
Catastrophes
Changes, sudden
Checks (patterns)
Clairvoyant
Colonise
Commoner
Communistic
Contradictions
Contrary
Convulsions
Co-operative
Cranks
Crisis
Cyclones
Defiance
Detours
Different
Dire
Disapproval
Disaster
Discard
Discovery
Disorder
Disruptions
Distributors
Divorce
Dynamic
Dynamite
Dynamo
Earthquakes
Eccentric
Electric
Electricians
Electricity
Electron
Electronics
Elevators
Elopement
Emancipation
Engineers, electrical
Errant
Erratic
Estrange
Exile
Experiments
Explosive
Extraordinary
Extremist
Expurgate

119

Fanatics
Filibuster
Firecrackers
Fitful
Flashes
Flying
Foreign
Fraternal
Freakish
Freedom
Freelance
Free thinker
Fugitives
Gales
Gamin
Garage
Garish
Gases
Generators
Genius
Grotesque
Hangars
Hazard
Helicopters
Hiccups
Hippies
Hobo
Homosexual
Humanitarian
Hurricanes
Illegal
Illegitimate
Impromptu
Impulses
Incompatible
Incongruous
Independent
Indiscretion
Informal
Ingenious
Innovation
Interruptions
Intuitive
Inventive
Inversion
Jilted
Kilowatt
Kinetic
Lawless
Liberal
Liberty
Liberation
Libertine
Lightning
Linesman, electrical
Lines, power
Madcap
Magnetic
Manoeuvre
Metamorphosis
Metaphysics
Microphones
Microscope
Miracle
Miscarriage
Mixed
Modern
Motorman
Motley
Mutiny
Nomadic
Nonconformists
Notorious
Novelties
Now
Oblique
Obstreperous
Obtrude
Occultism

Originality
Oscillate
Oust
Outbreak
Outlaws
Outrageous
Overturn
Panic
Paradoxes
Peculiarities
Pioneers
Piquant
Plaid patterns
Precipitate, to
Premature
Prodigies
Progressive
Quaint
Quandary
Queer
Quest
Quiver
Quizzical
Radar
Radiators (electrical)
Radical
Radio
Radio-active
Radium
Rapid
Raving
Rebellion
Rebels
Reform
Rejecting
Repellent
Repulsing
Research
Revolts
Revolutionising
Revulsion
Roving
Runaways
Satire
Saucy
Schism
Scientists
Sedition
Seismic
Separations
Shocks
Socialism
Sonar
Spark plugs
Spasmodic
Spasms
Spectacular
Stereograms
Strange
Strangers
Strikes
Sudden
Surprises
Switchboards
Tantrums
Telegrapher
Telepathic
Telescope
Television
Tornadoes
Transformers
Transposing
Trespassing
Turbines
Turbulent
Twitching
Unconventional
Unexpected
Uninvited

Unorthodox
Unusual
Upheavals
Upsets
X-rays

Neptune

Absorption
Abstract
Abstruse
Accomplice, an
Acting
Actors
Adaptable
Addicts
Adoration
Adrift
Adulteration
Alchemy
Aesthetic
Alcohol
Aliases
Alibi
Ambiguous
Anaesthetic
Apparitions
Aqueducts
Aquariums
Artifice
Artificial
Asphyxiation
Assuming
Astral
Asylums
Baths
Bays
Beaches
Befog, to
Beguiling
Benzine
Bewildering
Bigamy
Billowy
Bleach
Bluffing
Bogus
Bohemian
Bootlegging
Breweries
Bribery
Cajole
Cameras
Camouflage
Canals
Canneries, fish
Cataleptic
Chaos
Charlatans
Cheats
Chicanery
Chloroform
Cigarettes
Cinemas
Clairsentient
Clairvoyance
Clandestine
Clouded
Clouds
Coffee
Collusion
Communism
Confidence tricks
Confidential
Confound, to
Confusion
Conspiracy
Counterfeit

Coral
Dampness
Debauchery
Deception
Defile
Delusions
Dilute
Disguise
Dissolve
Distillers
Distraught
Divers
Divination
Docks
Double dealing
Doubtful
Drains
Dreams
Dreamy
Drink (alcohol)
Drowning
Drugs
Drunk
Dupe, to
Ecstasy
Elusive
Embezzlement
Emotional
Enchanting
Enervating
Engulf
Enigmas
Enigmatic
Enticing
Escape
ESP
Evade
Exotic
Fables
Fairies
Fakes
Fanciful
Fantasy
Fascination
Fawning
Feet
Fictitious
Fiddle (as in cheat)
Film industry
Films
Fish
Fishy
Floods
Fluids
Fluorescence
Flying
Fog
Fountains
Fraud
Fumes
Gases
Gasolene
Gelatine
Germicides
Gin
Glamour
Glass
Graft
Guile
Gullible
Half-wit
Hallucinations
Harbours
Haze
Hazy
Heroin
Hidden
Hoax
Hospitals

Hydraulics
Hydrotherapy
Hypnotism
Hypochondria
Hypodermic
Hypocrisy
Idealism
Illimitable
Illusion
Imagination
Imitation
Immaterial
Impalpable
Impersonation
Imposters
Incense
Incomprehensible
Indefinite
Indulgent
Inflate
Inspiration
Intangible
Intoxication
Intrigue
Intuition
Inundation
Irrigation
Inveigle
Kelp
Kerosene
Latent
Lather (as in washing)
Leaks
Lethargy
Limpid
Liquid
Liquor
LSD
Lubrication
Lure
Magic
Marine
Mariners
Marooned
Mazes
Mediums, psychic
Melodious
Mermaid
Mirages
Mirrors, reflections in
Misrepresent
Mist, misty
Morons
Morphine
Mountebank
Music
Mystery
Mysticism
Mythology
Myths
Naive
Namby-pamby
Narcotics
Nautical
Naval
Nebulous
Necromancy
Nightmares
Nudists
Nymphs
Oceans
Odours
Oil
Omens
Opium
Paradise
Perfume
Periscopes
Perverted

Petroleum
Phantoms
Photography
Pilots
Poison
Ponds
Prediction
Premonitions
Pretence
Prophecy
Pseudonyms
Psychic matters
Puzzles
Quacks
Quandary
Questionable
Quiescent
Quintessence
Quixotic
Rainbows
Receptive
Recondite
Rendezvous, secret
Reverence
Reveries
Riddles
Rubber
Scandal
Scheming
Scurrilous
Sea
Seafaring
Seances
Seclusion
Secret
Seduce
Seer
Seraphim
Showers
Simulative
Skulking
Sleep
Sleep walking
Smuggling
Sorcery
Spectres
Spies
Spiritualism
Sponges
Steam
Submarines
Subterfuge
Subversion
Swamps
Swimming
Synthetic
Tangle
Tea
Telepathy
Tenderness
Theurgy
Tobacco
Toxic
Trance
Transcendental
Transfigure
Transparent
Treachery
Trident
Uncanny
Undine
Undulating
Unmask
Vacillating
Vague
Vapour
Veils
Visionary
Visions

Volatile
Wade
Water
Waves
Weird
Wet
Whimsical
Whirlpools
Wiles
Wine
Witchcraft
Witches
Yachts
Yeast
Yoga
Yogis

Pluto

Abattoirs
Abduction
Abyss
Adulterate
Ambushes
Amnesia
Annihilation
Anonymous
Assassination
Assassins
Atomic
Atomic energy
Atrocities
Autopsies
Bad
Baffle
Bandits
Bequeath
Betrayal
Black magic
Blowflies
Bootlegger
Booze
Brimstone, fire and
Bulk goods
Calamities
Callous
Carrion
Cartels, powerful
Catastrophes
Cesspools
Chasms
Clubs
Combines, large
Compulsion
Conscience
Contempt
Convicts
Corruption
Covetous
Cremation
Crematories
Crime, organised
Criminals
Crowds
Death
Defiance
Defilement
Degenerate, to
Degradation
Demolition
Demonic
Demons
Depravity
Destruction, total
Destruction, self
Detectives
Dice
Dictators
Embalming

Enigmas
Epidemics
Eradicate
Evil
Evolution
Expunge
Expurgate
Fanatical
Fanatics
Felons
Fetid
Fiendish
Filth
Foul
Fumigate
Gangland
Gangsters
Gargantuan
Genocide
Gigantic
Godless
Graves
Groups
Guillotine
Guilty
Gunman
Hades
Hag
Havoc
Hell
Holocaust
Hoodlums
Horrors
Huge organisations
Immoral
Immortal
Impelling
Impure
Indifferent
Infernal
Infernos
Insatiable
Inscrutable
Intemperate
Kidnapping
Laser beams
Lawlessness
Lice
Looting
Lust
Maggots
Magic, black
Malefactor
Malevolent
Mammoth
Marshes
Massacres
Menace
Mephistopheles
Metamorphosis
Mobs
Mob violence
Mire
Miscreant
Moll
Monster
Monstrous
Murder
Murder, mass
Nefarious
Nihilist
Nudism
Null
Nullify
Obliteration
Obscure
Odious
Organised Crime
Orgies

Outrageous
Passionate
Perdition
Perpetration
Plagues
Plutonium
Pollution
Prostrate
Pungent
Purgatory
Purge, to
Purification
Putrid
Racketeers
Ransom
Rape
Ravage
Readjustment
Recuperation
Regenerate
Regimentation
Reincarnation
Relentless
Renewal
Reprobate
Reproduction
Reversion
Rogue
Rotten
Rotting
Rubbish
Sadistic
Savage
Savages
Scavengers
Scorn
Scorpions
Sedition
Septic, tanks
Severe
Sewerage
Sewers
Sexual
Sinister
Siren
Slime
Slough
Smut
Spoil
Stolen
Stoolpigeon
Subconscious
Subnormal
Sulphurous
Superphysical
Swag
Taciturn
Tapeworms
Teams
Terrible
Terror
Terrorists
Terse
Trade unions
Transformation
Treachery
Tyranny
Tyrants
Underworld
Ungodly
Unknown, the
Unscrupulous
Vampires
Vanish
Vast
Venom
Vermin
Vice
Victimisation

Victims
Vile
Vindictive
Violence
Voodoo
War
Waste
Wicked
Wreckers
Wrecks
Wretched

Calendar of star patterns

Note. EST indicates Eastern Standard Time

August 1992

Date	Favourable star patterns
1............ Jupiter-Uranus
             Moon-Uranus: 5pm to 7pm, EST
             Moon-Jupiter: 5.15pm to 7.15pm, EST
2............ Jupiter-Uranus
3............ Sun-Mercury
             Sun-Moon: 11.40am to 1.40pm, EST
             Moon-Saturn: 7.10pm to 9.10pm, EST
4............ Moon-Venus: 1.40pm to 3.40pm, EST
7............ Mercury-Mars
8............ Jupiter-Neptune
9............ Jupiter-Neptune
10.......... Moon-Uranus: 6.30pm to 8.30pm, EST
             Jupiter-Neptune
15.......... Moon-Uranus: 7.20pm to 9.20pm, EST
17.......... Moon-Mercury: 4.10pm to 6.10pm, EST
             Mars-Saturn
18.......... Mars-Saturn
19.......... Venus-Uranus
20.......... Venus-Neptune
21.......... Venus-Neptune
23.......... Venus-Jupiter
24.......... Venus-Pluto
             Jupiter-Pluto
25.......... Jupiter-Pluto
             Moon-Jupiter-Pluto: 12.20pm to 2.20pm, EST
             Moon-Venus: 3.30pm to 5.30pm, EST
26.......... Jupiter-Pluto
27.......... Jupiter-Pluto
29.......... Moon-Pluto: 12 noon to 2pm, EST
             Moon-Jupiter: 12.40pm to 2.40pm, EST
30.......... Mercury-Mars
             Moon-Mars: 4.45pm to 6.45pm, EST
             Moon-Mercury: 7.40pm to 9.40pm, EST

August 1992

Date	Adverse star patterns
3............ Moon Uranus: 6.20pm to 8.20pm, EST
5............ Moon-Mercury: 12.30pm to 2.30pm, EST
7............ Sun-Saturn
8............ Sun-Saturn
12.......... Moon-Mercury: 1.15pm to 3.15pm, EST
             Sun-Pluto
13.......... Sun-Pluto
15.......... Moon-Mars: 4pm to 6pm, EST
18.......... Moon-Neptune: 11am to 1pm, EST
20.......... Moon-Saturn: 4.15pm to 6.15pm, EST
             Venus-Mars
24.......... Mercury-Saturn
25.......... Mercury-Saturn
27.......... Mars-Jupiter
29.......... Mercury-Pluto
             Moon-Mars: 2pm to 4pm, EST

September 1992

Date	Favourable star patterns
1............ Sun-Moon: 8.40pm to 10.40pm, EST
2............ Moon-Pluto: 4.30pm to 6.30pm, EST
             Moon-Jupiter: 6.50pm to 8.50pm, EST
3............ Moon-Venus: 3.45pm to 5.45pm, EST
6............ Sun-Uranus
7............ Sun-Uranus
             Moon-Pluto: 12.10pm to 2.10pm, EST
             Moon-Jupiter: 4.45pm to 6.45pm, EST
8............ Sun-Neptune
9............ Sun-Neptune
10.......... Mercury-Uranus
11.......... Mercury-Uranus
             Venus-Saturn
12.......... Mercury-Neptune
             Moon-Pluto: 1.30pm to 3.30pm, EST
13.......... Sun-Pluto
14.......... Mercury-Pluto
15.......... Sun-Mercury
16.......... Mercury-Jupiter
17.......... Moon-Jupiter: 6.20pm to 8.20pm, EST
             Sun-Jupiter
18.......... Sun-Jupiter
22.......... Sun-Moon: 12.15pm to 2.15pm, EST
24.......... Moon-Venus: 12.10pm to 2.10pm, EST
25.......... Moon-Uranus: 12.30pm to 2.30pm, EST
             Moon-Neptune: 4pm to 6pm, EST
26.......... Mercury-Saturn
29.......... Moon-Uranus: 2.30pm to 4.30pm, EST

September 1992

Date	Adverse star patterns
5............ Moon-Mars: 11am to 1pm, EST
             Venus-Pluto
12.......... Venus-Uranus
14.......... Venus-Neptune
21.......... Moon-Neptune: 2pm to 4pm, EST
22.......... Mercury-Mars
27.......... Moon-Uranus: 12.30pm to 2.30pm, EST
             Moon-Neptune: 4pm to 6pm, EST
             Mercury-Uranus
28.......... Mercury-Neptune
29.......... Mercury-Neptune
             Sun-Pluto
             Moon-Saturn: 11.10am to 1.10pm, EST

October 1992

Date	Favourable star patterns
1............ Moon-Saturn: 4.30pm to 6.30pm, EST
5............ Sun-Saturn
             Venus-Mars
             Moon-Jupiter: 11.30am to 1.30pm, EST

122

6 .... Venus-Uranus
8 .... Venus-Neptune
9 .... Moon-Neptune: 11.15am to 1.15pm, EST
              Moon-Venus: 1pm to 3pm, EST
11 .... Moon-Saturn: 1.50pm to 3.50pm, EST
17 .... Mercury-Uranus
19 .... Mercury-Neptune
20 .... Mercury-Mars
21 .... Mercury-Mars
              Venus-Jupiter
22 .... Venus-Jupiter
23 .... Mercury-Pluto
              Moon-Mercury-Pluto: 10.40am to 12.40pm, EST
27 .... Moon-Mars: 1.20pm to 3.20pm, EST
28 .... Moon-Jupiter: 10.50am to 12.50pm, EST
29 .... Venus-Saturn
30 .... Venus-Saturn
              Mars-Pluto

October 1992

Date   Adverse star patterns
5 .... Venus-Saturn
              Sun-Mars
6 .... Moon-Saturn: 2pm to 4pm, EST
7 .... Sun-Uranus
9 .... Sun-Neptune
              Mars-Uranus
10 .... Mars-Uranus
14 .... Mars-Neptune
15 .... Mercury-Saturn
19 .... Sun-Moon: 1.15pm to 3.15pm, EST
              Venus-Uranus
20 .... Moon-Saturn: 4.10pm to 6.10pm, EST
31 .... Mercury-Neptune

November 1992

Date   Favourable star patterns
4 .... Mercury-Jupiter
5 .... Sun-Moon: 12.20pm to 2.20pm, EST
              Moon-Uranus: 4.10pm to 6.10pm, EST
              Moon-Neptune: 7.40pm to 9.40pm, EST
6 .... Moon-Mars: 11.15am to 1.15pm, EST
7 .... Sun-Uranus
              Moon-Mercury: 12.30pm to 2.30pm, EST
10 .... Moon-Uranus: 12.20pm to 2.20pm, EST
              Moon-Neptune: 3.30pm to 5.30pm, EST
12 .... Moon-Saturn: 2.15pm to 4.15pm, EST
15 .... Sun-Pluto
              Moon-Sun-Pluto: 1.20pm to 3.20pm, EST
              Mercury-Jupiter
16 .... Moon-Mercury: 12.40pm to 2.40pm, EST
              Moon-Jupiter: 1.50pm to 3.50pm, EST
18 .... Moon-Venus: 2pm to 4pm, EST
19 .... Sun-Mars

22 .... Sun-Mercury
23 .... Moon-Uranus: 12.40pm to 2.40pm, EST
              Moon-Neptune: 3.15pm to 5.15pm, EST
24 .... Mercury-Mars
25 .... Moon-Saturn: 1.40pm to 3.40pm, EST
27 .... Mercury-Pluto
28 .... Venus-Neptune

November 1992

Date   Adverse star patterns
2 .... Sun-Moon: 6.10pm to 8.10pm, EST
3 .... Moon-Pluto: 6.50pm to 8.50pm, EST
4 .... Sun-Saturn
11 .... Venus-Saturn
17 .... Moon-Pluto: 4.30pm to 6.30pm, EST
              Sun-Moon: 8.40pm to 10.40pm, EST
18 .... Moon-Mercury: 12.20pm to 2.20pm, EST
20 .... Venus-Jupiter
              Venus-Pluto
              Mercury-Neptune
21 .... Moon-Neptune 11.45am to 1.45pm, EST
              Jupiter-Pluto
              Mercury-Uranus
22 .... Jupiter-Pluto
              Sun-Uranus
23 .... Jupiter-Pluto
              Sun-Uranus
24 .... Sun-Neptune

December 1992

Date   Favourable star patterns
1 .... Sun-Jupiter
2 .... Sun-Jupiter
              Mercury-Venus
3 .... Venus-Pluto
              Moon-Venus-Pluto: 6.10pm to 8.10pm, EST
5 .... Mercury-Pluto
              Sun-Saturn
6 .... Mercury-Pluto
              Sun-Saturn
8 .... Moon-Mars: 7.15pm to 9.15pm, EST
9 .... Mercury-Mars
              Moon-Jupiter: 8pm to 10pm, EST
16 .... Moon-Uranus: 2.10pm to 4.10pm, EST
              Moon-Neptune: 3.50pm to 5.50pm, EST
18 .... Moon-Saturn: 2.15pm to 4.15pm, EST
19 .... Sun-Moon: 11.50am to 1.50pm, EST
              Venus-Jupiter
20 .... Mars-Pluto
21 .... Mars-Pluto
              Moon-Mars-Pluto: 11.20am to 1.20pm, EST
22 .... Mercury-Jupiter
24 .... Mercury-Saturn
25 .... Moon-Uranus: 2pm to 4pm, EST

123

Calendar of star patterns

Note. EST indicates Eastern Standard Time.

        Moon-Neptune: 3.40pm to 5.40pm, EST
27 .... Moon-Jupiter: 4.30pm to 6.30pm, EST
29 .... Mercury-Venus
30 .... Mercury-Venus
        Moon-Uranus: 2pm to 4pm, EST
        Moon-Neptune: 3.30pm to 5.30pm, EST

December 1992

Date	Adverse star patterns
5	Moon-Uranus: 2.40pm to 4.40pm, EST
6	Moon-Mars: 12 noon to 2pm, EST
	Venus-Mars
7	Moon-Saturn: 7.40pm to 9.40pm, EST
8	Moon-Pluto: 1.30pm to 3.30pm, EST
	Mercury-Jupiter
12	Moon-Neptune: 11am to 1pm, EST
18	Moon-Uranus: 5.30pm to 7.30pm, EST
	Moon-Neptune: 7.15pm to 9.15pm, EST
22	Sun-Saturn
	Venus-Saturn
28	Moon-Pluto: 3.30pm to 5.30pm, EST
30	Venus-Pluto
31	Sun-Pluto

January, 1993

Date	Favourable star patterns
9	Sun-Neptune
12	Moon-Mercury-Mars; 7pm to 8.30pm EST
15	Sun-Pluto
17	Venus-Mars
	Moon-Mercury: 3.15pm to 4.15pm, EST
19	Moon-Saturn: 2.15pm to 3.15pm, EST
22	Venus-Uranus
	Venus-Neptune
27	Moon-Pluto: 1.20pm to 2.20pm, EST
28	Sun-Moon: 3.20pm to 5.20pm, EST
	Venus-Pluto
30	Mercury-Jupiter

January 1993

Date	Adverse star patterns
4	Sun-Jupiter
5	Moon-Venus: 1pm to 3pm, EST
	Mars-Neptune
6	Mars-Neptune
7	Mars-Uranus
8	Sun-Mars
	Sun-Uranus
12	Mercury-Jupiter
13	Mercury-Mars
16	Mars-Jupiter
29	Moon-Uranus-Neptune: 1.30pm to 3.30pm, EST

February, 1993

Date	Favourable star patterns
3	Moon-Mercury: 11.50am to 1.50pm, EST
	Sun-Jupiter
4	Sun-Jupiter
9	Moon-Uranus-Neptune: 10.45am to 1pm, EST
11	Sun-Moon: 3.50pm to 5.50pm, EST
12	Moon-Mercury: 6.30pm to 8.30pm, EST
	Moon-Mars: 7.20pm to 9.20pm, EST
	Mercury-Mars
13	Moon-Uranus-Neptune: 3pm to 5.30pm, EST
15	Moon-Jupiter: 11.30am to 1.30pm, EST
16	Sun-Moon: 12.30pm to 2.30pm, EST
21	Mercury-Neptune
	Mercury-Uranus
	Mercury-Neptune-Uranus
23	Moon-Mercury: 1.30pm to 3.30pm, EST
25	Moon-Venus: 1.50pm to 3.50pm, EST
27	Moon-Mars: 12 noon to 2pm, EST
28	Sun-Mars

February, 1993

Date	Adverse star patterns
1	Moon-Pluto: 11.30am to 1.30pm, EST
2	Mercury-Saturn
5	Moon-Uranus-Neptune: 11am to 1pm, EST
	Mercury-Pluto
9	Sun-Saturn
	Venus-Saturn
10	Sun-Saturn
11	Moon-Uranus-Neptune: 11.30am to 1.30pm, EST
13	Venus-Mars
14	Sun-Pluto

March, 1993

Date	Favourable star patterns
2	Moon-Venus: 2.20pm to 4.20pm, EST
4	Sun-Moon: 10.50am to 12.50pm, EST
6	Mercury-Uranus
	Moon-Jupiter: 11.30am to 1.30pm, EST
7	Mercury-Neptune
9	Sun-Mercury
11	Sun-Neptune
	Sun-Uranus
12	Sun-Uranus
15	Mercury-Mars
16	Sun-Pluto
25	Moon-Saturn: 2.50pm to 4.50pm, EST
27	Moon-Neptune: 4.15pm to 6.15pm, EST
29	Moon-Venus: 12.30pm to 2.30pm, EST
30	Moon-Saturn: 11.40am to 1.40pm, EST

March, 1993

Date	Adverse star patterns
5	Mars-Pluto
12	Mars-Jupiter
17	Moon-Venus: 12.50pm to 2.50pm, EST
20	Saturn-Pluto
	Moon-Saturn-Pluto: 12.50pm to 2.50pm, EST
23	Jupiter-Saturn
25	Venus-Mars
30	Sun-Jupiter
31	Sun-Jupiter

April, 1993

Date	Favourable star patterns
1	Sun-Venus
2	Moon-Jupiter: 3.20pm to 5.20pm, EST
5	Moon-Neptune: 10.50am to 12.50pm, EST
	Moon Uranus: 12.15pm to 2.15pm, EST
9	Mercury-Mars
	Mercury-Uranus
	Moon with either Neptune, Mercury, Mars or Uranus: 11.30am to 2.15pm, EST
10	Moon-Venus: 1.50pm to 3.50pm, EST
17	Mars-Pluto
18	Sun-Saturn
	Mercury-Venus

April, 1993

Date	Adverse star patterns
6	Venus-Jupiter
7	Moon-Uranus: 11.45am to 1.45pm, EST
8	Mars-Neptune
10	Mars-Uranus
11	Sun-Neptune
12	Sun-Uranus
13	Sun-Mars
21	Moon-Neptune: 11.40am to 1.40pm, EST
	Moon-Uranus: 1.40pm to 3.40pm, EST
24	Moon-Saturn: 12.45pm to 2.45pm, EST
29	Mercury-Neptune
	Mercury-Uranus
30	Mercury-Uranus

May 1993

Date	Favourable star patterns
3	Mercury-Saturn
	Moon-Mars: 2.30pm to 4.30pm, EST
9	Mars-Jupiter
12	Sun-Neptune
	Sun-Uranus
13	Sun-Uranus
14	Mercury-Neptune
	Mercury-Uranus
16	Sun-Mercury
	Moon-Sun-Mercury: 3pm to 5pm, EST
19	Moon-Saturn: 12.10pm to 2.10pm, EST
20	Mercury-Jupiter
21	Mercury-Jupiter
22	Moon-Mercury: 2.10pm to 4.10pm, EST
24	Mercury-Mars
26	Sun-Jupiter
29	Mercury-Venus

May, 1993

Date	Adverse star patterns
6	Mercury-Mars
15	Mercury-Pluto
18	Mercury-Saturn
21	Sun-Saturn
27	Venus-Neptune
28	Venus-Uranus

June 1993

Date	Favourable star patterns
2	Mercury-Saturn
7	Venus-Saturn
12	Moon-Neptune: 1.10pm to 3.10pm, EST
	Moon-Uranus: 2.45pm to 4.45pm, EST
15	Moon-Mars: 11am to 1pm, EST
16	Moon-Venus: 3pm to 5pm, EST
18	Sun-Mars
20	Mercury-Pluto
21	Sun-Saturn
	Moon-Venus: 2.40pm to 4.40pm, EST
22	Sun-Saturn
26	Moon-Pluto: 11.10am to 1.10pm, EST
27	Venus-Neptune
	Venus-Uranus
30	Moon-Neptune-Uranus: 12.45pm to 2.45pm, EST

June, 1993

Date	Adverse star patterns
5	Mercury-Jupiter
11	Mars-Pluto
12	Mars-Pluto
17	Mercury-Neptune
	Mercury-Uranus
23	Mars-Saturn
24	Mars-Saturn
27	Sun-Jupiter
28	Sun-Jupiter
29	Venus-Pluto

Calendar of star patterns

Note. EST indicates Eastern Standard Time.

July, 1993

Date	Favourable star patterns
1	Moon-Jupiter: 4.10pm to 6.10pm, EST
3	Moon-Saturn: 10.40am to 12.40pm, EST
4	Mercury-Venus
9	Sun-Moon: 2pm to 4pm, EST
13	Venus-Jupiter
14	Mercury-Pluto
15	Sun-Mercury
	Sun-Pluto
	Mercury-Pluto
16	Moon-Venus: 11.50am to 1.50pm, EST
17	Moon-Saturn: 8.50pm to 10.50pm, EST
23	Moon-Neptune-Uranus: 12 noon to 2pm, EST
24	Mercury-Mars
	Moon-Jupiter: 7pm to 9pm, EST
26	Mars-Neptune
	Mars-Uranus
31	Mars-Pluto
	Venus-Saturn

July, 1993

Date	Adverse star patterns
1	Moon-Mars: 1.30pm to 3.30pm, EST
6	Venus-Saturn
7	Moon-Pluto: 2.15pm to 4.15pm, EST
12	Sun-Neptune
	Sun-Uranus
19	Mercury-Uranus
20	Mercury-Neptune
21	Venus-Mars
25	Moon-Mercury: 11am to 1pm, EST
	Moon-Neptune-Uranus: 1.30pm to 3.30pm, EST
30	Mercury-Neptune
31	Mercury-Neptune
	Mercury-Uranus

August, 1993

Date	Favourable star patterns
1	Moon-Mars-Pluto: 12.30pm to 2.15pm, EST
2	Sun-Jupiter
4	Mercury-Pluto
9	Mercury-Mars
13	Sun-Moon: 2.30pm to 4.30pm, EST
17	Mercury-Jupiter
19	Moon-Neptune-Uranus: 6.45pm to 8.45pm, EST
21	Venus-Pluto
22	Venus-Pluto
29	Sun-Mercury
30	Moon-Jupiter: 12.20pm to 2.20pm, EST

August, 1993

Date	Adverse star patterns
6	Moon-Mars: 4.30pm to 6.30pm, EST
7	Moon-Venus: 11.40am to 1.40pm, EST
8	Moon-Neptune-Uranus: 2.20pm to 4.20pm, EST
11	Moon-Saturn: 7.10pm to 9.10pm, EST
12	Venus-Jupiter
15	Sun-Pluto
16	Sun-Pluto
18	Venus-Neptune
	Venus-Uranus
20	Sun-Saturn
23	Mercury-Pluto
24	Mercury-Saturn
25	Mercury-Saturn
27	Moon-Mars: 5.10pm to 7.10pm, EST

September, 1993

Date	Favourable star patterns
5	Mercury-Uranus
	Mercury-Neptune
6	Mars-Jupiter
7	Mercury-Pluto
9	Moon-Venus: 12.15pm to 2.15pm, EST
	Moon-Jupiter: 3.50pm to 5.50pm, EST
11	Venus-Jupiter
	Sun-Uranus
	Sun-Neptune
15	Venus-Mars
16	Sun-Pluto
	Moon-Pluto: 12.15pm to 2.15pm, EST
18	Moon-Mars: 12.40pm to 2.40pm, EST
	Moon-Saturn: 2pm to 4pm, EST
19	Mars-Saturn
24	Mercury-Jupiter
25	Sun-Moon: 5.45pm to 7.45pm, EST
27	Mercury-Saturn
29	Moon-Uranus: 12.45pm to 2.45pm, EST
	Moon-Neptune: 1pm to 3pm, EST

September, 1993

Date	Adverse star patterns
4	Moon-Mars: 12.15pm to 2.15pm, EST
	Moon-Jupiter: 2.15pm to 4.15pm, EST
	Moon-Uranus-Neptune: 7.50pm to 9.50pm, EST
9	Mars-Uranus
10	Mars-Neptune
	Mars-Uranus
	Moon-Mercury: 12.20pm to 2.20pm, EST
14	Moon-Pluto: 12.30pm to 2.30pm, EST
	Moon-Saturn: 3.30pm to 5.30pm, EST
16	Jupiter-Uranus
	Jupiter-Neptune
17	Jupiter-Uranus
	Jupiter-Neptune
	Venus-Saturn

20 .... Moon-Saturn: 3pm to 5pm, EST
23 .... Mercury-Uranus
             Mercury-Neptune

October, 1993

Date   Favourable star patterns
2 .... Moon-Saturn: 1.30pm to 3.30pm, EST
4 .... Moon-Uranus: 2pm to 4pm, EST
             Moon-Neptune: 2.15pm to 4.15pm, EST
5 .... Mercury-Mars
6 .... Venus-Uranus
             Venus-Neptune
8 .... Moon-Mars: 1.50pm to 3.50pm, EST
11 .... Venus-Pluto
12 .... Jupiter-Saturn
13 .... Jupiter-Saturn
17 .... Sun-Saturn
             Mercury-Uranus
             Mercury-Neptune
             Moon with either Mercury,
             Uranus or Neptune: 2.30pm to 4.30pm, EST
18 .... Sun-Jupiter
19 .... Sun-Jupiter
23 .... Moon-Venus: 12.50pm to 2.50pm, EST
24 .... Mars-Uranus
             Mars-Neptune
29 .... Mercury-Mars

October, 1993

Date   Adverse star patterns
8 .... Saturn-Pluto
9 .... Saturn-Pluto
11 .... Sun-Uranus
             Sun-Neptune
12 .... Sun-Uranus
             Sun-Neptune
15 .... Moon-Uranus-Neptune: 2.45pm to 4.45pm, EST
30 .... Venus-Neptune
31 .... Venus-Uranus
             Mars-Saturn

November, 1993

Date   Favourable star patterns
2 .... Mercury-Uranus
             Mercury-Neptune
             Mars-Pluto
4 .... Venus-Saturn
6 .... Sun-Mercury
9 .... Venus-Jupiter
11 .... Sun-Neptune
             Sun-Uranus
14 .... Mercury-Venus
18 .... Sun-Pluto

24 .... Venus-Neptune
             Venus-Uranus
25 .... Venus-Uranus
30 .... Mercury-Neptune
             Mercury-Uranus
             Venus-Pluto

November, 1993

Date   Adverse star patterns
5 .... Moon-Neptune: 4.30pm to 6.30pm, EST
             Moon-Uranus: 4.45pm to 6.45pm, EST
7 .... Moon-Mercury: 11.30am to 1.30pm, EST
             Sun-Moon: 3.40pm to 5.40pm, EST
8 .... Moon-Mars: 4.40pm to 6.40pm, EST
16 .... Sun-Saturn
17 .... Sun-Saturn
21 .... Sun-Moon: 11am to 1pm, EST
25 .... Moon-Neptune: 4.30pm to 6.30pm, EST
             Moon-Uranus: 5.15pm to 7.15pm, EST
28 .... Moon-Venus: 2pm to 4pm, EST
             Moon-Saturn: 3pm to 5pm, EST
             Venus-Saturn
29 .... Venus-Saturn
             Sun-Moon: 3.30pm to 5.30pm, EST

December, 1993

Date   Favourable star patterns
1 .... Moon-Jupiter: 7.30pm to 9.30pm, EST
4 .... Mercury-Pluto
8 .... Moon-Venus: 2pm to 4pm, EST
9 .... Moon-Mars: 3.45pm to 5.45pm, EST
10 .... Moon-Jupiter: 3pm to 5pm, EST
14 .... Mars-Saturn
17 .... Moon-Mercury: 7pm to 9pm, EST
             Sun-Saturn
18 .... Sun-Saturn
23 .... Moon-Mercury: 11.10am to 1.10pm, EST
             Moon-Venus: 12.45pm to 2.45pm, EST
24 .... Venus-Saturn
             Mercury-Saturn
25 .... Mercury-Venus
             Moon-Neptune: 2.30pm to 4.30pm, EST
27 .... Sun-Mars
29 .... Moon-Jupiter: 11.50am to 1.50pm, EST
31 .... Sun-Jupiter

December, 1993

Date   Adverse star patterns
3 .... Mercury-Saturn
5 .... Moon-Saturn: 2.45pm to 4.45pm, EST
9 .... Moon-Neptune: 12 noon to 2pm, EST
             Moon-Uranus: 1pm to 3pm, EST
21 .... Moon-Mars: 11am to 1pm, EST

Index

A
AQUARIUS
- Career paths 51
- Characteristics 29
- Child's personality 57
- Colour associated with the star sign 67
- Compatibility with other star signs ...... 33, 35 - 43
- Herbs linked to the star sign 81
- On the ascendant 21
- The Aquarius home 101

ARIES
- Career paths 46
- Characteristics 26
- Child's personality 54
- Colour associated with the star sign 64
- Compatibility with other star signs .... 32 - 34
- Herbs linked to the star sign 78
- On the ascendant 13
- The Aries home 98

C
CANCER
- Career paths 47
- Characteristics 27
- Child's personality 54
- Colour associated with the star sign 65
- Compatibility with other star signs .... 33 - 38
- Herbs linked to the star sign 79
- On the ascendant 15
- The Cancer home 99

CAPRICORN
- Career paths 51
- Characteristics 29
- Child's personality 57
- Colour associated with the star sign 67
- Compatibility with other star signs ...... 33, 35 - 43
- Herbs linked to the star sign 81
- On the ascendant 20
- The Capricorn home 101

G
- GARDENING, see Planting by the Moon 70

GEMINI
- Career paths 47
- Characteristics 27
- Child's personality 54
- Colour associated with the star sign 64
- Compatibility with other star signs ...... 32, 34 - 36
- Herbs linked to the star sign 79
- On the ascendant 15
- The Gemini home 99

L
LEO
- Career paths 48
- Characteristics 27
- Child's personality 55
- Colour associated with the star sign 65
- Compatibility with other star signs ...... 33 - 34, 36 - 39
- Herbs linked to the star sign 79
- On the ascendant 16
- The Leo home 99

LIBRA
- Career paths 49
- Characteristics 28
- Child's personality 56
- Colour associated with the star sign 66
- Compatibility with other star signs ...... 33 - 34, 36 - 40
- Herbs linked to the star sign 80
- On the ascendant 18
- The Libra home 100

O
ORIENTAL ASTROLOGY
- Earth 86
- Fire 86
- Metal 85
- Table of astrological elements and animals ... 94
- The Dog 92
- The Dragon 89
- The Horse 90
- The Monkey 91
- The Ox 88
- The Pig 93
- The Rabbit 89
- The Rat 87
- The Rooster 92
- The Sheep 91
- The Snake 90
- The Tiger 88
- Water 85
- Wood 86

P
PISCES
- Career paths 52
- Characteristics 29
- Child's personality 57
- Colour associated with the star sign 67
- Compatibility with other star signs ...... 34 - 36, 38 - 43
- Herbs linked to the star sign 81
- On the ascendant 22
- The Pisces home 102

PLANTING BY THE MOON
- Moon sign chart for 1992 75
- Moon sign chart for 1993 76
- Phases of the moon 74

R
RACING
- Calendar of star patterns 122
- Dictionary of keywords 114
- Star patterns 110
- The moon's star patterns 113

S
SAGITTARIUS
- Career paths 50
- Characteristics 28
- Child's personality 56
- Colour associated with the star sign 66
- Compatibility with other star signs ...... 33, 35 - 42
- Herbs linked to the star sign 81
- On the ascendant 19
- The Sagittarius home 101

SCORPIO
- Career paths 50
- Characteristics 28
- Child's personality 56
- Colour associated with the star sign 66
- Compatibility with other star signs ...... 33, 35 - 41
- Herbs linked to the star sign 80
- On the ascendant 18
- The Scorpio home 101

TAURUS
- Career paths 46
- Characteristics 26
- Child's personality 54
- Colour associated with the star sign 64
- Compatibility with other star signs 32, 34, 35
- Herbs linked to the star sign 79
- On the ascendant 14
- The Taurus home 98

V
VIRGO
- Career paths 48
- Characteristics 27
- Child's personality 55
- Colour associated with the star sign 65
- Compatibility with other star signs ...... 33 - 34, 36 - 40
- Herbs linked to the star sign 80
- On the ascendant 17
- The Virgo home 100

SHELVING YOUR INVESTMENTS

Here's the perfect way to keep your Home Library books in order, clean and within easy reach. More than a dozen books fit into this smart silver grey vinyl holder.

Phone now for your Home Library Holder Yours for just $A9.95 each (including postage and handling)

☎ Sydney (02) 260 0035
Elsewhere (in Aust.)
008 252 515 (free call)
Have your credit card details ready (Mon - Fri, 9am - 5pm)
or Fax your details to Sydney (02) 282 8254
or write to AWW Home Library GPO Box 7036 Sydney NSW 2001

Please allow up to 21 days for delivery within Australia. Overseas residents, please add $A10 per holder for postage. **OFFER VALID WHILE STOCKS LAST.**

HLMH91

The Dates Of The Zodiac

♈ **Aries** March 21 – April 20	♌ **Leo** July 23 – August 23	♐ **Sagittarius** November 23 – December 21
♉ **Taurus** April 21 – May 21	♍ **Virgo** August 24 – September 23	♑ **Capricorn** December 22 – January 20
♊ **Gemini** May 22 – June 21	♎ **Libra** September 24 – October 23	♒ **Aquarius** January 21 – February 19
♋ **Cancer** June 22 – July 22	♏ **Scorpio** October 24 – November 22	♓ **Pisces** February 20 – March 20